DE NIRO

By the same author

King of Fools
The Princess Royal
Five for Hollywood
The Trial of Rock Hudson
Prince Philip: A Critical Biography
The Joker's Wild: the Biography of Jack Nicholson
The Queen: the New Biography
At the Heart of Darkness
Elvis: The Secret Files
Sean Connery
Polanski
Michael Douglas: Acting on Instinct

DE NIRO

John Parker

VICTOR GOLLANCZ

LONDON

First published in Great Britain 1995
by Victor Gollancz
An imprint of the Cassell Group
Wellington House, 125 Strand, London WC2R 0BB

A catalogue record for this book is
available from the British Library.

ISBN 0 575 05876 5

Photoset in Great Britain by
Rowland Phototypesetting Ltd,
Bury St Edmunds, Suffolk
Printed and bound in Great Britain by
Mackays of Chatham plc,
Chatham, Kent.

Contents

1

New York, New York

Truman Capote once wrote that New York was made out of modelling clay. It was a city, he said, that 'can become anything you want. You can hide, have secrets and have friends that your friends don't know that you have.' Robert De Niro was born into its artistic hub at a time when Capote's own star was rising and the clay was perhaps at its most pliable. It has remained De Niro's home, and often his inspiration, to the present day. So, half a century after Capote, he is well qualified to make his own assessment of the place and explain why he not only continues to live there but returns with great haste as soon as his business elsewhere is concluded: 'New York's the centre of something. I don't know what, really, but the centre of a lot of things. With all its problems, chaos and craziness, it's still for me the only place to live.'

It became the focus of his life from the moment his memory clicked into action, and he has not strayed far from the street where he was born on 17 August 1943, in wartime Greenwich Village. It would become his own long-term stamping ground, and the area upon which he would draw heavily for some of his most successful work. A dozen of his movies, almost a third of his output, have been set there. If it is possible that a town, a city or the kind of environment that only real New Yorkers supposedly know and love can really affect the mind and the thinking of a person who expresses himself through art, then it is demonstrably true in De Niro's case. Not only that, he has himself taken on some of that city's deep complexities, and perhaps that is to be expected.

At the time of his birth, Greenwich Village was in the middle of a revival of literary, artistic and theatrical talent on a scale not seen since the turn of the century. On account of his family background De Niro would be exposed to this activity throughout his childhood. Apart from America's home-grown writers and artists there were many who had arrived, to escape the war in Europe, from Paris, Berlin, Prague, Budapest, Moscow and elsewhere. Impious thinkers and irreverent practitioners abounded. The village was positively bristling with aspirants and tutors, mentors and maestros whose work right across a broad spectrum of the arts would reverberate in its influence down the rest of the century, and in due course upon De Niro himself.

Broadway too was at the beginning of a revolution. A new breed of writers, directors and actors were taking on board daring and, for the most part, exciting new techniques of presentation and style, emanating largely from the experimental styles imported from Europe and Russia in the late 1930s. They were turned into a very special way of American acting by a new young set who surrounded what was then known as the Group Theater.

They were a passionate bunch of young intellectuals, actors and writers, who formed around the likes of Lee Strasberg, Franchot Tone, Luther Adler, John Garfield and Clifford Odets. Their movement was transformed into what became known as the Actors Studio, which created a style that turned American film and theatre on its head and produced some of the most distinctive names in American acting history: Marlon Brando, James Dean, Marilyn Monroe, Montgomery Clift, Paul Newman and, eventually, Robert De Niro himself. This particular era would be the starting point of his professional research, the point where the influences that would become so apparent in his own style of acting were emerging. Director Elia Kazan, one of the prime movers of the new thinking and who would later select De Niro for the lead in his movie version of F. Scott Fitzgerald's *The Last Tycoon*, was, for example, making his name in the New York theatre. Kazan had also just discovered a young actor who would lead the revolution in stance and delivery: Montgomery Clift. In that year of 1943 when De Niro was born Clift was Broadway's newest matinee idol, appearing in Thornton Wilder's *The Skin of Our Teeth* and Lillian Hellman's *The Searching Wind*.

There was another coincidence, in Robert De Niro's actual birth date. It was the day that the Allied forces, following a route laid out by Mafia chieftains, finally captured Sicily, home of the mythical Vito Corleone. Years later he would be portrayed by Robert De Niro in Francis Ford Coppola's *The Godfather Part II*, for which he won his first Oscar. Thereafter he became tagged as an Italian-American, though he had more Irish in his ancestry than Italian, with a touch of Jewish thrown in. His father, Robert De Niro senior, was of Italo-Irish stock, a handsome young man with dramatic features and long, dark hair that curled at the bottom in a style befitting the atmosphere of Greenwich Village, which had become his adopted home.

Born in Syracuse, New York State, in his youth Robert senior had shown talent as an artist and, encouraged by his parents, went on to study under the renowned German-born painter Hans Hofmann who himself had been influenced by Matisse and the Cubists in Paris just before the First World War. Hofmann emigrated from Germany in 1932, settled in New York and opened an art school. He rose to some notoriety through the technique he developed of dripping paint on to a canvas and applying bright colours in broad strokes.

De Niro senior first came under the Hofmann influence in Provincetown, Rhode Island, where the student set his course on becoming an Abstract Expressionist. It was there, in Hofmann's tutorials, that he met Virginia Admiral, an equally talented, highly intelligent and independently minded young woman from Oregon. They went on to continue their studies at Hofmann's studio in the heart of Greenwich Village, on West 8th Street, and within a year they were married.

They set up home in a second-floor apartment in Bleeker Street, just a few paces from Broadway and on the edge of Little Italy and the Lower East Side, which later became a social magnet in their son's life. The De Niros moved among a wide circle of friends and fellow painters, brought together through the bonds of hope and hard times. The young couple were poor, but better off than many of their fellow artists, and by the time their only child arrived they were living frugally but in relative comfort.

Both Virginia and her husband were considered to be among the more talented of Hofmann's protégés, and fellow students talked of them in envious terms. They would both have their work hung at the Peggy Guggenheim Gallery in Venice, and in New York would find themselves being exhibited alongside such important contemporary American artists as Jackson Pollock and the Latvian-born Mark Rothko, who at the time was in his Surrealist phase. Years later, when Robert De Niro junior was hitch-hiking around Europe, he went to see the Guggenheim Collection and there proudly discovered some of his mother's paintings on display.

Virginia was also the only one in her group to receive the patronage of the Museum of Modern Art. Set up in 1929 by the Rockefeller Foundation to introduce New York to the Paris School, it had recently broadened its scope to present important and controversial new trends in modern art. To have a painting bought by MOMA, as it was affectionately known, was recognition indeed. Virginia also edited a review which published the little-known Henry Miller, along with the then unknown English novelist, playwright and travel writer Lawrence Durrell, who in 1957 would make his name with the four novels known as the *Alexandria Quartet*, and Anaïs Nin, the novelist and artist who became a seminal figure in the new feminism of the 1970s.

The De Niros began to offer a sort of open house to their artist friends, running a modest 'salon' in their apartment, later extending it with visits by well-known writers and artists at soirées which would go on until late in the night. These salon meetings were very popular in America at the time, much to the later chagrin of Senator Joseph McCarthy who, during his witch-hunt against 'Un-American Activities', imagined that such gatherings, particularly in the arts world and in Hollywood, were the breeding ground of Communism.

Talk at the De Niros' was serious, highbrow and artily snobbish. Concepts and ideas were exchanged. The De Niros and their friends viewed it as a coming together of kindred spirits in an important period of so-called 'purist thought', in which any reference to personal success or ability was frowned upon as a distraction from the pursuit of art. De Niro senior, a romantic and fiercely volatile character, was also highly critical of anyone whom he believed, as an artist, to be less than absolutely dedicated. 'That is the main weakness of young artists,' he would say. 'They lack dedication. They will stick to art as long as it doesn't cost them anything, when in fact they must stick to it whatever the cost.' Such uncompromising attitudes would, in due course, be instilled into their son to beneficial effect − but they could also become a heavy burden upon personal and family relationships, as time would show.

In many respects the De Niros lived in a heady, artificial world because their views about what was important were shared only by a small group of similar-minded artistic intellectuals. They were easy meat for social butterflies and another new breed of socially adept professionals, psychoanalysts: at the time there was great fascination in the writings of Sigmund Freud, who had died in 1939. It was becoming fashionable to talk about visiting one's analyst for mind-straightening sessions to illuminate day-to-day problems, and even life itself, so that this terrible world which had recently witnessed such horrors in Europe could be seen more clearly.

Montgomery Clift, as a typical example, had himself already fallen into the clutches of such a person. At a party given by Truman Capote he had met one of the many foreign-accented 'doctors' whose credentials could not be checked, and who, sadly for Clift, was a charlatan. Far from curing his client of his tendency towards drug and alcohol excesses, he encouraged and even joined him. He also attempted to solve Clift's sexual confusion by jumping into bed with him. Monty's closest friends blamed this self-proclaimed doctor for the shambling wreck that the actor had become by the end of the forties.

Such people, some more qualified than others but most with ideas that were as bizarre to the outside world as Abstract Expressionism was to devotees of Rembrandt, proliferated in the new social whirlpool of post-war New York. Greenwich Village became a magnet to them and a profusion of analysts, curers and carers offering every kind of spiritual guidance to those whose professional loneliness or search for the ultimate in perfection had driven them to distraction.

One of those who fell into the category of the blind leading the partially sighted came into the circle of artists who surrounded Hofmann and the De Niros. His medical qualifications were dubious and it was more likely that he was a failed artist who, with his own sanity barely intact, had given up and decided to go for the easy money instead. With his daring talk about relationships, virtually unheard of outside the privacy of the bedroom in the mid-forties, he encouraged his 'patients' to be open and honest about their aspirations and bold in their quest for sexual satisfaction.

The De Niros found themselves examining their own young marriage and not long afterwards, in the spring of 1946, stunned their friends by splitting up. With her two-year-old son Virginia moved into a small apartment on West 14th Street. The marriage was over, and in two years' time would be finalized by divorce; friends blamed the meddling of the Freudian fraud. Virginia's career as an artist was put on hold, largely due to the need to earn a living to support herself and her son in the knowledge that she could not necessarily count on her husband. She immediately went into business as a small secretarial unit, offering typing and proofreading service to writers and publishers. A little later, film-writer Manny Farber moved in. However he did not stay long, and when he met De Niro in Hollywood years later and asked: 'Don't you know who I am?' De Niro merely grunted and walked away.

Robert De Niro senior kept his home in the vicinity, although, as with most artists, survival took second place to his work. He would eventually achieve moderate fame in the city but at the time, and throughout his son's early years, he lived a hand-to-mouth existence in lofts and attic apartments around Greenwich Village. At times his circumstances were so reduced that during his travels he lived variously in barns, a coal-house and a tent. His own personality remained at best erratic. For a long time he had an obsession with Greta Garbo, which had begun way back in his younger days. He painted numerous studies of her as Anna Christie, from her 1929 movie. He wrote dozens of poems to her, and his volume of seventy-six poems, written over the years since 1941 and privately published in 1976, contained twelve which were dedicated to Garbo in *Camille*. It is a point of reference, and speculation, for his son's own Garbo-like love of total privacy today, although that could be seen in his mother, too. After she had earned some attention in the art world she was questioned about her early years and responded with a quote that her son would repeat time and again down the decades: 'I want to keep my life my life.'

The family had an amicable relationship after the divorce, and there was a degree of father-and-son bonding which usually took the form of walks or cheap seats at the cinema. It was not until later, however, that they became close – although that adjective is apparently debatable. In his now famous oblique responses to questions of a personal nature, De Niro once told an interviewer who had asked him about his relationship with his father: 'Close? In some ways I was and in some ways I wasn't. I don't know. In some ways I was very close to him, but then. . . .' And the voice trails away.

There is evidence of unhappiness and great loneliness. Friends of his mother would tell that from quite early on she had a tendency to push him out of the house, giving him a book to read and letting him find his own amusements. Again, De Niro himself would never speak of her in terms that were in any way affectionate.

Further evidence of this unhappiness emerged in 1989, when De Niro was doing the classic *Playboy* interview from which few stars have emerged without the feeling that they have just spent a week on a psychiatrist's couch. In De Niro's case it was more like being in a dentist's chair and having a deep-rooted molar extracted – he absolutely refused to disclose details of his past to anyone, always insisting that

12

his upbringing, his schooldays and his hobbies, are not only no one else's concern but are matters of trivia which have no place in a discussion about his work.

He succumbed to the interview under protest and only at the request of the studio with which he had just made a movie. After several false starts he finally turned up to meet Lawrence Grobel, well known for his persistence and analytical questioning. Even so, De Niro turned off the tape recorder on eleven occasions, looked at his watch seven times and said he had to leave five times. Grobel pressed on:

'What kind of kid were you?' he asked. 'Introverted, extroverted, shy, loud?'

'It's hard to talk about yourself, about what kind of kid you were. So I don't feel disposed to it,' came the reply.

'Why is it hard?'

'It just is. That's why I don't do interviews. I think it's self-evident. It's a personal thing and it's really nobody's business.'

'Is your past something you've decided to shut out?' asked Grobel. 'Was it a happy past or an unhappy past?'

'No, it's not that. It's. . . .' De Niro stopped and leaned forward to switch off Grobel's tape recorder and said he did not want to talk about his childhood, becoming, in Grobel's words, 'emotional and angry'.

'This has nothing to do with you,' De Niro continued. 'I'm just feeling angry about this . . . being pressured into doing an interview. . . .'

'So,' said Grobel picking up the question once again, 'you had an unhappy childhood?'

De Niro was now angrier than ever. He stood up and began pacing around the room, looking at his watch and saying he had to leave.

'Why turn off the tape recorder to say you don't want to talk about your childhood?' Grobel asked him. 'Why not just talk about why you don't want to?'

'I'll just say this . . . I'm not good at editing how I feel. And those personal things that I feel, like maybe who I would talk to in the past or something . . . are not something that I care to let anybody know about. That's my own personal thing.'

After this continued lack of answers – only talk about the questions, which was no good for a *Playboy* interview – Grobel was struggling. 'Then why not talk about your privacy? Brando felt the same way and was articulate about it, saying he wouldn't hang his private laundry out in public. How about you?'

13

'I can't even make a clear statement about that. . . .'

So Grobel gave up and changed the subject. He never did discover, from the man's own mouth, what kind of childhood he had or why he became so emotional and angry when the topic was raised.

There are other clues and other reasons, which will become apparent as his story unfolds, which explain to some degree why there are areas of his childhood that he does not ever discuss. Even today they still evoke strong emotions, time and time again, as if they were fresh in his mind – those who have tried to get him to unload childhood memories have on occasion noted that his eyes well up with tears.

Such emotions probably make him a better actor, but also one who appears vulnerable and ill suited to being a personality of the kind that Hollywood requires its stars to become. 'His mother was a quiet, intellectual woman and his father was inarticulate and spoke in half-sentences. Bobby became both of them,' said one who knew the De Niros in their most difficult times.

Family friends also recall that De Niro senior remained a temperamental and self-obsessed man who was devoted to his work, arrogantly defensive about his style and ability. He would never sell a painting to anyone whom he did not think would appreciate it, so in the early days he was very hard up for long periods of time and he remained virtually unknown for many years. This side to his nature became evident when his son wanted to give two of his paintings to Francis Ford Coppola on his fiftieth birthday in 1989 – first he had to convince his father that the recipient was worthy of receiving the gift. 'He was very touchy about that stuff,' De Niro admitted.

There were long periods of little or no contact between father and son, especially in the early fifties when the boy was in his formative years. In 1951, on the advice of Tennessee Williams whom he met while working as a waiter in the Beggar's Bar in Greenwich Village, De Niro senior moved to France and stayed for four years. He returned quoting Picasso, that 'painting is love made visible', and continued to succumb to his obsessive meanderings, apparently unconcerned about his lack of wealth or material effects.

This, then, was the background to the upbringing of the son of a couple who were initially dominated by their dedication to art above all else. Out of this grew a kind of Freudian self-examination and uneasy self-expression in their striving for perfection that Robert De Niro himself inherited. Deepness of thought, too, was evident from an early age. It may well have resulted in part from being the son of this intense couple, contemplating his own situation slotted between them, and often their only point of contact.

And so Bobby De Niro continued his childhood in the heart of New York's most colourful bohemian district, a loner who would wander the streets around his home and disappear into the regions of Little Italy and the Lower East Side which border the southern reaches of Greenwich Village. A frail, pale kid, taciturn and shy, he received a local education at Public School 41 in the Village. Here he became friendly with other boys and joined them in the then safer streets around his home. He usually plumped for single friendships, particularly with anyone who shared his developing passion for the cinema, born out of the visits he made there with his father. Not until years later did he realize that it was as a boy that he had first met Martin Scorsese, who in later life became his director, collaborator and friend. Scorsese lived not far away, but it would be almost two decades before they would meet professionally.

De Niro's own earliest interest in acting came at school, when he was cast as the cowardly lion in a production of *The Wizard of Oz*. Soon afterwards, his mother arranged for him to attend speech and drama classes because he showed something of an aptitude for it. She was doing typing work for Marie Ley-Piscator who, with her husband, had founded the modernist Dramatic Workshop. Like his mother's earlier mentor Hans Hofmann, the couple had come out of Germany and favoured Abstract Expressionism. The husband eventually went back, but Marie stayed on and formed a workshop that attracted some high-profile students. Both Marlon Brando and Rod Steiger studied with her for a time, before they moved on to the Actors Studio. In lieu of payment for Virginia's typing work, Marie took Bobby into her Saturday youth classes. So, for two years from the age of ten, De Niro was given an early taste of workshop experience in the style that was to be classically termed New York acting, and for quite a long time spoken of in derogatory fashion over on the West Coast by the products of the Hollywood studio system who encountered it among their co-stars.

By the time he was entering his teens, however, he had lost his interest and left. He became an indifferent student at school, more noted for his truancy than for any academic progress. As a result, when he was thirteen his mother sent him to a progressive private school. He had by then begun to run with a local gang who gave him the nickname of Bobby Milk because he was such a pallid, thin boy.

Once, while kicking around with some of his friends in Washington Square, the centre of Greenwich Village, he happened upon his father who berated him and said: 'Get away from those young hoods!' Father and son did not speak again for many months. But De Niro was never really a young gangster – contrary to popular opinion which arose after the appearance of some of his movies in collaboration with Scorsese, notably *Mean Streets* (1973) and *Taxi Driver* (1976). He was never a tough kid anyway, and one of his friends at the time confirmed that 'he used to wander around with a book under his arm, which was hardly teenage gang stuff. Then he'd get shy, and go off somewhere and read.'

In any event, his surroundings as a boy and a youth were not in the heart of New York's socially deprived regions, where the real mean streets and knife-wielding, community-threatening gangs were to be discovered. Life in Greenwich Village in the fifties and sixties was positively genteel compared to that in the bad boroughs of greater New York. And, even though they had little money, his parents were certainly middle-class in their outlook and in their aspirations for their son, which was sufficient to retain control over him.

These years continued to be a time of great activity in music and the arts in general. New York nightlife was featuring the vanguard of modern jazz, such as Dizzy Gillespie, Gerry Mulligan and the Modern Jazz Quartet. Carnegie Hall was presenting its most varied programme of visiting orchestras since before the war, the opera was booming and Broadway was alive with innovative productions. But though Bobby De Niro had shown an initial interest in acting, it had passed for the moment. He certainly paid no heed to, and probably had no knowledge of, the developments in the performing arts not far away in midtown Manhattan, which would in time become the greatest influence on his career.

The now famous Actors Studio, formed in 1947, had come to rest in its permanent home, a white-painted church-like building on West 44th Street, which became the mecca of both aspiring and working young actors hoping for a chance to study there. Those who ran the studio were the founders of that most contentious of contemporary American acting styles, based upon the Stanislavski Method. In its infancy at the time of De Niro's birth, it was now attracting an adventurous new breed of actors, directors and playwrights.

Clift and Brando, the earliest graduates of Method tuition, were already big stars in the early fifties when De Niro began his Saturday acting classes. Clift was first to make it, initially on Broadway and then in movies such as *A Place in the Sun, I Confess* and *From Here to Eternity*. Brando, whose career would have a curious intertwining with De Niro's, set Broadway alight in 1947 in Kazan's production of *A Streetcar Named Desire* and was immediately whisked away to Hollywood to do the same in the screen version, followed by *The Wild One* and *On the Waterfront*. James Dean, living in squalor not far from De Niro's house, was doing the rounds of New York auditions. He finally got noticed in a Broadway play; then, like Clift and Brando before him, he was discovered by Kazan and flown to Los Angeles, where he starred in *East of Eden* in 1954. And so in the early fifties three of De Niro's future icons, and others besides, became famous with a style of acting that he would later develop for himself.

He would, in fact, prove to be a far more dedicated and proficient student that those earliest exponents whose style became such a focus of attention. Much had been made of their Method training, though it was exaggerated. 'Clift and Brando did not rigorously involve themselves at the Studio,' said Elia Kazan, 'but perhaps they did not need that kind of training by then. Jimmy Dean didn't work much either. He would sit and watch and then develop his own exercises, privately. He hated criticism.'

They were ranged before De Niro at his most impressionable age in movies that broke new ground. At the time, as these young stars found international acclaim, the potential of the Method style and the work of its main tutors – Kazan, Bobby Lewis, Stella Adler and Lee Strasberg – was neither fully appreciated nor understood by audiences. The critics treated it with utter disdain, accusing its exponents of mumbling and stuttering and of unnatural behaviour. It fired one of the greatest debates ever to take place among the critics and the acting establishment, most of whom abhorred the Method and preferred the accepted practice of 'speaking your lines loud and clear'. Even Laurence Olivier led a delegation of actors from Britain to visit the studio to see what the fuss was about. Olivier did not like it either, but many British actors, including Sean Connery and Kenneth Haigh, would adopt a form of the Method in their own work.

Younger cinema audiences of the day were, however, impressed – but for different reasons. The new breed brought something completely fresh to the cinema. They gave the disorientated youth of the early fifties, in search of idols to replace the now greying stars of the Golden Age, a whole new repertoire of sayings, postures and gestures. In doing so, they tapped into a goldmine and quickly became diverted from their original serious course as actors. They were carried away on a wave of celebrity, that aspect of American culture that turns its performers into commercial products known as superstars – with all the accompanying problems.

Most of this passed over the head of the young Bobby De Niro. He was only eleven when the most controversial of these early Method movies, Brando's *The Wild One*, appeared, and only twelve when James Dean caused a sensation in *Rebel Without a Cause* in the autumn of 1955 – largely because by then Dean had already died in his car crash. The early work of Brando, undoubtedly his best, and that of Clift would have to be rediscovered later when De Niro was himself studying the Method. At the time it was more spectacular entertainment that made a more lasting impression on him, and he has always picked out one movie in particular, from 1960. It was *Can-Can*, starring Shirley Maclaine and Frank Sinatra, which he enjoyed so much that he said to a friend as they left the cinema, 'I'm going to do that.'

'What?' said his friend.

'Act in the movies.'

His friend laughed and they walked on home.

2

Method and Madness

Robert De Niro's first steps to acting were far from sure-footed. At sixteen, he more or less ended his formal education when he dropped out of high school after one semester and, while still enjoying his street life, began to move towards the dramatic arts. His mother encouraged this new direction. Another form of inspiration came from watching Dennis Hopper in the stage version of *Mandingo*, a Jack Kirkland play from the novel by Kyle Onstott.

Hopper had been a James Dean acolyte, appearing in *Rebel Without a Cause* and *Giant*, and one of Dean's best friends. His brooding, post-Dean presence in Hollywood had made him unpopular with the establishment there and he was on the brink of a long period in exile, exacerbated by his own erratic character and his experimentation with drugs. He had now made this brief return to the stage with Franchot Tone. De Niro was sixteen when he saw him, thought he was brilliant and would go backstage to watch.

At the time Bobby had just enrolled at the Stella Adler Conservatory of Acting, which he attended for almost three years and with which he maintained a long association afterwards. Adler was an important influence, as she had been on a number of major stars of the previous generation. De Niro arrived on the scene at a particularly fraught time among the Method-ists of New York. Adler had been one of the original importers of the Stanislavski school to New York, although her version of the technique was different from that of Elia Kazan, Lee Strasberg and most of the others who taught at the Actors Studio. The daughter of a Jewish actor named Jacob Adler, in 1934 she had gone to Paris to meet Constantin Stanislavski. She had returned to New York with a chart system which she had devised after her talks with the great man; this she used as the basis for her own study and tuition for years to come, and it was still in use during De Niro's period at her conservatory. Lee Strasberg accused Adler of totally mis-interpreting the words of Stanislavski, and their ongoing battle had recently flared into a very public row.

Maureen Stapleton, who studied alongside Brando and Clift at the Actors Studio when Adler was teaching there, told me:

> Stella was a very formidable lady by then. There had always been a lot of rows and fallings out over whose version was correct. Lee Strasberg emerged as the driving force at the Studio, but you could not say he was always right. Strasberg taught his system. Adler taught hers. But in the end it didn't matter about the specifics, or who was right and who was wrong. You don't even have to study the Method to become a good, or even a great, actor. But to those of us involved at the time it was a very intense and studious form of tuition, quite rigidly imposed. The Method was supposed to be a natural form of helping to learn your craft, bring your inner senses to the surface and improvise on all your feelings. You could not get two better examples than Clift and Brando, but theirs was also an innate talent. To watch Marlon and Monty, both very quiet in their delivery, was breathtaking. The tuition helped them bring it out without overdoing it. They always exercised restraint in vocal expression, which is a keynote of much of De Niro's work.

The student De Niro was immediately confronted by the basic tenet of Method tuition, which centred around character creation. The training was based upon a controversial system of exercises and experi-mentation to enable the actor to forage among his own emotions. Students were encouraged to search for and draw upon every detail of their past lives, experiences and sexuality, in whatever form it took – from suffering and private demons to great joy. The exercises were many and varied: some verged on the obscene to make the would-be actors totally open about themselves, while others, like becoming a tree, were aimed at developing their ability to become completely inanimate.

Established Hollywood actors of the day often dismissed it as useless mumbo-jumbo – 'like masturbating: fun but it gets you nowhere,' was how Charlton Heston described it to me – but with the benefit of hindsight we can see that those who trained in the Method were among

20

the most successful actors of the fifties, sixties and beyond. Even so, many famous names of the old school found working with Method actors incredibly tiresome, though occasionally amusing. Julie Harris told me that, when she was co-starring with James Dean in *East of Eden*, Raymond Massey, who played Dean's father, was driven almost to apoplexy. He protested loudly to Elia Kazan about Dean's preparation techniques – the young star would stand on set emitting a stream of foul words. Once Massey walked off the set, declaring: 'I have never experienced such behaviour in my entire life.' Kazan did not intervene. He felt that the animosity which had arisen between the two actors would help their scenes as they played out their screen roles of father and son. Dean himself explained: 'To me, acting is the most logical way for people's neuroses to manifest themselves in the great need we have to express ourselves.' All these were events and statements that influenced De Niro in his extensive research of the period.

It might also be said that the Method was a uniquely dangerous form of tuition, since many of those who went through it developed severe emotional problems in their personal lives. This may, of course, have been mere coincidence and might have happened anyway, but there is a theory that the exercises performed at the Method schools could well have brought latent psychological forces to the surface. Suicides and mental breakdowns among Method actors were not unusual.

Stanislavski's principle was that the role, the character, should be created out of the actor's own emotions. Tutors, and Stanislavski himself, always warned their students not to confuse themselves with the characters they had created. It became absolutely central to De Niro's own development. Method preparation verged upon the mystical and was in some ways almost like witchcraft. Some students, including several who became famous stars, found it impossible to avert the flow of fiction into reality, so that the emotions of the imagined character spilled over into their own. It soon became apparent that many actors, perhaps suffering an imbalance in their own mind or bodily chemistry, could become overtaken by the persona of the created character, especially if they were cast repeatedly in similar roles. An actor totally immersed in his work would then find a severe conflict of personalities between the real and the imagined. It was known as the existential fallacy.

Monty Clift, for example, went into self-destruct mode with the help of his so-called psychotherapist. Brando went off into all kinds of diverse activities with quite evident anguish, especially in matters sexual. He talked constantly of quitting almost from the moment he became famous. He too resorted to therapy for many years. James Dean was said to have developed a death wish, and his closest friends reckoned that a disturbing guilt over his mother's death – she actually died of cancer – was aroused during his Method training, which he practised daily. His sexuality, like that of Clift, became confused. All dabbled with homosexual encounters – which was, in any case Clift's only preference. Elia Kazan admitted that Dean had become a 'pudding of hatred', torn and twisted. 'Frankly, I didn't like him much,' he confided. Once Dean's inner emotions had been released, he became what his former girlfriend Barbara Glenn described as 'a very destructive person' who could seriously affect the lives of those around him.

Marilyn Monroe, already of ultra-frail temperament, became involved with the Method in an attempt to find a level of acting ability of which many people thought she was incapable. Although she proved them wrong, her confidence became destroyed and in her last years Paula Strasberg, her Method tutor, was in virtually constant attendance. Monroe once said of Method stardom: 'Every weakness is exaggerated. So this industry should behave to its stars like a mother whose child had just run out in front of a car. But instead of clasping the child to their bosom, they start punishing the child.'

Warren Beatty, too, sought therapy from an early stage in his career, almost immediately after his work with De Niro's tutor Stella Adler. Beatty talked often about her tuition, and about how he had been given the key to searching among the deepest regions of his own psyche. Leslie Caron, who was very close to Beatty while he was wrestling with his acting techniques in the mid-1960s, told me: 'Warren came to rely heavily on his therapist and became very fond of him. He was a brilliantly witty man and he never stopped going. He also used to send all of us [his girlfriends] to see a psychoanalyst. He believed the experience was very beneficial to us, personally and professionally.'

So what of De Niro, product of mercurial parents and an unusual home life, whose guidelines to life had come through a philosophy that might be termed as early existentialist? Stella Adler was considered by some of her students as a woman whose directives might only add to the confusion in the impressionable brain of a young man in his mid-teens. She promoted the use of what she described as external physical stimulation to achieve the desired character improvisation, so that the actor stepped outside of himself and into the world created by the author of the play or script. The actor was supposed to analyse not himself but 'the externals', such as the clues that the author had given him and the realities of the situation in which that character had been placed. In other words, an Adler student created the character from the outside in, absorbing in every detail all that had been set around that character by the author.

It was there that Adler clashed with Lee Strasberg at the Actors Studio. His teachings emphasized the internal 'discovery' of the character, drawing from the actor's own soul and creating that character from the inside out. Adler would argue that, in doing so, Strasberg students would always play themselves because the character was created out of their own genes, which might well be true of certain famous actors who only ever played themselves – regardless of the part written in the script. It was an important point, which De Niro himself would pick up on.

He would, in time, become exposed to both sets of directives, combining them to develop over several years his own very unique style. But, like Warren Beatty and many others before him, the teachings of Adler were very evident in his early performances. Leslie Caron, Beatty's companion at his most volatile period of acting, explained: 'Stella Adler had an immense influence on her students . . . it was all aimed at a particular intellectual level. The phenomenon of Method happened as with the Impressionists, who all have a common denominator in their painting. The Method, with its inevitable abuse, was an open challenge to the somewhat facile acting that was practised previously.'

Adler ran the newcomers' classes which De Niro attended strictly. No sloppily dressed students were admitted, and they broke the rules at their peril. The men had to wear white shirts, pressed trousers and polished black shoes with no scuffs. Hair had to be trimmed neatly and, for women, swept off their faces. The reception of new students and the daily commencement of classes was a well-performed ritual.

Adler students would get three days' preparatory tuition from one of her assistants; then, on the fourth day, she herself would appear, dressed entirely in black and heavily made up, at the door of the classroom with an assistant on either side. The students would all stand and recite: 'Good morning, Miss Adler. We are pleased to meet

23

you and look forward to embarking with you on a journey to discover our art.' Adler would then enter, ascend the tutorial platform and place herself on the single leather chair, which looked for all the world like a throne. Her two assistants remained on either side like bodyguards, and it was they who would begin the tuition sessions – which she would interrupt at virtually every pause for breath with her own interjections, in language more fitting of a drill sergeant commanding a company of raw recruits.

She would instruct students to remember: 'Your life is one millionth of what you know. Your talent is your imagination. The rest is lice.' She always encouraged her class to use extrovert physical action and props to enable them to become their characters, to free themselves from the dictates of the script and from themselves. These were the keys to her whole principle of Method tuition. 'Acting is action, action is doing. Find ways to do it, not to say it,' she would say.

De Niro went into the Method process at the Adler conservatory and studied with her, on and off, for more than three years. He would study intermittently with Adler and later other tutors, as well as doing group work at the Actors Studio, over the next fifteen years; there is no question that during this time he produced some of his best work, just as Clift and Brando had done when they were doing workshops and exercises with Lee Strasberg.

Round about this time there was a foreign interlude which is couched in some mystery. De Niro went to France to seek his father, who had decided to move back to Paris in the hope of a change in his fortunes – one of many trips abroad to find peace in the continued turmoil of his work. In deep moments he continued to write poetry, which served as a diary of events and influences in his life. But he found no greater success in Montmartre than he had in the USA or elsewhere. Indeed his son found him broke and barely surviving, though still committed to his art.

De Niro has always been typically tight-lipped about the episode, but did admit to a friend: 'It was an absolute nightmare.' He brought his father back to New York where eventually he re-established himself in Greenwich Village – although the area was already on the decline as the hub of the city's artistic life. Even so, he had better luck. He continued to lead what his son described as the classic artist's life – 'struggling, for want of a better word' – and received some decent reviews for his work. Eventually his work was exhibited at the classier uptown galleries.

When young Bobby had become famous and wealthy he published his father's poems under the title A *Fashionable Watering Place*. Their mixture of harsh realities and touching sentimentalism contained colourful Kiplingesque images of the life and times and inspirational travels of a struggling artist, although in the intervening years he had enjoyed considerably more success and ultimately more tranquillity. Bearing in mind that he was now considerably better known than his father, De Niro junior wisely and tactfully included a note that read: 'These poems are by Robert De Niro, the painter, not to be confused with Robert De Niro, the actor, his son.' The painter went on to establish a comfortable and stable existence and a relationship with his actor son that went through a patchwork of phases. When he died in 1993 his estate was valued at $2 million, mostly in personal property and paintings. His son dedicated the first movie he ever directed, A *Bronx Tale*, to his father.

Virginia De Niro, in the meantime, had also become very active again in the art world. Young Bobby could not fail to have been both impressed and influenced by his parents' dedication to their art, which would ultimately reveal itself in his own absolute commitment to his roles and his observance of ideals. But perhaps more importantly, it was the basis for the learning acquired from Stella Adler that a sense of remoteness could be not only beaten but exploited through the craft of acting. As with Dean, also at first a very quiet young man, it offered him chameleon-like possibilities to escape from his terrible shyness by subliminating his own personality in favour of those characters he was to portray.

At nineteen years old, these possibilities were already beginning to occur to him. They became evident to his friends via the growing collection of hats and other wardrobe items that he gathered at home for his private rehearsal of the make-believe world that had been instilled into him by Stella Adler. Sally Kirkland, an actress friend from those early days, remembers that when he first began doing the rounds of auditions, in the early sixties, he carried a portfolio of photographs of himself in various disguises. 'He told me he just wanted to prove to directors that he wasn't an ethnic,' said Kirkland, 'but of course it went much deeper than that.' He was already making a point of his commitment, and his ability to sublimate his own character for any role he was auditioning, thus stepping out of himself into the guise of that character. As well as the portfolio, he had a composite of four photographs of himself in different disguises, each of which appeared to be a picture of a completely different person. He was unrecognizable.

One casting director, Marion Dougherty, was an early witness of his portfolio: 'One of them, I remember, was particularly striking. He was made up as an eighty-year-old man. In other shots, he was wearing costumes of all kinds. I had never seen anything like that in any of the portfolios young actors carry around, which are for the most part glamour shots.' Later, he himself would make a rare admission that he saw acting as a way of doing things 'that you would never dare do yourself'. This possibility continued both to inspire and to intrigue him. He scoured the trade press for audition dates, and it was from this research that he found his first movie role. Hearing that a new young director was looking for actors willing to work for practically nothing on an experimental new movie, he went eagerly to be tested.

The project was the first-ever movie to be made by Brian De Palma, who in the mid-sixties was ranked among a select group of film-makers, including Martin Scorsese, Francis Ford Coppola, Steven Spielberg and George Lucas, who were dubbed the Movie Brats. Later he was to become famous for a string of controversial films, verging on the sensational and occasionally the pornographic, which, with heavy accusations of voyeurism, would earn him as many brickbats as they did acclaim. It was the first of several encounters with De Niro as their careers progressed and their friendship developed, and De Niro's entry into that circle would have future benefits because it brought him to the attention of other thrusting young movie-makers.

Then, in 1963, when De Niro was just leaving his teens, De Palma had nothing to his name except a series of shorts which he made while studying at Columbia University, and then later at Sarah Lawrence College, where he had been awarded an MCA scholarship. It was there that he met a wealthy student named Cynthia Moore who used the pseudonym Cynthia Munroe. She rashly agreed to put up $100,000 to finance his first feature movie, entitled *The Wedding Party*, which he co-wrote and directed. Cynthia was also co-director, co-producer, co-writer and co-editor with De Palma and Wilford Leach, who taught at the university.

Hearing the grapevine buzz about actors being required, De Niro got an audition but was disappointed to discover that his reading consisted of speaking lines written on a few scraps of paper. This he completely messed up. He knew immediately that he had not done it well, and hung around until he caught De Palma's attention. De

Palma said the young De Niro was desperately shy and barely capable of talking, but managed to ask if he could do something else. When the budding director agreed, De Niro went outside to prepare and was away for some time. 'Then he burst in,' said De Palma, 'chest puffed out, face red and exploding into a speech from *Waiting for Lefty*. He was terrific.' He recalled: 'I decided at that moment he was going to be a major star in the future.' So De Niro was given a part in the film and promised a flat fee of $50. For that he would co-star with another unknown but later famous actress, Jill Clayburgh, who was also making her debut.

Filming began very soon afterwards. *The Wedding Party* barely had a plot, but was made up of a series of improvisational scenes based upon a wedding in Long Island. De Niro played a friend of the groom and Clayburgh was the bride. The actors were given key lines for each scene and were then supposed to ad-lib the remainder, having immersed themselves in the scenario as described by De Palma. It was an interesting experiment, and one which was, given the inexperience all round, surprisingly successful.

It was not successful enough, however, to find a company willing to distribute it into the cinemas, even though it was billed to reach the American youth market at the start of the hippie era. It lay on the director's shelf for two years before he even attempted to edit it, and was not finally accepted for release until 1969. The movie then received a scattering of mini-reviews which were largely dismissive, and De Niro was deservedly mentioned only in passing. *The Wedding Party* might have disappeared from view completely had not De Palma, De Niro and Clayburgh become famous in the meantime. In 1983 it was released on video-cassette with packaging that hinted of better things. Even so, it remains an interesting piece of cinematographic history as the debut of people who later achieved significance.

After that, De Niro went for months without working again. It was a chance meeting with a famous graduate of the Method culture which helped him on his way once more. Shelley Winters, whose yo-yo career as America's busiest female character actress was in the doldrums, met De Niro when he was just past his twenty-first birthday and took him up as her protégé.

They were introduced by Sally Kirkland, whose room-mate had dated De Niro on occasions. Kirkland, later to become a busy Hollywood actress with roles in *The Sting*, *The Way We Were*, *Private Benjamin* and *JFK*, took him to Jimmy Ray's bar on Eighth Avenue.

Winters remembers him as a skinny youth, very quiet and obviously with no money. He rode around New York on an old bicycle. If she had taken a guess then, Winters would not have put him in the class of superleague possibles, or anywhere near it, though she was soon to change that opinion and in fact became a lifelong friend who today calls herself his Jewish Mama. In fact she became well known for the helping hand she gave to a number of young actors and actresses – 'my theatrical waifs', she called them.

In the sixties, with a colourful romantic past and some spectacular affairs, including Brando, Burt Lancaster and a failed marriage to Italian actor Vittorio Gassman fresh in local memories, there was talk that she and De Niro were romantically involved – the term 'toy boy' was not in common use then – in spite of their twenty-one-year age difference. Winters denies it. She says she just took a shine to the kid with the dark, watchful eyes and soft voice, and began taking him to parties and introducing him around. With her influence at the Actors Studio, where it was still no easy task to get accepted into those hallowed halls, she arranged for him to become an observer. 'He would never do an audition for Lee Strasberg,' said Winters. 'He just didn't want to do it.' Observer membership, however, allowed him to watch Studio members at work, staging plays, doing readings and receiving words of wisdom from Strasberg and his co-tutors.

As at Adler's conservatory there was an air of formality at the Studio, where students would gather in the lobby to wait for Strasberg to arrive. They would then follow him upstairs to the lecture hall for a two-hour discussion and tuition period in which all enrolled members would participate. The pride in past members was prominently displayed, especially when the studio opened its Californian branch, where huge posters of Monroe, Brando and Dean adorned the walls. There was always a kind of starry-eyed aura permeating the Studio's declared serious intent of becoming a mirror of contemporary art and then changing it.

De Niro was able to join workshop sessions to gain first-hand experience, although he was never a student of Strasberg himself. Sally Kirkland went along, too. They took their newly gleaned Strasberg Method-isms back to De Niro's place and spent hours rehearsing scenes in the kitchen. 'It was real kitchen-sink drama,' Kirkland recalls. 'He could beat up a terrific rage in the confines of his own home.' Apart from his immense character 'wardrobe' he used books for inspiration. 'He had a stack of paperback novels,' said Kirkland, 'and these were the source of his ideas for his characterizations. He was always talking about writing his own screenplays.' They spent hours acting out their scenes, talking about hopes and possibilities. As always, he was very intense.

His contact with the Actors Studio continued for many years, although he never became a member. Later, Lee Strasberg offered him full membership without an audition after they had appeared together in *The Godfather Part II*, although long before then he had concluded that De Niro had the ability to match the Studio's most outstanding old boy, Brando.

But at this time his career was still moving very slowly. *The Wedding Party* had helped him not a jot because no one had seen it. He took virtually any role he could, ranging from appearing in Chekhov's *The Bear* with an acting group touring schools to playing a part in a German Expressionist drama called *Cry in the Streets*. He took jobs in dinner theatres, waiting on tables as well as appearing on stage. He acted in *Cyrano de Bergerac*, *Compulsion* and *Long Day's Journey into Night*.

Then, out of the blue, in 1968 he won another audition. It was a bizarre off-Broadway – and in this case well off – production of a play entitled *Glamour, Glory and Gold*, in which he would play no fewer than five characters. Written by transvestite Jackie Curtis, the play was the slender tale of an actress from Chicago who becomes a star but then loses all through addiction to drink. He had written it for his friend Andy Warhol's personal discovery, the transvestite celebrity Candy Darling, so that he/she could do her Marilyn Monroe impressions. Few serious reviewers bothered to show up, but De Niro at last received some mentions as a welcome newcomer and entered the magic circle of famous names surrounding Warhol himself. Sally Kirkland recalled: 'I thought he was electrifying, and afterwards in his dressing room I told him I'd never seen anything so brilliant and that he was going to be a big star.'

Face to face, De Niro appeared embarrassed and coy. Next day, from the distance permitted by the telephone, he called her up and kept asking: 'Do you really think I'm any good? Do you really?'

Meanwhile, with this minor success under his belt, another expedition abroad beckoned. He had apparently become obsessed with finding his roots and had raised enough money to get to Ireland. From there he travelled across Europe, partly hitch-hiking, to discover the origins of the Italian branch of his family. He located them, it is said, in Campobasso, sixty miles north-east of Naples. He was away for

29

four months and ended up in Paris, where he discovered the dubious delights of cheap hotels.

He went back to minor stage work and also played a walk-on role in Marcel Carné's *Trois Chambres à Manhattan*, literally one day's work that was barely noticed in the finished movie. Thus the first time the filmgoing public would have the opportunity of seeing Robert De Niro was in 1968, in another Brian De Palma film called *Greetings*. It was followed the next year with a sequel entitled *Hi, Mom!* Both were mini-budget affairs and, like *The Wedding Party*, dealt with the currently fashionable topic of the concerns of young people. They were counter-culture movies which in spite of the obvious lack of funds – *Greetings* was made for just $43,000 – produced good vibes for both director and star.

Greetings was quite significant. It was produced by Charles Hirsch, in his early twenties but recently hired by Universal Pictures as a talent director, charged with scouring New York for new actors, writers and directors. He met up with De Palma, and before long they had a script and a star and were producing a picture that helped change the attitude of the Hollywood moguls to small, independently made movies – particularly those aimed at the younger audience but which did not pander to the biker brigade in the wake of *The Wild One*.

In *Greetings*, De Niro played a militant right-winger who suddenly enlists in the army. De Palma recalls that, when he turned up to shoot the scene, he did not recognize him. 'It was make-up and clothes that changed his looks, but it was more than that,' said De Palma. 'He had inhabited the character and become different physically.'

The movie proved to the doubters of the mainstream that it was possible to show a profit with surrealism and slightly eccentric productions, and De Palma's star began to rise. *Greetings* and *Hi, Mom!* were not in that financial league of the surprise independent blockbuster *Easy Rider*, with which Peter Fonda, Dennis Hopper and Jack Nicholson shocked Hollywood by making a movie that cost $400,000 and grossed $35 million. But they were important for the career development of both De Palma and De Niro, arousing interest in their techniques and styles that rose above the serious flaws of the movies themselves.

Hi, Mom!, originally entitled *Son of Greetings* before they had a sensible change of mind, was financed by the producer Martin Ransohoff of Filmways. Ransohoff had just given another trend-setting director, Roman Polanski, his head in the movie that starred his future wife, Sharon Tate – a spoof horror called *The Fearless Vampire Killers*. Polanski later turned on him and called him an 'absolute prick'.

Ransohoff, however, doubled the budget that De Palma had had for *Greetings*, and, as with all Ransohoff pictures of that era, sex and violence were well to the fore. De Niro picked up the character where he had left off in *Greetings*, and now portrayed him as a flamboyant voyeur. At last he became the focus of reviewers, whose reaction was positive, if a touch apprehensive. One critic highlighted his 'terrifying capacity for the depiction of violence-prone individuals', which would become a feature of reviews of De Niro's work in the future.

Both pictures showed freshness, vitality and a good deal of controversy, and the two roles allowed De Niro a free-ranging opportunity to experiment with his Stella Adler-inspired approach. It was the beginning of what would become a feature of his work; whereas many stars remain almost unchanged from one movie to the next, regardless of the role they are playing, he was clearly working at changing himself, not only in personality but also physically, as De Palma had noticed. Even these early efforts in that direction were so convincing that they drew attention to the most practised part of his talent – to move freely into characterizations, which, he would admit, had a direct bearing on his success.

In one of his few interviews, given early in his career before he brought down the shutters on his inner thoughts, he spoke revealingly about what most saw as an obsession with self-immersion. He admitted, in complex language that sounded like a lecture from the Stella Adler conservatory:

> I see each part as a mathematical problem. The character on screen is the solution. What I do is to visualize that end result and then trace it back to the roots to discover how it is arrived at, and that is the point of truth. To totally submerge into a character and experience life through him, without having to experience the real-life consequences . . . well, it's a cheap way to do things that you would never do yourself.

These sequences of backward movement towards reaching the character he was playing were confirmed by playwright-actress Julie Bovasso, who had known De Niro since he was a boy. She would later cast him in her off-Broadway comedy *Schubert's Last Serenade*, and for a time had grave misgivings about having done so. 'During

31

the first week of rehearsals,' she recalls, 'I kept thinking to myself, "Oh, my poor play." But he arrives at his characterizations by a very circuitous route . . . and eventually I could see him making the connections, and in the end he was terrific.'

There was to be one more example of De Niro's early efforts before the end of the sixties, a little-known work that is seldom mentioned and which few have seen. Entitled *Sam's Song*, it was a belated end-of-an-era movie that was made by and starred a clutch of enthusiastic unknowns, most of whom has never been heard of since apart from De Niro himself. It was, as one reviewer complained, 'a bit of a mess' – which was also a bit of an understatement. Somehow or other, a studio had coughed up some decent money to an independent company to get it made, and was probably attracted by its hefty sexual additives. Although filmed in 1969, *Sam's Song* was put on the shelf and lay there gathering dust for years. Two attempts to release it in the 1970s were aborted and it did not see the light of day until 1980, when someone remembered that they had a movie with the now famous Robert De Niro locked away in the vaults. It came out that year but quickly fell by the wayside when the truth became known.

The film then had a second life. It was cut up and used for flashback sequences in a second movie called *The Swap*, with contemporary scenes played by an entirely new cast. Released on video, it was heavily promoted to take advantage of De Niro's presence with a confusing promotional line which read: 'He's tough. He's cool. He's murder on women and they're death on him.' De Niro was furious, but there was nothing he could do. For true De Niro fans, however, it was actually an interesting piece, providing further early examples of the themes and styles he would introduce in later work.

So his entry into the world of the cinema had hardly been a smooth ride. As the seventies dawned he had appeared in four movies and yet was still an unknown, although his mother-hen benefactor, Shelley Winters, was at that very moment attempting to rectify that situation.

3

Momma's Boy

Like his father, who had for years remained locked in his world of surrealist art with his high principles and low income, Robert De Niro had become the classic struggling actor. Almost a decade had passed since his first tentative moves into acting through the Stella Adler conservatory, and there were still no real signs of a breakthrough. He continued to trawl the possibilities of work, mainly in New York, taking minor roles in small halls well off Broadway and occasional television work. His self-imposed apprenticeship continued to dominate him, and it was Brian De Palma who identified it as one of De Niro's built-in flaws.

Although he was obsessively attentive to the detail of his characters, he had little personality in real life. He remained a quiet, retiring young man who spoke little and whose main topic of conversation, to the point of eyelids snapping shut, was the work itself. He would stand back at parties and let others take the high ground, he had no romances of the kind that had made Warren Beatty famous before he even made a picture, and he had not managed to attract the attention of anyone of note in the hierarchies of Broadway or Hollywood. He only came alive, said De Palma, when he was acting, and his opportunities to display this talent had been slender.

Elia Kazan, who had yet to work with De Niro, would make an interesting point in comparing him with the more famous actors of the day. De Niro had to prove himself twice over: first to show that he did possess what was, like it or not, the key to success for most stars – sexual attraction and charisma, and second to show that he could act. Brando, Clift, Dean and the next generation like Paul Newman, Robert Redford and Steve McQueen all had it and went quickly to stardom. They had all known hard times, but their apprenticeship lasted only three or four years and the charisma picked up from audience reaction or through the lens of a camera had as much to do with jolting them out of their obscurity as did their acting ability.

As Kazan noted many times, those stars had a presence which could be felt even in a crowded room. Heads would turn inexplicably towards them. They attracted media attention, which was another crucial ingredient. To be 'a good actor' was a one-dimensional state in Hollywood; casting directors were looking for charisma as well.

De Niro was not alone in this problem. Michael Douglas, a year younger than De Niro, had just arrived in New York in the search for work after graduating from the University of California at Santa Barbara. Douglas found rejection a way of life and only finally broke through in television, with a little help from friends of his father. Even so, it took him years to make it to the big screen with any substantial role, and even then it was more through his own initiative than because he was selected by others. Jack Nicholson, similarly, had been in Hollywood fourteen years and had made twenty films before he became an 'overnight' star in *Easy Rider*. Up to that point, you could walk into any bar on Sunset Strip and ask: 'Is Jack Nicholson here?' and the reply would come back: 'Who?'

Oddly enough it was Roger Corman, king of the cheap exploitation movie made for second features or drive-ins and on which Nicholson and a clutch of other modern film-makers, including Coppola and Scorsese, cut their teeth, who provided De Niro's entrée to Hollywood. Corman's format was well known. He used to boast that he could make a movie in two weeks, though most took a little longer, sometimes even stretching to six weeks. Setting unknown actors, writers and directors who worked for the basic rate alongside low-paid former stars like Vincent Price, Peter Lorre and Boris Karloff, he turned out pictures targeted at particular audiences, moving largely with the market. Corman produced a series of horror movies which included some classics like *Little Shop of Horrors*, biker movies aimed at the youth market, and then hippie era, druggie movies.

In late 1967, in the wake of Warren Beatty's surprise runaway blockbuster *Bonnie and Clyde*, he had a script hurriedly written for a cheap imitation. Based loosely on the outlaw family of the notorious Ma Baker of the 1930s, it was predictably packed with sex, drugs and violence but was equally hurriedly shelved in the wake of the assassinations of Martin Luther King and Robert Kennedy. The project was

34

resurrected a year or so later when Corman was kicking himself that he had turned down *Easy Rider*, sending Peter Fonda and Dennis Hopper into the arms of another independent producer and thus missing a share of $35 million. At the end of 1969, as *Easy Rider* was rattling the box office tills and Warren Beatty had become a millionaire through *Bonnie and Clyde*, he rushed ahead with his gangster movie, entitled *Bloody Mama*, for which he signed Shelley Winters as the star leading a fairly decent cast of experienced actors.

At the time Winters was in one of the less auspicious periods of her career. She had made more than fifty movies and won two Oscars, the first for her role in *The Diary of Anne Frank* in 1959 and the second in 1965 for *A Patch of Blue*. Since the last award she had appeared with Michael Caine in *Alfie* (1966), Paul Newman in *Harper* (also 1966), José Ferrer in Neil Simon's *Enter Laughing* (1967) and with her former lover Burt Lancaster in *The Scalp Hunters* (also 1967), plus three or four other movies.

She had successfully transferred from sexy leading lady to character actress, loud and plump, and made it clear to all who asked that her only wish was to keep working, which in turn sometimes clouded her judgement in selecting scripts. *Bloody Mama* fell into the category of her less prestigious roles, though she fully appreciated that she had been approached to give weight to a straightforward second-bill movie of the kind that had earned Corman his lively cash flow. Exploitative he may have been, but Corman was one of the few producers in Hollywood who could claim that he had never yet lost money on a picture.

Winters agreed, on the proviso that Corman test her protégé Robert De Niro to play one of her four psychopathic sons. She told the director: 'This kid's going to be a big star. When I first saw him on stage, I had tingles down my spine. The way he moves and speaks . . . I haven't seen anything like that since Brando in the 1940s.' When Winters telephoned De Niro with the news she built it up as a major chance – which of course it was for an out-of-work New York actor who had never worked inside a fully functioning film studio, either in Hollywood or anywhere else. Corman's company, American International Pictures, was no MGM or 20th Century-Fox, but, as she pointed out, a lot of people who were now famous had passed through its doors.

Corman duly tested him, and gave him the role of Ma Baker's son Lloyd, the most sadistic of the bunch, who is addicted to morphine

35

and dies before the end. They then had a row over how much De
Niro was being paid – always a delicate matter with Corman, as Jack
Nicholson would readily confirm. De Niro was getting rate pay which
was as low as it could possibly be, but Winters' intervention succeeded
in getting him a rise.

De Niro was ecstatic at landing the part and immediately began
what would become his legendary preparations before playing any role.
He set off alone for Arkansas where the location filming would take
place, carrying with him a tape recorder and notebook to record local
dialects and perfect the accent and speech patterns. Corman said De
Niro put him in mind of Jack Nicholson, who was one of the few
actors to tackle a role with that kind of background research. De Niro
impressed him. By the time the unit was ready to go on location De
Niro had acquired so much local knowledge that Corman, who both
produced and directed the film, used him as a dialogue coach. But
according to Winters, De Niro had overdone his quest for reality by
trying to look like a drug addict.

> It was mostly with the things he did to his body. He can flush
> or turn white just like that, but he also broke out in sores
> which he picked at to make worse. He refused to eat and drank
> only water – he must have lost thirty pounds. Just to look like
> an addict. It made me a nervous wreck. His character, Lloyd,
> was supposed to deteriorate physically, but Bobby got so frail we
> all became alarmed. At night we'd all go out and stuff ourselves,
> and Bobby would just sit, drinking water. When he gets to
> the soul of a character, he refuses to let it go.

In fact, he kept it up to the last. When his character died in *Bloody
Mama*, he gave his fellow actors a huge shock when they gathered
around an open grave in a burial service for him. He had secretly
climbed into the grave and covered himself with earth, so that when
they looked down they would give an honest reaction.

The fact that Winters, who had worked with some of Hollywood's
finest, had taken De Niro under her wing was apparent to all on the
six-week shoot. If the publicists were looking for an angle they had one,
and perhaps it was no surprise that rumours of a romantic involvement
between them started up again. She in turn says that, to her, De Niro
was the son she never had.

Like most Corman cheap and cultist movies, *Bloody Mama* had a successful run. Never intended as an A-list movie, it found its niche in drive-ins and on double-bill features. It also attracted the cries of scorn that often greet Corman productions over its lack of morals, poor attention to authenticity, violence and gratuitous sex. Corman was well used to being dismissed merely as a maker of quick-flicks. But he usually laughed all the way to the bank because in reality his movies were all carefully planned and meticulously, if cynically, tailored and executed. Quality was never the top priority. It was a form of pop art that thumbed its nose at the expensive pretentiousness of the Hollywood establishment, brazenly used sex, sleaze and sadism as selling points, and never overestimated the entertainment require-ments of an audience who for the most part were glimpsing scenes between back-seat clinches.

De Niro was well pleased by the experience and, given the limita-tions of a Corman movie, deserved applause for his harrowing perform-ance of the drug addict Lloyd. Once the reviewers had performed their usual demolition job on Roger Corman, several mentioned him as a young man to watch. A *New York Sunday Times* writer went so far as to say that 'Academy awards have been given away for lesser efforts' than those of De Niro in *Bloody Mama*. So De Niro came away from this movie pleased, not least from the experience of working with Shelley Winters. He would sit talking shop with her for hours. She was a fund of stories and experience, a woman of immense recall in terms of her career and personal life, as she eventually demonstrated with her volumes of autobiography. Since the late 1940s she had covered pretty well every section of the American cinema and theatre, and worked or studied with all the major personalities, directors and moguls. It was Winters who advised more theatre experience and, after filming *Bloody Mama*, De Niro would join the Theater Company of Boston for the 1969–70 repertory season.

Meantime, she continued to act as his patron and, ignoring the toy boy jibes, brought him back to New York to appear in her own theatri-cal production which had been a personal ambition for some time. It was a semi-autobiographical project consisting of three loosely connec-ted but separate plays based upon particular phases of an actress's life. She had entitled it *One Night Stands of a Noisy Passenger* and cast De Niro as the male lead in the third play, called *Last Stand*.

He was to play opposite Diane Ladd, who was cast as an Oscar-winning star whose career was fading. The irony was that for Ladd in real life it was the reverse situation. She was virtually unknown outside

New York. Then thirty-one, she had been around long enough to have dated Warren Beatty on his way to Hollywood ten years earlier, but had yet to make her first picture. Her own arrival in Hollywood still lay in the future, when she was cast in *Chinatown* (1974) by Beatty's chum Roman Polanski. But it was Martin Scorsese, by then De Niro's friend, who shot her to fame in *Alice Doesn't Live Here Anymore* (1975), for which she won an Academy Award nomination for best supporting actress. At the time of her selection for the Winters play in the autumn of 1970 she, like De Niro, was pleased to see any work that came along. As De Niro said, they were both accepting anything and everything offered.

De Niro was cast as Ladd's lover, a bisexual Method actor and karate expert with whom she ends up in bed after an acid trip. He immediately went into preparation mode and within three weeks had become sufficiently expert in karate to be able to chop a board in two with his bare hand for real (instead of having a sawn prop) – all for a fifteen-second sequence on stage.

Rather like Corman, Winters had included samples of the current trends in society as shock tactics for her audience. They included an apparently excessive smattering of expletives, drug scenes and an abundance of sex, as befitting any Hollywood-linked saga. The play opened at the Actors' Playhouse in December 1970. No one disgraced themselves and the notices were rather good in recording individual performances, especially those of De Niro and Diane Ladd, who clearly benefited from scenes with him. 'I worried to start with,' she said, 'because he was such an unusual guy. It was difficult to know what to make of him because he did not give much away. He did not come across at all ebullient or over-confident. He kind of built up to it, like a bricklayer building up his blocks.'

Winters, as enthusiastic as ever, declared that De Niro's perform-ance could be likened to 'watching sexual lightning on stage. Every night was a different performance.' Sadly, however, the New York critics, notorious for their ability to kill a play stone dead, put the boot in. They had never shown any mercy to Hollywood stars returning to Broadway, as Kirk Douglas discovered in 1963 when he presented his own stage version – the original – of *One Flew Over the Cuckoo's Nest*, which attracted the most hostile of reviews. Monty Clift and Maureen Stapleton did not fare well in their revival of *The Seagull*, which is why Brando had avoided going back on stage since he left *A Streetcar Named Desire* to go to Hollywood.

Shelley's under-rated play was given an uneasy reception and, when the midnight editions came in after the preview performance, she declared: 'I've been clobbered and I'm in a daze. Nobody understands my plays.' One critic complained that even the most ardent voyeur would be turned off by 'this trio of tawdry peepshows', while another said Shelley was a terrible dramatist. De Niro consoled her, but the play was further troubled by industrial action in the New York theatres and it closed after seven performances. 'I was so bitter about the experience,' said Winters, 'I have not written another play since.'

De Niro would return intermittently to the stage, though never in a major Broadway production. Between film work in 1971 he performed two one-act plays written by Merle Molofsky, presented under the title of *Kool-Aid* by the Repertory Theatre of Lincoln Center. In 1972 he appeared at the prestigious American Place Theatre in *Billy Bailey and the Great American Refrigerator* and had a leading role in a play written by his friend Julie Bavasso, an absurdist comedy entitled *Schubert's Last Serenade*, which was staged at the Manhattan Theater Club in June 1973. By then, however, his film work was becoming more regular and the theatre was relegated almost to the point of non-existence.

He appeared in three more movies, all filmed during 1971, that did nothing other than give him experience. They were all embarrassing flops, but at last put him on the payroll of mainstream studios. The first one, called *Jennifer on My Mind*, looked on the face of it a promising proposition, one of those Hollywood ventures that have an air of confidence at the beginning but which slowly slip into oblivion by the time they reach the cinema.

Producer Bernard Schwartz called a press conference to announce that he had paid $50,000 for the film rights to a first novel by Roger Simon, entitled *Heir*. 'I am so impressed,' he said, 'I want to make *Heir* the way it is – a real story about two youngsters born into money but who grow up without family affections and go on drugs. It is a story of today. . . .' And cynical, heard-it-all-before representatives of the media put their hands to their mouths to stifle their yawns. Drugs as a topic had already been widely and perhaps definitively covered in *Easy Rider* and Arthur Penn's *Alice's Restaurant* the year before.

Schwartz promptly hired Erich Segal of *Love Story* fame to write the screenplay and changed the title to *Jennifer on My Mind*, thus disassociating it from the novel. An embarrassed De Niro's role was cut to a bit part, and he received nineteenth billing on the credits.

Nothing more needs to be said. The film was a complete disaster, was tried out in just a few cinemas by United Artists and then taken off and dumped, never to be heard of again.

It must be a constant source of wonder to actors who are approached to appear in this kind of project – not to mention the cinema audiences who are expected to turn out – exactly how some of these movies get past the conception stage, let alone to the point where someone in the hierarchy begins writing large cheques. The same applied to De Niro's next, called *Born to Win* – whose title at least had thankfully been changed from the original, *Scraping the Bottom*.

Yet another saga of drug addicts on heroin, it starred Karen Black and George Segal, who was also involved in the management side as co-producer. It was a black comedy with potential that once again was somehow lost *en route*. Czech-born director Ivan Passer, who received over-the-top acclaim for his *Intimate Lighting* in 1965, failed to hit the mark. De Niro's role was a brief contribution and he was probably glad.

His third picture that year looked more promising, if only because his role was more substantial. It too was based upon a novel which had been well received: *The Gang That Couldn't Shoot Straight* by Jimmy Breslin, a reasonably clever ethnic black comedy about a New York Mafia gang who start a cycle race which ends in mass murder. It appealed to De Niro because it was set in Little Italy, an area of New York with which he was thoroughly familiar; but equally enticing was the fact that Al Pacino was originally wanted for the role. Pacino had turned it down in favour of playing Michael Corleone, son of Brando's Vito Corleone, in *The Godfather*. This movie had just gone into production at Paramount, and coincidentally would enable De Niro, in the fullness of time, to be cast as Pacino's father when a young man.

Any similarities between the two projects, however, ended with the word 'Mafia'. *The Gang That Couldn't Shoot Straight* turned out to be a farce and a failure. De Niro was to play the role of a gang member imported from Italy. Although it was by no means a major role, it did not stop him doing major preparatory work. Incredibly he immediately threw a few clothes in a bag, along with his tape recorder, and set off for southern Italy with the sole purpose of perfecting the accent of an English-speaking hood from the lower regions of the Italian boot. It seemed an extravagant way of rehearsing himself, and few people apart from Italians originating from that region would have noticed the difference had his accent slipped. It was more to do with personal satisfaction, and once again he had demonstrated his determination to achieve as near perfection as possible regardless of cost and importance. What mattered to De Niro was getting into the character and knowing that, when he saw himself on screen, it was as authentic as anyone could get.

Actually, it might have mattered more than it did if the movie had been anywhere near decent. But despite a screenplay by Waldo Salt, who had just collected an Oscar for *Midnight Cowboy*, it strayed well away from the book and was turned into a weak and witless production that sank to the lowest form of ethnic comedy and was virtually racist. It drew protests from the Italo-American community who, though quite prepared to laugh at themselves, came out of the cinemas feeling insulted. The critics gave it a deserved roasting, and even the book's author, Jimmy Breslin, was critical too.

There was only one consolation prize, and that was awarded to De Niro himself with another small collection of decent notices; this time, unusually they spelled his name right. His well-prepared, well-rehearsed performance was duly noted, not merely by the critics but by other film-makers too. It would have implications for the future.

As for the trio of duff movies that had fallen to his lot in 1971, he would admit that *The Gang That Couldn't Shoot Straight* was probably the low point of his work to date. He did not become entirely disillusioned, however, and had decided that at worst he would make a decent living as a journeyman actor while at best he might go on to a higher level of achievement. He had the patience to accept that nothing was going to fall into his lap and, in spite of everything, he was sure he was on the right track. There is no question, according to his friends, that the intensity of his study of acting techniques continued to dominate his life above all else, just as his father's determination to follow a particular course in his life had endured his struggle for survival.

De Niro's personal life was quiet by theatrical standards, his relationships few and brief and, to put it mildly, he was still considered to be something of a social oddball. 'He just wasn't showbiz, not at all,' New York character actor Billy LaMassena told me. An old friend of Monty Clift, who for years lived a couple of streets away from De Niro's apartment, he saw him often around the city and at the Actors Studio.

He was not one of the fast crowd. I mean, who could he be, rattling around on a beat-up old bike? He didn't even look like he might be connected with theatre or film, other than perhaps on the technical side. He was so quiet and unassuming, kept out of sight almost. He was the only man I ever knew who seemed as if he had to think before he smiled, as if he was saying to himself, 'Is that funny? Shall I laugh or what?' His laughter never seemed spontaneous, which I always found rather curious.

The personal curiosities were part of the emerging De Niro. They would never leave him, and some of the traits he was displaying then would become more pronounced – like his ability to slip in and out of a crowd without anyone noticing, or to turn up at a party, chat a while and then, when someone said, 'Where's Bobby?' he would be gone. But there was also an element of deliberation in his actions, as if he was forming a character for himself as well as for his screen persona, one he could run with and be comfortable with and even hide behind if he ever became famous. This possibility emerged in several conversations with those who knew him back then, when the dark and slightly mysterious complexities in his character were no less evident than they are thirty years on. De Niro was going to be different, not a Brando clone but a one-off, and if those early observers were right it would be no accident that his public image would become, over the years, as much a product of rehearsal as his screen roles.

The pieces of his personal jigsaw finally began to fall into place in the autumn of 1971, after his year among the turkeys. At that time a husband and wife team of independent producers, Lois and Maurice Rosenthal, were casting their net for a movie called *Bang the Drum Slowly*. Although they had the distribution backing of Paramount Studios they had a fairly modest budget and could not afford A-list actors, so they began looking around New York for their players.

There was a history to *Bang the Drum Slowly*. It first appeared as a novel by Mark Harris in 1956, and a year later was turned into a television playhouse special starring Paul Newman. Since then, the film rights had passed through several hands before ending up in the ownership of the Rosenthals. The story concerns the relationships in a baseball team as one of their number, the dim-witted, tobacco-chewing Bruce Pearson, is diagnosed as suffering from Hodgkin's disease. The producers and the director, John Hancock, were more than meticulous in choosing their cast: given the financial constraints, De Niro read for the Pearson role seven times. He read for the director, the producer, the producer and his wife – and finally got the part, his first leading role in a mainstream movie.

De Niro plotted his course like a chess player, as if knowing from the outset that this was the film that would finally launch him. He decided he had to avoid stereotyping and sentimentality. In doing so, he served up a convincingly unsympathetic character who gradually won everyone's heart. The film was overloaded with tear-jerking scenes, but there was also great potential for subdued comedy. De Niro gave a cool but emotion-drawing performance that attracted many decent notices. He also won the admiration of those with whom he worked, though it was kept strictly on a professional level: they described him as a standoffish personality who, during filming, pretty well kept himself to himself. Director John Hancock recalled, 'He reminded me very much of the way Alec Guinness submerged himself in his roles. Guinness isn't a personality actor, he's a character actor who is also a star, and that's Bobby. The only difference is that De Niro also has evident sexuality, which Guinness never had.'

The media were now beginning to take an interest, and to start with he was relatively calm about giving interviews – though right from the beginning he shied away from personal questions. The magazine *American Film* dropped in to ask how he had managed to give such a convincing performance that had captured the hearts of cinema audiences everywhere. In reply he revealed a few of his trade secrets:

> I went down south with a tape recorder and got local people to go over the whole script with me. I was always watching for little traits that I could use. And then I did all the baseball. We practised in [New York's] Central Park for I think three weeks to a month. When I was in Florida, I practised a lot, even with the batting machines. I also watched ball games on television. You're looking right at the catcher all the time and you can see how relaxed he is, in a sense.

There was other evidence of this intense preparation from Mark Harris, author of both the original novel and the screenplay. Apart from noting De Niro's dedication in learning to play baseball, Harris watched him closely during particular scene takes and was astounded by his actions in one, which required De Niro to have tears in his eyes. He achieved this by plunging his fingers down his throat, practically to the point of making himself vomit. 'He did this not once,' said the

43

writer, 'but forty times to accomplish every "take" and every trial shot.'

Harris also made an interesting comparison between De Niro and his co-star Michael Moriarty, another young actor of the day who showed great promise but then temporarily faded from view. Moriarty, an accomplished pianist, was tall, handsome and gregarious. After work, beside the pool or at the tavern during happy hour, he would be the centre of attention, always drawing a small crowd to him because, said Harris, he was reachable and touchable. People enjoyed his friendliness.

During the evening viewing of the day's rushes Moriarty would be there, attentive, discussing, enquiring. But where was De Niro? Said Harris,

> From De Niro's point of view, a roomful of tense people watching the rushes was the gateway to hell. He cared nothing for all that jabbering, all that speculation. Such a scene was pointless. Superfluous. Whether De Niro had sufficient confidence to ignore the rushes, or too little to risk exposure to torrents of talk, I could not decide. For whatever reason, he remained in his room studying. If not studying, alone. If not alone, fabulously discreet.

Though filming was completed by early 1972, the movie was not released until 1973. In March that year De Niro won his first major accolade: the New York Film Critics' Award for best supporting actor for his performance in *Bang the Drum Slowly*, and at the presentation people spoke in glowing terms about how much more was expected of him.

By then, that promise was already a certainty. De Niro was about to explode upon the screen in the movie that gave him international status, and it came about almost by accident. At Christmas 1971 writer Jay Cocks and his actress wife, Verna Bloom, gave a party at which the guests included Robert De Niro and Martin Scorsese. Although they had both spent most of their youth and adult lives close to each other in Greenwich Village and the wider village that is Manhattan, Scorsese and De Niro had only come across each other briefly in their early teens, and the memories were vague.

'Hey,' said Scorsese, 'I know you . . . didn't you used to run with a gang on Kenmare Street?'

'Yeah . . . well . . . perhaps . . . I don't know,' said De Niro.

'Yeah . . .' said Scorsese, 'I remember you.'

But Scorsese had to admit that he had never seen any of De Niro's films. He had never seen him act. Nor for that matter did De Niro know much about Scorsese. Up to that point in his career he had not made a feature film, but he was in fact working on a project at that very moment – called *Mean Streets*.

De Niro's eyebrows rose slightly, '*Mean Streets*, huh?'

4

Enter Scorsese

Martin Scorsese was, like De Niro, on the brink of coming to fame in 1972, the year of his thirtieth birthday. To look back upon his output from a distance of thirty years is to view the work of a man who had contributed much to modern cinema with movies that are uniquely distinctive in style and form. His list of credits is impressive and influential and, although few have been as commercially successful as Hollywood blockbusters or the output of contemporaries such as Steven Spielberg, George Lucas or Francis Ford Coppola, none of his films can be considered unworthy of acclaim or merit. Furthermore, they are movies that generally stand the test of time, to be brought out again and again down the decades.

From that standpoint, Scorsese's meeting with De Niro at Jay Cocks' Christmas party marked the beginning of an important collaboration from which both men would profit, and De Niro especially would derive great benefit in his progression as an actor. In fact, their very first project together took them both from obscurity to moderate fame in one move. It was a coming together of two men of similar minds who, in the coming years, became, in Scorsese's words, as 'close as Siamese twins emotionally and professionally'.

Scorsese admits that, like De Niro, he is an obsessive man who pursues his goals on a very personal level; mainstream Hollywood directors, on the other hand, want to please the money men and always have one eye on the box office. From his youth he formed a view of movie-making that would evolve around his fascination with characters rather than with stories. It was born out of being glued to the television and cinema screens in his childhood, and although his movies feature flawed, violent and freakish characters, his personal background did not put him in touch with such people.

46

The young Scorsese was a sickly child whose chronic asthma kept him confined to home and seldom allowed him to roam the smoggy fifties' streets. His parents bought their first television set when he was six and, through his situation, he became addicted to it. The family, like De Niro's, was of Italian immigrant origin. Scorsese himself was born in Flushing, New York, in 1942, but his family returned to its roots when he was ten and he spent his adolescence in the Little Italy quarter of New York, not far from De Niro's home.

Unlike De Niro's bohemian parents the Scorsese family were deeply religious. At the age of fourteen Martin decided to become a Catholic priest, although he was unable to pursue that ambition because of his poor school record. Catholicism and religion would instead become a regular theme of his films, and, turning to what he knew best through the 'education' he had given himself, in due course he enrolled as a student of film at New York University. He wrote scripts for and directed a number of award-winning shorts. His first full-length feature, *Who's That Knocking at My Door?* (1969) was a mini-budget picture which, in spite of its crudity and amateurish attempt to follow the styles of the European New Wave directors Truffaut and Godard, contained the promise that he later fulfilled. After working as assistant director on the classic pop music documentary *Woodstock* (1970), he too went for some postgraduate training with Roger Corman, who was producing yet another imitation of *Bonnie and Clyde*, his 1972 *Boxcar Bertha*.

Just as De Niro had his first screen hit with Corman's *Bloody Mama*, Scorsese turned in a very competent directorial debut with this tale of Depression era train robbers with a twenty-three-year-old Barbara Hershey in the title role, and elevated it beyond the normal B-movie status of Corman's output. Corman was so happy with the result that he offered Scorsese another movie to direct, called *I Escaped from Devil's Island*. But Scorsese turned it down because he wanted to do his own, more personal portraits. By then he was also working on an idea for what would become his first style-setting movie, the one that would show his hand completely. While at New York University he had made a short film in 1964 entitled *It's Not Just You, Murray*. It was about an Italian street kid, and it was this theme that he developed as he wrote the first draft of a screenplay called *Mean Streets*, a sequel to *Who's That Knocking at My Door?*

He had completed the script with co-writer Mardik Martin five years earlier, but had been unable to find a backer until Coppola's first

47

instalment of *The Godfather*, with Brando leading its all-star cast, revived interest in Mafia stories. He was, however, still unable to find money through the conventional Hollywood circles and eventually convinced Bob Dylan's manager, Jonathon Taplin, to put up the bulk of the cash. The financial constraints were still the same as working for Corman. In order to keep within the modest budget of $400,000, filming had to be completed in under thirty days – a feat of which even Corman would have been proud.

Scorsese was in the middle of the planning stages when he came across De Niro at that Christmas party. He found him, as others had done, standoffish and reticent. But as soon as Scorsese began talking about *Mean Streets* De Niro opened up, and the two of them haven't stopped talking since. Scorsese believes that the rapport came from an understanding born out of their background. 'We were both brought up in the same area, and we see things the same way. I think, also, we both had a sense of being outsiders.'

The characters of *Mean Streets* became the focal point of that first conversation. Scorsese outlined the leading character, Johnny Boy. Within seconds, De Niro was describing to him what kind of hat the character would wear and the way it would tilt on his head. But actress Julie Cameron, then Scorsese's wife, believes that the two men discovered a common bond that went much deeper than the mere location of their upbringing: 'De Niro found in Martin the one person who would talk for fifteen minutes on the way a character would tie a knot. That's what drew them together, and since then I have seen them go at it for ten hours virtually non-stop.'

And so began one of the most enduring and significant actor–director partnerships in modern cinema history. Their first movie together would also be an important signpost for the future, and its styles and acting would be widely mimicked and plagiarized in the ensuing years.

Although he had managed to prise only $400,000 out of backers, Scorsese's little movie, along with Peter Fonda and Dennis Hopper's *Easy Rider* which was made for the same sum, hammered the final nails into the coffin of the old Hollywood studio system. The great and the good of the movie industry were both angry and fascinated by the work of these subversive upstarts from the film schools and the independent production companies that were sprouting like wild grass. Dennis Hopper would not be taken seriously for years because of his eccentric social habits, but some of the more stable talents were already being courted by mainstream Hollywood. Coppola, who won an Oscar for his script of *Patton* in 1969, was the Trojan horse of the new wave of American film. With *The Godfather* he unlocked the gates to the Hollywood sanctuaries and let the rest of them in.

It was also ironic that in Scorsese De Niro had found a collaborator who would never pander to the Hollywood expectations of conformity to the star syndrome and to the well-tried and -tested theories of movie-making which centred around the art of the star-spangled spectacular. Even Coppola's outstandingly successful *The Godfather* had merged older stars, such as Brando, Sterling Hayden and Richard Conte, with the new breed represented by Al Pacino, James Caan and Diane Keaton, and splattered the whole with a hefty measure of spectacle plus a multi-million dollar budget.

Scorsese's technique followed the more minimalist style of the French New Wave, and to some degree Roman Polanski at his best – *Knife in the Water* or *Chinatown*, in that he focused on the movie as a whole, to be read like a book. The stars were important, true, but less for who they were than for their skill at achieving the characterization required by the story.

This is what De Niro found so enthralling about working with Scorsese, as indeed did Jack Nicholson with Polanski. It provided the opportunity for total immersion; this was fine for the actor, of course, but could be deadly boring for the viewer if the movie, like a slow novel, didn't come alive. In this case it would. *Mean Streets* consumed both them and Harvey Keitel, De Niro's co-star, who had played the lead in *Who's That Knocking at My Door?* In that film Keitel's character, Charlie, was on the brink of life as a minor gangster. Now, with all his guilt complexes stemming largely from his Catholic upbringing (about which Scorsese would write with authority), he is plunged into a world of confusion as he pursues his upwardly mobile 'business' activities. De Niro preferred that role to his own character, but Scorsese wanted to offer some continuity to those who might remember the previous movie. In reality, therefore, De Niro was the supporting actor to Harvey Keitel, although he eventually stole the picture. In their roles as two young mafiosi Keitel is the foil to the violence and ruthless desperation of De Niro's character, the ignorant, fast-tempered Johnny Boy. Unlike Brando, Caan and Pacino in Mario Puzo's hugely expansive *Godfather* saga, they play two small-time hoods in a strictly localized story in an area of New York that was very familiar to De Niro and Scorsese.

Mean Streets was never going to be a straightforward gangster movie, but concentrated on the small-world environment in which the characters evolve in their macho male bonding at Tony's Bar, the location of all the drinking, womanizing, brawling and hustling. The movie becomes a penetrating, sensitive and at times sympathetic account of the seedy low-life that operates beneath the level of activity portrayed in *The Godfather*. The result is not so much a conventional dramatized story as a fly-on-the-wall observation of the daily lives of the principal characters. Scorsese's cameras create visual impact through the realism of ordinary locations – sleazy nightclubs, bars, houses, immersed in almost lurid lighting effects with garish colours and accompanied by loud rock 'n' roll music from the sixties.

What made this aspect of the movie even more of an achievement was the fact that, because of budget limitations, Scorsese was able to spend only six days filming on location in New York. The rest was shot in just over three weeks in the sets constructed on a Hollywood soundstage, using virtually the same crew that Scorsese had used on Corman's *Boxcar Bertha*. He even gave Corman a subtle tribute in his portrayal of a 42nd Street cinema where a Corman double bill was always playing.

The rush to film produced some obvious jerky flaws, but, though it could be criticized in this and a number of other directions, especially for its lack of a core story and its relentless sordid melodrama, *Mean Streets* was an original of its time. It was a totally naturalistic movie which would take on the aura of a famous painting to be emulated and imitated by fakers and copyists. But for all film buffs, and for fans of De Niro and Scorsese in particular, it became essential viewing.

The performances of the principals were outstanding, and De Niro's pathological, maniacal Johnny Boy positively exploded on to the screen. But the reviewers were not unanimous in their praise, and New Yorkers themselves did not flock to see it. The city's social problems were evident enough. Crime on the streets was increasing as the drug scene, created largely by the Mafia, took off with the massive importation of heroin via the French Connection and the Sicilian gangs. Scorsese's movie was perhaps a little too realistic for some palates, as indeed was the language which shocked audiences still unused to such a torrent of four-letter words.

Coppola's *The Godfather*, which had come to the screens the previous year, was a shadowy, distant reality to the viewing public, like the Mafia itself. They always knew it was there, but for most people it was a subject to be read about or as seen on TV. *Mean Streets*, on the other hand, was real urban violence as it happened, real language, real settings, real decay, right in the heart of their city; and most New Yorkers did not, at that time, want to confront or even acknowledge it.

As the movie made its way around the world, the realism had less meaning. In Britain it was viewed more or less as an art film, and, given only a limited release in April 1974, looked as if it would disappear without trace. It might have done but for the tenacity of a one-man distribution company run by Peter Hayden, who saw *Mean Streets* at the Cannes Film Festival and was deeply moved by it. He sold virtually everything he possessed, including his home, to raise money to buy the British rights, and then spent almost a year trying to get it back into mainstream cinemas. It wasn't until late 1976 that he succeeded and, to the great joy of Scorsese, managed to secure a re-release. It then ran for twenty-five weeks in central London.

This mixed reaction to the realism of *Mean Streets* did not, however, detract from the reception of De Niro, finally, as an outstanding actor of the modern age. Praise was heaped upon him from most quarters: 'intensely appealing', 'wild and strong' and 'bravura acting'. Inevitably there were detractors, and some critics who examined De Niro's performance compared him unfavourably with other exponents of naturalism. Foster Hirsch, in the *New York Sunday Times*, insisted:

De Niro is a virtuoso actor, but as Johnny Boy, he's not an original. The territory has already been staked out, classically, by Marlon Brando in *On the Waterfront*. De Niro uses the same slum-drenched diction, the same restless, shifting movements, the same distracted sidelong glances . . . but his work, for all its terrific pace and energy, for all its bravura histrionics, is marked indelibly as Brando imitative. [His] performance is too studied, too influenced by too many movies.

There were a number of back-handed compliments in the *Times* piece, and for De Niro it was the first of many comparisons with one of his own idols, Brando. There was every reason to make such comparisons. Their acting tutorials had followed much the same course, and often with the same tutors. It was, though, a golden rule at the schools of Method acting that there should be no attempts to imitate star performers. When Brando saw James Dean in *East of Eden* he remarked memorably: 'That kid is using my last year's clothes and my last year's talent.' Even so, for De Niro to be compared to Brando at all demonstrated the quantum leap De Niro had made with that picture, and the fact had not been missed by those who had the power to promote him further.

Brando had been through a bad patch in the sixties, and Francis Ford Coppola's invitation to take the lead in *The Godfather* came when he was low on cash and being offered fewer and fewer good scripts because of his 'attitude' and expanding waistline. He had taken on several dire movies and treated them all with complete cynicism, seldom bothering to learn his lines: he had to have cue cards plastered everywhere, in one famous instance stuck to another actor's forehead. The magnetism that had set Broadway alight in 1947 as Stanley Kowalski in *A Streetcar Named Desire*, and then in Kazan's movie, was a memory aroused only occasionally by the reshowing of the movie on television. Before Coppola made the call he was being written off as a mixed-up has-been. But *The Godfather* provided him with the opportunity to demonstrate his powers through a character whose physical appearance matched his own, and it arrived at just the moment when he needed a return ticket to commerciality and credibility. The point at which all this affected De Niro was in the aftermath of *The Godfather*, when the sequel was being planned following the international success of the first movie.

Between his debut as a writer/director in 1961 and *The Godfather* Coppola had made half a dozen movies; none, however, had set the world alight, apart from his Oscar-winning script for *Patton*, aided by the performance of George C. Scott. Probably the best known of Coppola's directorial efforts was *Finian's Rainbow*, a screen version of the Broadway hit musical which flopped in every respect. As the 1960s ended Coppola was determined to go his own way and, with George Lucas, opened a studio called American Zoetrope – Greek for 'life in movement'. The aim was to establish a film company run by creative talents and free of business and bureaucrats – a philosophy which, according to the Hollywood establishment, was a recipe for bankruptcy.

It was a wonderful ideal, of course, and one shared by Scorsese, Spielberg, half a dozen other young film-makers and eventually De

Niro himself. But for Coppola, then thirty-three, the dream was put temporarily on hold when Robert Evans, thrusting new production head of Paramount Studios, made him an offer he could not refuse. Evans, brought in by the new owner of Paramount, Charlie Bludhorn, to bring the studio back into profit and among the Oscars, was keen to acquire the assistance of several New Wave directors so long as they more or less conformed to his requirements. This Polanski discovered on *Rosemary's Baby* and *Chinatown*, as did Sidney Lumet when making *Serpico* with Al Pacino, and Coppola on *The Godfather*. In return, Evans provided ample budgets and stars aplenty. Despite all the ballyhoo about setting up his own untainted production company, Coppola insisted that signing for Evans was not a sell-out – 'not commercialism at all'.

By the time *Mean Streets* appeared Evans and Coppola were talking about the *Godfather* sequel, which would include flashback sequences to the early life of Vito Corleone as a reaction to audience interest in the origins of the story. What Coppola had now realized was that his first movie had given a far too romantic image to the gangster family of Vito Corleone, whose character Brando had equipped with a noble, almost irresistible charm. The flashbacks would be used to balance this image.

In *The Godfather*, for instance, Corleone's youngest son, Michael, played by Al Pacino, was the war hero whom his father did not want to enter the family business, but was forced into it by the activities of a corrupt police chief whom he assassinated. This scene was heavily milked to give the audiences cause for sympathy, and again later when Michael found true love while hiding in Sicily, only to see his new wife blown up. Brando himself portrayed the Mafia chief as an almost reluctant gangster who wanted nothing to do with the burgeoning drugs trade and who, after the assassination attempt on him by rivals, became the epitome of a venerable old New York gentleman living out his last days doing nothing more dangerous than pruning the apple trees and playing hide and seek with his grandson.

Elements like this, in spite of the overwhelming violence that ran through the movie, combined to provide a highly romanticized portrayal of a leading Mafia family which, as more modern history has shown us, could not have been further from the truth. Coppola recognized this and had already decided to correct this impression in *The Godfather Part II* by recounting the early life of the central character Vito Corleone. This in turn would need an actor who in style and presence could be considered a young Vito, in other words a young Brando.

Coppola was originally very keen that Brando himself should play the role; he had no doubts that, if it was within Brando's capability to play a much older man, likewise he could turn the clock back. But by then Brando, whose fading career Coppola had rescued, was back in demand again; restored to his usual cantankerous self, he was demanding a hefty fee. Coppola felt badly let down. 'When we discussed the sequel early on the project really excited him. He came up with some terrific ideas. Then he and Paramount had a big falling out on money, and he was no longer available.'

Evans and Coppola ran through many names. Warren Beatty, who had turned down the Al Pacino role in the first movie, was always a contender. So was Jack Nicholson, especially given his current acclaim in *The Last Detail*, and just possibly Dustin Hoffman, who had also been in the running for the Pacino role first time around. After that, the names began to dry up. De Niro was on the list by virtue of his performance in *Bang the Drum Slowly*, which was distributed by Paramount, but the great question mark over him was that he was still virtually unknown: critical reaction to *Bang the Drum Slowly* and then *Mean Streets* had not yet filtered through. In fact, he too had been considered for one of the lesser roles in *The Godfather*, but had asked to be released when he was offered the lead in *The Gang Who Couldn't Shoot Straight*, which Pacino had just turned down in favour of *The Godfather*.

Coppola and Evans had a private viewing of *Mean Streets*, after which Coppola called his friend Scorsese who told him De Niro was a natural; so he got the part without so much as a screen test. It was the biggest moment of De Niro's life, and he immediately threw himself into the preparation. Coppola himself was faced with a tight filming schedule, to be completed in eight months in various parts of the world including several locations in America. While he began the initial scenes with Al Pacino, De Niro took himself off to Sicily with his tape recorder and began his own search for the character he was to portray.

He flew first to the capital, Palermo, and then travelled up into the hills to the town of Corleone which had given its name to the family. A place of twelve thousand inhabitants, it truly gave birth to the most virulent clan of mafiosi in criminal history, who provided the real-life supreme head of the Mafia in a blood-soaked period of Sicilian history which was already in full swing when De Niro arrived. The Corleonesi were bidding for total domination of the Mafia and the international heroin traffic. A man named Luciano Liggio was about to be given several life sentences, having been found guilty of dozens of murders. His right-hand man, Salvatore Toto Riina, would succeed him and eventually force the Mafia worldwide into recognizing him as its head.

While his own experiences on the fringes of Little Italy had played a part in his ability to take on these ethnic qualities, his experiences in Sicily would provide him with a dimension of fear that he had never experienced before. The *Godfather* movie was already well known in those parts, and De Niro perhaps did not realize the extent of the danger he was in. His visits to the province of Trapani and the coastal town of Castellamare del Golfo brought him to the birthplace of some of the American Mafia's most famous gangsters, and indeed to the heart of the Mafia bosses who ran Sicily. 'I told people honestly why I was there,' De Niro would say later. 'And although they are very cordial to tourists, Sicilians have a way of watching without appearing to watch. They scrutinize you, and you don't even know it.'

But the watchers were being watched by De Niro. He was making notes of their facial expressions, the eyes and mouths of those to whom he spoke, and, as always, taping to get the dialect. When he returned to America he stunned the Sicilian consultant on the movie, Romano Pianti, by his command of the language and the nuances he had picked up.

Next, he studied Brando himself. Whereas some actors might have been tempted to disregard the original characterization of Don Vito Corleone and start afresh, De Niro chose to do the opposite. He began dissecting Brando's performance by replaying *The Godfather* over and over, and switching back to particular scenes to find the threads of his own character creation. It enabled him in the end to play Vito Corleone, not Brando playing that role. The Brando nuances were important, but they were to be absorbed into his own immersion into the character. He would explain: 'I did not want to do a Brando imitation, but at the same time I had to make the character realistic enough to be viewed as Brando/Corleone as a young man.'

Coppola's view was sympathetic to what De Niro had in mind, and they held constant discussions to the point that the director himself wondered if the actor was going too far. His screen time in *The Godfather Part II*, after all, comprised only a relatively short sequence. It was, however, a pivotal part from which the whole of the *Godfather* story really flowed: the audience were now to discover how this fictional figure entered his life of crime at the turn of the century when the Mafia, then known as the Black Hand, emerged among the Italian ghettos of New York.

The result was a spellbinding performance, noted particularly for the scenes in which he spoke in Sicilian dialect. He did so with a fluency and ease that convinced audiences that he was a natural-born Sicilian, at the same time dealing with his English-speaking lines in the precise and cautious manner of a man for whom it was not his first language.

His performance was heightened by the superb production qualities achieved by Coppola and his cinematographer Gordon Willis, in which De Niro's Vito came to life in a setting which brilliantly captured the atmosphere of the period. De Niro, like Brando, would be accepted by the audience as he began his career of Mafia Godfather not as a gangster but as a local hero, whose clinical killing of the existing Godfather would be seen as quite defensible. And in that respect, the romanticism that Coppola had established in the original *Godfather* movie would be perpetuated. It would be left to the sequences involving Al Pacino, as Michael, gradually to dismember that notion as the film weaves its way through its three hours and twenty minutes' running time.

The De Niro sequences in *The Godfather Part II* remain among the most memorable of all in the *Godfather* trilogy, and the critics heaped generous adjectives upon him. There were detractors who complained that the shadow of Brando hung over his performance to the degree that it turned into an impersonation, yet that was never true.

Although less successful at the box office than the first of the three, *The Godfather Part II* received an equal number of nominations for Academy Awards, nine in all, and gained twice as many Oscars. And the necessity to compare Brando and De Niro continued as far as the 1975 awards ceremony. The role of Vito Corleone remained an attraction to the selectors: Brando had won Best Actor in 1972, and De Niro was nominated for Best Supporting Actor for the sequel.

In fact it was a vintage year for modernistic talent, a kind of coming together of some of the most distinctive film-makers and actors of that era. Coppola himself, for example, had two films in the nominations for Best Picture: *The Godfather Part II*, which he produced and directed, and *The Conversation*, the absorbing, Kafkaesque suspense drama starring Gene Hackman which he had written, produced and directed that same year. He was vying in the category for Best Picture with his good friend Roman Polanski (after whom he named his son) who was in the list with *Chinatown*, starring Jack Nicholson – who was nominated as Best Actor.

That year the list of nominations for Best Director included Coppola, Polanski, John Cassavetes with *A Woman Under the Influence*, Bob Fosse for *Lenny* and François Truffaut for *Day For Night* – a veritable feast of directorial talent won by Coppola. Even Martin Scorsese was represented, when Ellen Burstyn won an Oscar for her leading role in his squalid, foul-mouthed but absolutely captivating slice of Americana, *Alice Doesn't Live Here Anymore*. Seldom has such a diversity of influential movie-makers been brought together at one time in that establishment arena.

There was strong competition in De Niro's category. Fred Astaire was up for Best Supporting Actor for his role in *The Towering Inferno*, while Jeff Bridges was listed for his performance in *Thunderbolt and Lightfoot*. But most interestingly, De Niro was also up against two actors from his own movie: Michael V. Gazzo, who played Frankie Pentangeli, and Lee Strasberg for his role as the ageing crime boss Hyman Roth.

Thus Strasberg, mentor of the Method whose work at the Actors Studio had influenced Brando and De Niro himself, found himself competing with one of the 'young punks' who used to sit before him as an observer of his acting classes. And it was something of a consolation to him that, if he had to be beaten, it would be by one of his own – and so it would be. Strasberg bowed to the new young master and applauded his talent, telling him, 'You did right not to try to imitate Brando.' He said it was evident that De Niro had gone back to zero, creating mannerisms and expressions that would later have evolved into those used by Brando. 'It required an incredible precision, but he did it,' he said.

Two further similarities between Brando and De Niro were recorded that night. First, neither turned up for the ceremony – though, unlike Brando, De Niro did not reject the award, which was collected on his behalf by Coppola. Even so, his reaction was typically low-key: 'A lot of people get Oscars who don't deserve them,' he told an interviewer, 'so it makes you a little cynical. Thrilled? I don't know . . . but it can change your life.' Brando himself added a footnote to the whole business. After watching *The Godfather Part II* he told an associate: 'De Niro is the most talented actor working today. I doubt if he knows how good he really is.'

5

Roman Adventure

As author Mark Harris had observed during the making of *Bang the Drum Slowly*, Robert De Niro's private life was conducted with discretion and even decorum. Although his name was becoming more widely known among the New York media, he provided virtually nothing in the way of gossip, shunning the brash film people who populated the avenues of Manhattan in the early seventies. His was a close circle of friends, made up largely of people whom he had met in recent times as his movie career began to take off. He maintained a fairly anonymous lifestyle centred on a cheap apartment in Greenwich Village, and it was only these close friends who were aware of his relationship with a young, aspiring black actress, singer and model called Diahnne Abbott, whose own career so far had been more of a struggle than her lover's.

Diahnne had the looks of a classic Afro-American beauty, and the familiar adjective 'stunning', used of her later by the media barely did her justice. Tall and willowy, she walked like a ballerina and had a singing voice that ought in itself to have won her fame. But, as she herself explained, it was harder for women to get a break than men, especially so for black actresses, because mainstream movies were at that time about white people; blacks were usually a token inclusion, seldom in star roles. Even in the so-called enlightened nineties, the number of black actresses who hit the major league can be amply accommodated on the fingers of one hand.

When she and De Niro first met, they were both struggling. She was supporting her then six-year-old daughter from a previous marriage by working as a waitress between jobs, and it was at a restaurant off Washington Square that she met him. She recalls:

At first, it was a very offhand situation. I did not take to him at all. But I was attracted by his quietness, a very gentle approach. It was one of those developing things of mutual attraction, born out of his persistence. He kept ringing up for dates. When I was trying to get work as a model, the girls in that business were obsessed by meeting men with money. It was a nice thought, but I wasn't into that, otherwise I would have turned Bobby down flat. Whatever our friendship was based upon, it certainly wasn't a starry-eyed, romantic vision of a Hollywood lifestyle. At the time, that wasn't even on the horizon for either of us.

Friends say that what especially attracted De Niro to Diahnne, apart from her exotic beauty, was her commitment to her career, which had continued in spite of some hard times that had made her better known on Tenth Street as a waitress than as an actress. She also understood that he had to spend a lot of time alone pursuing his work, and she was never possessive. 'From the beginning it was a fairly casual, open arrangement,' she admits. 'We both had our own views on life, and they did not mean we had to pin each other down.'

By the very nature of De Niro's priorities their relationship was spasmodic, but it was passionate in their sexual attraction. He would go off on his preparation jaunts and she would not see him for weeks. And then he would turn up, 'in character . . . so wrapped up in a role that you would not know him; he was capable of changing even his physical appearance'. Diahnne adds: 'Although I thought he was marvellous, I'll be frank and say that when I first knew him I did not expect him to become a star. But gradually, I could see he was so obsessive about his work that he just had to succeed.'

That success was signposted even before he had won his Oscar for *The Godfather Part II*. Word travelled quickly. At the end of 1974 Robert De Niro found himself in the 'star' arena, and from then on never stopped working. Scripts and offers were coming in fast, and from people he did not even know.

He was particularly intrigued by one project which fascinated him beyond measure, a script for *Taxi Driver* which would ultimately become his second collaboration with Martin Scorsese. At the time it was in an embryonic stage. Producers Julia and Michael Phillips were still trying to raise the money to finance the movie that everyone said would never get made. They even had to be talked into hiring De

Niro and Scorsese by the author of the screenplay, Paul Schrader. Months of horse-trading lay ahead before they were able to proceed.

Mike Nichols, currently trying to recapture his earlier success, also wanted him for a Neil Simon screenplay entitled *Bogart Slept Here*, while the famed Hollywood producer Sam Spiegel sent him a script based upon F. Scott Fitzgerald's unfinished novel *The Last Tycoon*, which was to be directed by Elia Kazan. Other projects landed on his doormat with increasing frequency. He had to abandon his philosophy of accepting any work that came along, because he had suddenly become an actor with choices and the opportunity to work with some of the most acclaimed directors of the era.

One of them, the brilliant and stylish Bernardo Bertolucci, had already booked his services for his own long-awaited new film. It followed the outstanding and controversial success of his *Last Tango in Paris*, the movie best remembered for its scenes with Marlon Brando and Maria Schneider which introduced audiences across the world to male–female buggery with the aid of a dollop of best butter. The new movie, too, would co-star Maria Schneider, although that's where the similarity ended. The prospect of working with Bertolucci held an obvious appeal for De Niro, not least because of the Brando connections which added a kind of intrigue to the whole project.

Bertolucci himself was a director well studied by modern mainstream actors, although the Hollywood money-men were wary of his politics and the 'art' prefix to his work. His most outstanding venture prior to *Last Tango* had been *The Conformist*, a gripping if occasionally confusing drama set in 1938 which told of a young man trying to conform to Fascism.

His new project, *Novecento (1900)*, was a mixture of elements from both movies, historical and explicit. As a member of the Italian Communist Party Bertolucci used his craft to explore the tension between politics, sex and violence, those three fashionable topics of the 1970s at a time when political corruption was the subject of a glut of Hollywood movies in the wake of Watergate and when the boundaries of explicitness were being pushed ever outwards.

The success of *Last Tango* allowed Bertolucci the freedom to pursue what otherwise might have been a difficult project to launch. It was a huge Marxist epic for which, as well as his two stars, he put together a package of top names including Orson Welles, Donald Sutherland and Sterling Hayden as well as French newcomer Gerard Depardieu. Then he trotted off to Hollywood in search of financial backing.

Impressed by a sex-ridden script that had possibilities of out-shocking even *Last Tango*, and by the financial results of that movie, three Hollywood studios, Paramount, 20th Century-Fox and United Artists, agreed to cough up $2 million each. Bertolucci was up and running, with a confidence which may well have been somewhat misplaced. As he later admitted: 'After *The Conformist*, I was convinced I could make anything that came into my head. I was swamped with ideas and projects . . . and *Novecento* exploded within me.'

The script, co-authored by Bertolucci himself, was an extravagant, studious documentary of Italian history from the turn of the century, spiced by an abundance of sexual activity. The focus was on two boys born in the year 1900: Alfredo, played by De Niro, is the scion of a wealthy landowning family, while Olmo (Depardieu) is an illegitimate peasant child. They become the best of friends, and then bitter enemies. Through their lives Bertolucci sets out to chart the social turbulence of twentieth-century Italy, with all its internal strife and political upheaval. And, as a man with a vision of this historical pageant fixed in his own mind, he naturally wanted to see it portrayed with precision. In doing so, he overloaded both De Niro and Depardieu with heavy political baggage.

It was, sadly, one of those works that hover somewhere between genius and disaster, undermined in part by a troubled production followed by terrible squabbling over money and the final cut. For De Niro it provided an insight into the machinations of European cinema – a situation that many of his colleagues have explored and walked away from with considerable unease.

Indeed, that unease was evident among the assembled cast from the outset of what Bertolucci described as 'my great adventure'. Daily script rewrites and clashes of temperament brought early casualties. Orson Welles, strong-willed and never short of expletives, was replaced by Burt Lancaster, who arrived with memories of playing the Sicilian nobleman in Luchino Visconti's 1963 movie *The Leopard*, a work of brilliance in its original form but later massacred by re-editing and commercialization in the USA. Lancaster was said to be so pleased at the opportunity that he offered to work for nothing.

Soon afterwards Maria Schneider, whom Bertolucci had plucked from nowhere and turned into a reluctant star, found the demands of the script all too much. Weighing heavily on her mind also was the one thing she feared so much about her new life of dubious notoriety – that she should be perceived as a sex symbol. Already in emotional turmoil as a result of the clamouring media circus which had tracked her every move since *Last Tango*, she had become a virtual recluse and loudly proclaimed that Bertolucci was guilty of gross exploitation of her body. In spite of his spirited defence in the name of art – always a debatable topic when big money is at stake – she marched off the set and never returned. Bertolucci replaced her with Stefania Sandrelli, who had featured in his film *The Conformist*.

They finally went into production in June 1974 on location at Parma and then at Rome's Cinecittà studios. De Niro found the experience – if not the movie – an education. Unlike some of his colleagues, he enjoyed Bertolucci's intensity, although their opinions often differed over De Niro's meticulous character creation techniques. Bertolucci admitted, as other directors have done, that initially he had some grave misgivings about the actor's ability. 'The first few days were a nightmare,' he said, 'and I had to keep telling myself that what I felt about him when I first met him was so strong that I could not possibly be wrong. This was certainly true. You cannot judge him by the first few days. He's a very sensitive actor and probably a neurotic person, so a director can be fooled. But if one has patience, well, it's worth it.'

Bertolucci would often call a halt and rewrite the script overnight to accommodate the 'realism' that emerged as the actors played their roles. In Gerard Depardieu De Niro found a kindred spirit in almost every respect. He too was a new star in his homeland whose acting, like De Niro's, relied more on ability than charisma. He had none of the good looks of some of his French counterparts, and possessed those maverick qualities that set him apart and eventually brought him to the attention of mainstream US film-makers.

Depardieu and De Niro were also willing students of Bertolucci's own techniques. This was especially important for De Niro, who has always maintained that he has to have dialogue with his director. On this film, much of which was in the director's head, it was doubly important. The interpretations of the historical background were entirely Bertolucci's, and the diversions such as the sex scenes were not only explicit but verged upon the psychologically disturbing.

De Niro and Depardieu, for example, were supposed to have sex with a girl who was suffering from an epileptic fit. In another scene, the characters of young Alfredo and Olmo are discovered naked in masturbation. Donald Sutherland is involved in a scene in which he sleeps with and then kills a young boy. Even Burt Lancaster is fondled by a young girl, and the female members of the cast, Dominique Sanda and Stefania Sandrelli, are variously revealed in nude sequences.

Another of Bertolucci's admissions on the making of his epic sent shivers down the spines of the Hollywood money men:

> *Novecento* turned from an epic into an interminable film
> because some films are destined to materialize the childish
> fantasies of omnipotence a director may hold . . . which favours
> the unstoppable accumulation of material. The history of the
> cinema is full of films that attempt to imitate life . . . and life
> went on and so did the film . . . as if it had developed a will of
> its own that would ensure its longevity . . . the film and my
> own life had become inextricably connected and, without
> realizing it, I just did not want the film to come to an end . . .

With all the script changes and the incessant need to go over scenes again and again to reach Bertolucci's vision of perfection, filming lasted eleven months and went $3 million over budget. The initial bonhomie between director and actors had long ago given way to a fractious tolerance that occasionally exploded into angry exchanges. Whereas De Niro had once applauded the director's willingness 'to discuss', as time wore on these discussions became instructions which verged upon the dictatorial as Bertolucci's obsession reached fever pitch.

De Niro and Depardieu, meanwhile, had become comrades up in arms, wary that their respective characters were not coming out as intended. Depardieu especially believed that he was being turned into some kind of comic-book hero. They spent many hours discussing their plight and shared a mutual fascination in each other's work. They both had a flair for taking on quirky characters and would do so, in the future, with delight. Depardieu believed that De Niro would become a heavyweight, prolific actor, but not even their joint gifts would persuade Bertolucci to trim the marathon shoot.

It went on even after shooting had ended. A year after he had finished filming, De Niro was called back to dub a number of scenes in which Bertolucci was not happy with either the words or the sound quality. This caused a problem. When filming began De Niro had spent weeks preparing, in his now customary manner, to act out the role of a high-born aristocrat, achieving a high level of accuracy with accents and intonations. By the time he came to dub over the poorly recorded scenes, that preparation had long been forgotten. He often slipped into his own Lower East Side dialect; that apart, the flaws in synchronization were evident in the final product – and not just in De Niro's scenes.

De Niro's reaction to his work on the movie was one of declared admiration for the director, tinged with unspoken dismay at the emerging fiasco as it was presented for release. As he left the set for the last time to return to New York he was typically brief in his observations, although he offered the comment that he had witnessed 'a new way to make a political film'.

By then, controversy and animosity between film-maker and distributors were raging out of control in the United States. Bertolucci's first cut of the film ran to a daunting six and a half hours. It began marvellously, but then slowly descended into a political morass that prevented it being understood by anyone not familiar with the details of modern Italian history. It was described as Italy's *Gone with the Wind*, and those who saw it at a special showing at the Cannes Film Festival described it in terms which swung wildly from 'a masterpiece' to 'a mess'.

The producer, representing the amalgam of backers, decided that it might possibly be divided and shown in two parts, which by any standard was a fairly unsatisfactory way to present a movie in the cinema. Even so, that's the way it went in Italy, France and Germany, with the two sections being shown on consecutive nights. In Italy a great debate had already opened up after a Communist newspaper gave a special showing of the full-length version in one sitting, and Bertolucci found himself at loggerheads with his left-wing friends as various political interpretations were passionately challenged.

In America, a very public row developed between director and Paramount Pictures, now boycotting its own movie. The New York critics, having seen the full-length version screened at Cannes, signed a petition calling for this work of art to be shown in cinemas in its uncut version.

Barry Diller, then president of Paramount Pictures who held the US distribution rights, said that there was no way he would accept anything more than one movie of the agreed three hour twenty minutes in length – which was the maximum time that most cinemas in America could allow for a twice-nightly feature. Although the argument was commercially based, most people suspected that the movie's strong political element had an underlying effect: for the first time in history Hollywood had backed a movie which contained pro-Communist propaganda.

All this took place at a particularly sensitive period in relations between Italy and the USA. Italy was in the grip of a terrorist war led by the Red Brigades, and the USA, which had clandestinely funded the ruling Italian Christian Democrats since 1945, was furious that this party's leader, Aldo Moro, was considering an alliance with the Communist Party. This situation ended with the kidnap and murder of Moro in 1978, but the background was already firmly in place as Bertolucci flew across the Atlantic with his finished work.

Lawyers were summoned and Bertolucci ended up in court, pleading with a US Superior Court judge to order Paramount to release the movie. He said that cutting it to three hours fifteen minutes would represent a serious slur on his reputation.

The judge, who had had to sit through three versions of *Novecento*, was so nonplussed that the best he could do was suggest that the director and the studio should go away and attempt to reach a compromise. And so it was that director and studio eventually agreed to a four-hour ten-minute version. Then the critics turned on Bertolucci for sacrificing his film for the sake of commerce. But even this statement did not hold water. The movie was a commercial disaster, and Bertolucci accused Paramount of ensuring that it flopped 'just to prove they were right from the start'.

Nor did De Niro walk away without taking some of the flak. His character, Alfredo, was the central figure, the catalyst to so many important scenes in which imperfections or confusion arose, that he was bound to be involved. Above all, this role represented perhaps too rapid a change for De Niro for audiences which had only just become familiar with his work through *Mean Streets* and *The Godfather Part II*. De Niro's portrayal of Vito Corleone was restrained and quietly elegant, but he allowed the character's dark strengths to exude from within. In *Novecento* there was no such depth for him to get to grips with; or perhaps it was simply that Bertolucci had not allowed it, as he wanted to demonstrate in his political commentary the ineffectual nature of the landed class when pitted against the proletariat.

De Niro did not come out of the movie with much credit, except for the personal experience of working with Bertolucci which in itself was worth a great deal. Years later, as so often happens with such projects, *Novecento* was resurrected in its first-cut six-hour English version and audiences were given a chance to see the original. 'Until then,' Bertolucci told me, 'you had been looking at a different movie than that which had been shown in Europe. I had re-edited, recut and redirected the movie in the editing suite until it conformed to acceptability by Paramount. I was tied like an umbilical cord to that movie; I could not let it go, but also I could not allow it simply to be massacred, sliced up like a piece of salami.' Over the years it became a cult film, which is less than it deserves. Bertolucci said the experience left him tired and broken, but he and De Niro remained good friends.

The same could not be said about De Niro's brief experience with the equally controversial director Mike Nichols, who had signed him to play the lead in a new movie, *Bogart Slept Here*, which had the excellent pedigree of being scripted by Neil Simon. Nichols, the former cabaret entertainer and comic turned film director, was at the time having difficulties in a career marked with stunning early success but which now looked dangerously close to slipping down the other side of the peak. He had also just emerged from a battle in the Supreme Court where he had had to defend himself against accusations of gross obscenity in his film *Carnal Knowledge*, which starred Jack Nicholson, Art Garfunkel and Ann-Margret, so he might well have been forgiven if he was a trifle irritable.

Neil Simon, author of such famous works as *Barefoot in the Park*, *Sweet Charity* and *The Odd Couple*, outstripped all other writers of modern comedy, with plays running practically all the time on Broadway. The scenario seemed set fair for an adventure into comedy that would give De Niro a totally new slant: *Bogart Slept Here* was the tale of a struggling actor who is forced to share an apartment with a young mother and her child. There was much to-do in the trade press about the forthcoming production, and a two-page advertisement announcing the movie centred upon a drawing of De Niro at the Chateau Marmont Hotel, that famous dormitory of actors on temporary assignment to Hollywood. All in all, it seemed a highly promising prospect. But, as De Niro soon discovered, his personal style of preparation and improvisation did not suit Nichols.

Nichols himself had once been a struggling actor and had studied with Lee Strasberg in New York. After his directorial debut with the Broadway production of Simon's *Barefoot in the Park* he had become one of the hottest stage directors around. He made his name in film in 1966 with *Who's Afraid of Virginia Woolf?*, which resurrected the flagging careers of Elizabeth Taylor and Richard Burton, and followed it with a movie of its time, *The Graduate*, with Dustin Hoffman, thus becoming Hollywood's first director to achieve a million-dollar salary.

Things began to go wrong with his ambitious re-creation of Joseph Heller's stunning novel *Catch 22*, which was heavily panned. He had only moderate success with *Carnal Knowledge* and then hit a box office disaster with his direction of Jack Nicholson and Warren Beatty in *The Fortune* in 1975. So when he hired De Niro for *Bogart Slept Here* he was facing problems of credibility in a career that had suddenly taken a turn for the worse.

Known, like Bertolucci, as a man who sought absolute perfection, he also had a reputation for a strict, almost rigid sense of direction which gave actors little leeway for their own interpretations. He was heavily into line-readings and rehearsals, always demonstrated a firm idea of the way a part should be played, and had no interest in holding long discussions. All this, of course, was at complete variance to the way De Niro operated.

Very soon the two men clashed. The rows were hot and heavy, with Nichols storming round saying: 'This man is undirectable.' A mere two weeks after filming began Nichols and De Niro had their final confrontation, the actor was fired and the film was shut down. Nichols was, like De Niro, fairly unforthcoming in his relationship with the media, but inquisitive reporters gathered that there had been an almighty clash of temperaments, that he could not bring out the comedy in De Niro, and that basically Nichols thought that 'he simply wasn't funny'. As a former stand-up comic of fame, Nichols reckoned he was a fair judge of that! He also had some reservations about the script and said later that it suited everyone to call a halt.

De Niro's recollection of the event was relayed later in his *Playboy* interview: 'He fired me. They tried not to pay me. They did not succeed.' He told friends he had found it virtually impossible to work under the constraints that Nichols had imposed, and that had been the crux of the issue.

Sam Spiegel, waiting anxiously in Hollywood to secure De Niro for *The Last Tycoon*, noted the discomfort between the two men and commented: 'The plain fact is that, though he is a superb actor, De Niro was not suited for a Neil Simon comedy. Neil's work is all upfront – not hidden meanings or darkness. De Niro is not that kind of an actor; he needs the mystery.' This was a very perceptive portrait of an actor whose work so far had hardly been sufficient to enable such an accurate and enduring assessment to be made.

The producers of *Bogart Slept Here* cut their losses and shelved their much-hyped movie. The potential of the project was, however, to be confirmed two years later when producer Ray Stark revived it with a new title, *The Goodbye Girl*. It was handed to a new director, Herbert Ross, famed on Broadway and fresh from his success with another Simon play, *The Sunshine Boys*, with George Burns and Walter Matthau. Richard Dreyfuss took the role vacated by De Niro and won an Oscar in the process. The film also received Academy Award nominations for Best Picture, Best Screenplay, Best Actress (Marsha Mason) and Best Supporting Actress (Quinn Cummings) and thereafter would be known by the disgruntled De Niro as the one that got away. But at the time he was simply glad to be out of it.

6

'You Talking at Me . . . ?'

De Niro described being fired by Mike Nichols as 'coming from the darkest depths to light and inspiration'. This was a prophetic statement because he was poised, though he perhaps did not appreciate it at the time, to thrust himself into cinema history. As with many classic movies there was a long history to the making of *Taxi Driver*, and it began several years before a final draft of the screenplay was delivered to De Niro while he was making *Novecento* in Rome. It came heavily recommended by his pal Brian De Palma, who had been shown it by its author, Paul Schrader, and he wanted to direct the movie himself. De Palma reckoned it was the strongest, most sensational screenplay he had ever read, so much so that he doubted whether any major studio would have the courage to make it in its initial form, an opinion readily confirmed by producers Julia and Michael Phillips. They endured three years of false starts and flat rejections as they tried to raise the cash to put the film into production, and then suddenly things began to fall into place – but not with De Palma.

The story for *Taxi Driver* was born out of Schrader's own rock-bottom experiences on city streets at the beginning of the 1970s, when his own life was in turmoil. He had failed to get his first screenplay sold, he was broke, his wife had left him, he was drinking and popping pills and wandering aimlessly around the streets in desperation for weeks. At nights, sleepless, he would go into porn movie houses. 'That was when the metaphor for *Taxi Driver* hit me,' Schrader recalled. 'I was exactly the story . . . the man who moves through the city like a rat through the river; the man who is constantly surrounded by people yet has no friends, urban loneliness; the story about a man and a car: that was my symbol, my metaphor.'

Schrader's agent passed the script to Brian De Palma, who in turn gave it to the Phillipses. The then husband-and-wife team, later divorced, were part of the 'young' set of independent film-makers (she was thirty in 1975 and he was thirty-two) who came in the wake of *Easy Rider*. Their friends and associates included Scorsese, De Palma, Coppola and Spielberg. Later Julia Phillips would explode from the anonymity that is the lot of most producers when she wrote her 1991 best-selling memoir and Hollywood exposé *You'll Never Eat Lunch in This Town Again*. The early part of her book described this particular period in New York, when she was breaking into the big time. The book went on to chart her own cocaine-addled decline as a producer and was especially notable for its comments on her erstwhile colleagues: i.e., on Spielberg . . . 'I taught the little prick he deserved limos before he even knew what it was to travel in a first-class seat on a plane' . . . on Donald Sutherland . . . 'A top-ten brain fucker' . . . and on François Truffaut . . . 'Deep down I knew he was a prick.'

In the mid-1970s the Phillipses came from nowhere, hustled and bustled and struck gold on their first major-league production, *The Sting*, with Robert Redford and Paul Newman. It won an Oscar for Best Picture in 1974 and turned them into millionaires overnight. With box office receipts reaching blockbuster proportions, the Phillipses were the blue-eyed kids to Hollywood studios. Now they were working on several new projects including *Close Encounters of the Third Kind*, to be directed by Spielberg, and *Taxi Driver*, which Michael thought would go through the roof. Julia was unsure.

They were two entirely different movies. *Close Encounters* achieved immediate big-money hype following Spielberg's 1975 smash hit *Jaws*, but *Taxi Driver* was altogether more difficult to coax into production. A number of directors, both up-and-coming and well established, had shown an interest in the movie. Not least among them were De Palma and Martin Scorsese – the latter, according to Julia, 'sidles up to me at parties and tells me in intense undertone how much he wants to do this picture'. The Phillips duo took an option on the screenplay from Schrader and told De Palma, who had yet to make a serious impression in the movie business, that he was not a candidate. Similarly, Michael Phillips told Scorsese they were not prepared to consider him just 'on the strength of *Boxcar Bertha*', his only movie to have been released at that time.

They took the script to several major studio executives, most of whom held their hands high in horror. One, however, did agree to back it, suggesting – incredibly – the singer Neil Diamond, seeking his first screen role, for the lead. Another wanted to do it with Jeff Bridges, the new clean-cut young actor, in the starring role and Robert Mulligan as director – but with the proviso, as De Palma had predicted, that the script was toned down considerably. It was felt to be far too strong 'in language and anti-social consequence'.

Schrader objected. 'I was fighting that off,' he recalled, 'because it didn't make any sense to me. The whole basis of *Taxi Driver* was its social and psychological documentary content. Yet it was a deal and, God knows, I wanted to see the film made . . . what saved it was seeing *Mean Streets*. . . .' The Phillipses were dragged to a private screening of *Mean Streets* with Schrader, and Julia recalls: 'We came out of the screening prepared to commit to Scorsese – so long as he got De Niro for the lead.' Scorsese called back within the hour and said he had got De Niro and all that was needed now was money.

Another year passed. In the meantime De Niro had gone off to make *Novecento* while Scorsese went to Hollywood at Brando's invitation to talk about a new picture which came to nothing, and was then commissioned to direct *Alice Doesn't Live Here Anymore*. By the time they were both free, in mid-1975, the Phillipses had made Columbia an offer they could not refuse in order to get the film made the way everyone among that group felt it should be made. They offered the picture as a package – producer, director, screenplay and star all for a bargain basement price of $150,000 plus a percentage of the profits. De Niro accepted a mere $35,000 fee upfront at a time when he was being offered five times that figure – the biggest salary of his career – to appear in Richard Attenborough's star-studded *A Bridge Too Far*.

Paul Schrader recalled that De Niro and Scorsese were adamant about getting *Taxi Driver* on to the screens. De Niro called it a movie that 'people will be watching in fifty years' time' and that was why he was prepared to give up the chance of serious money to see it through.

The overall budget was set at $750,000, though later raised to $1.3 million, and the streets of New York were once again to be alive with the activity of a De Niro–Scorsese collaboration. Those streets provided everything that they needed for such a modern horror tale, from the atmosphere of an area known so well by director and star to the backdrop of real-life scenery which could never be created on any soundstage or studio lot.

The story is one man's living nightmare, set in New York in 1976. De Niro's character is the former marine Travis Bickle, an introverted loner and insomniac who takes a job driving cabs to fill his sleepless nights. The taxi becomes his own hell on wheels and, although he could have plied his cab anywhere in New York, he is drawn relentlessly to the sex-filled nightlife around 42nd Street, where pimps, prostitutes, junkies, drug dealers and porno freaks abound. The back of his cab becomes a microcosm of city filth, and gradually the burning anger wells up, feeding his own sexual frustration and searing hatred of the people he serves and obsessively observes. Travis's own passions do not lie with the seediness of the sexual freaks he drives around. He despises them and their life, and his abhorrence is edged towards psychotic reaction by the stuff he has to clean from the back seat of his cab. He hates the whores, but the women he desires are seemingly unobtainable to him.

Occasionally he secures a date, as he does with a beautiful blonde named Betsy (played by Cybill Shepherd) who works at the office of a presidential candidate. He persuades her to go out with him a couple of times, and then she rejects him in disgust when he takes her to see a hard-core porno film. He calls her for another date and he is seen suffering, once again, the pain of rejection which Scorsese identifies as the heart of the film. Rejection and suffering become the psychological base for the horrific developments as the story proceeds. 'He becomes a commando for God,' said Scorsese. 'And I say that because there was an obsessiveness to the character which is very religious to me. He takes baths, sips peach brandy, he eats very odd combinations of food and he ritualistically keeps a diary which is written like poetry. Above all he has this image of the woman as something she is not, the goddess.'

Travis has to hit back, and gravitates towards his first violent act. He arms himself with a small arsenal of weapons, experiences his first killing when he shoots a hold-up gunman at a store, and gradually launches himself into a bloodbath of violence that puts many previous boundary-breakers in the movies into the shade. He attempts to kill the presidential candidate, but fails. He tries to rescue a twelve-year-old prostitute, superbly played by Jodie Foster, from her street life but she eventually rejects his advice. And so he plots to murder her pimp, Sport, a role that once again brings Scorsese veteran Harvey Keitel into the action. It is Travis's slaughter of Sport that leads the film towards its bloody finale.

So that was the story. Now Scorsese had to scout the locations. Meanwhile, the star took himself off to City Hall and renewed his taxi-driving licence, acquired years earlier in his 'struggling' days, so that he could actually take a job driving a cab. For the next two weeks he cruised the streets of New York just as Paul Schrader had done, attempting to discover the isolation of a man surrounded by people in the sleaziest part of midtown Manhattan. He was apparently recognized only twice. One passenger commented, 'Jesus, it's De Niro, isn't it? Last year you win an Oscar, and now you're driving cabs. Guess it's hard to find steady work.' Scorsese recalled, 'I drove with him a couple of nights. He said he got the strangest feeling when he was hacking . . . that he was totally anonymous. People would say anything, do anything, in the back of his cab as if he wasn't there at all.'

The De Niro idiosyncrasies in preparation were rediscovered by make-up artist Dick Smith, who had worked with him on *The Godfather Part II*. Smith confirmed the man's almost paranoid quest for perfection. 'He is extremely difficult to work with. He would scrutinize every single line I drew on his face, sometimes making me do it over and over until he thought it was right. You have to have real patience.'

Scorsese's supporting cast had been meticulously selected. He already knew that Harvey Keitel and Jodie Foster were exactly right for their respective roles, but Jodie Foster in particular was to have mixed views about her selection. She was twelve years old in real life when Scorsese first plucked her from the Disneyesque roles she had been playing since childhood. In his *Alice Doesn't Live Here Anymore* she was the wine-swigging alley kid, but her chilling performance in *Taxi Driver* as the drug-addicted prostitute brought her attention which was both welcome and highly unwelcome; her role in the movie returned to haunt her for years as she became the victim of stalkers and phone-freaks who drove her to reclusiveness and almost to a nervous breakdown. Most famously, she was the obsession of John Hinckley junior, who claimed that *Taxi Driver* 'inspired' him to make his assassination attempt on President Ronald Reagan in March 1981.

Even Cybill Shepherd as Betsy, the girl out of Bickle's reach and for whom he tried to kill the presidential candidate, was for once properly cast, although there had been a good deal of anguish beforehand. Julia Phillips recalled, 'Marty's misogyny was apparent from his casting Cybill Shepherd. We interviewed just about every blonde on both coasts and still he kept looking. I liked Farah Fawcett for her aquiline profile but Marty picked Cybill – a retro Italian gesture, I always felt. In the end he had to give her line-readings and De Niro hated her.'

In fact, there was virtually no contact between De Niro and Shepherd offscreen. For one thing his girlfriend Diahnne Abbott was also in the movie, playing a small role as an usherette in one of the porno cinemas frequented by Travis Bickle. But that had no bearing on De Niro's lack of contact with his fellow actors: beyond the requirements of work, where they found him a considerate colleague, most of them barely managed to exchange more than a half-sentence in passing. Even Scorsese found himself having to explain away his star's apparent introversion: 'He just blocks out everything else when he's working. He has no time for socializing.'

Few directors understand De Niro the way Scorsese does. Whereas Bertolucci and Mike Nichols had found his techniques of improvisation quite trying, Scorsese gave him his head and admitted that several scenes were better because of it. Perhaps the best example was De Niro's own creation which became one of the most quoted lines in modern cinema history. Standing in front of a mirror, practising drawing his gun from his holster, he said, at his reflection: 'You talking at me? Are you talkin' to me? Who are you talking to? Well, I'm the only one here.' Scorsese's confidence in the De Niro magic was reflected in the audience reaction. Although they were stunned and shocked by the violence, he also managed to engender sympathy, which, Scorsese asserted, required an 'incredible talent'.

He was right. De Niro *was* Travis Bickle, and that fact is probably best confirmed by an incident unknown to De Niro that happened while he was filming a street scene. Michael Moriarty, his co-star from *Bang the Drum Slowly* and whose own career had since dipped, happened upon the Scorsese crew as they were filming at the Bellmore Cafeteria and stood watching for a while. One of the technicians recognized him and suggested he went over and said hello to De Niro. 'No, thanks,' Moriarty replied. 'I won't bother. The man I knew was named Bruce Pearson [De Niro's character in *Bang the Drum*]. I don't know Travis Bickle – or Robert De Niro, for that matter.' And he strolled wistfully on his way.

It was a sad moment. Two actors who shared the same kind of ambitions, had made such a heart-warming movie together and had the deepest respect for their craft were yet miles distant, and had so little in common that one of them did not feel able to contact the other. It says a lot both for De Niro and about him. He was utterly remote.

In an odd way, Moriarty's comment also upheld the Phillipses' original contention that there were few actors who could have made the character believable. 'I, who had never been particularly fond of this script, became extremely fond of this movie,' said Julia Phillips. 'It is a ground-breaker and I think Travis is someone people should know about. I know he's out there, created by American culture and etched in stone by the Vietnam War.'

Columbia Studios nervously put some weight behind the finished product. The film was led into the cinema by a promotional campaign showing De Niro walking down a dilapidated, burned-out city street where a triple-X porno movie was being advertised on a cinema hoarding in the distance. He was carrying a bottle in a bag and his eyes were vacant, his facial expression desperate. The promo-line read: 'On every street in every city in this country there's a nobody who dreams of becoming a somebody.'

Unfortunately there was one such person in the audience. John Hinckley junior, saw the movie fifteen times. His defence lawyers would claim that it was Travis Bickle's attempt to kill a presidential candidate that inspired him some time later to shoot President Reagan. The film was shown at his trial, and his lawyers sought to demonstrate how Hinckley had 'identified' with De Niro's creation of Travis Bickle and felt that the movie was speaking to him personally. It was not the first time, or the last, that such a claim would be made about art inspiring life (Mark Chapman had a copy of *Catcher in the Rye* in his pocket when he killed John Lennon) and it was easy, with hindsight, to take the movie's violence to task.

At the time, however, De Niro basked in the afterglow of a mass of fine reviews which were well deserved. *Taxi Driver* was, for its social commentary, a sickening film, awful yet unforgettable. De Niro was right in predicting that it would be talked about for years to come, and in the 1990s both the movie and the soundtrack have been discovered by another generation.

When *Taxi Driver* finally opened in New York in 1976, the group of friends who had made it went out to dinner. They drove around the streets to find cinemas where it was showing, saw queues were forming and punched each other's shoulders with pride. The movie was a box office hit, taking more than $25 million in the USA alone; everyone who was on a percentage began to receive large cheques, including Brian De Palma who got 1 per cent for having brought the movie to the Phillipses' attention.

De Niro's critical acclaim was greater than on anything he had done in the past, and *Taxi Driver* was also the first movie on which he received solo billing above the title. The accolade was apt because it was very much one man's movie. He was voted Best Actor by the New York Film Critics' Circle and, when Oscar time came around in the spring of 1977, *Taxi Driver* received four nominations: for Best Picture, Best Supporting Actress (Jodie Foster), Best Musical Score (Bernard Herrmann, who used to write the scores for Alfred Hitchcock movies) and Best Actor (Robert De Niro).

However, *Taxi Driver* was not one for the Hollywood establishment, nor for those who abhorred the current wave of liberalism demonstrated in the arts, the media and the profusion of radical groups springing up across the USA and elsewhere, covering everything from civil rights for Indians (Brando's pet topic) to feminism. In the wake of Vietnam and political scandals such as Watergate American society seemed to have been brought to the brink of a cultural catastrophe, and the Hollywood Republicans who at the time outnumbered the liberals were not fond of ground-breakers. Those erstwhile supporters of Richard Nixon and his corrupt administration viewed the work of film-makers such as Scorsese, Jane Fonda, Lumet and Coppola as dangerous and unacceptable, even if it was a portrayal of truth. And thus, to many among the powerful right-wing faction of the Hollywood elite, *Taxi Driver* was regarded disdainfully as the sole creation of New York liberals. It clearly struck a nerve at a crucial time in the social history of America.

Although it would be in the realm of conspiracy theory to suggest that *Taxi Driver* was blackballed by people in the powerhouses of Hollywood, there was none the less a blatant omission from the official history of the Academy Awards, published at the time of the Academy's sixtieth jubilee. It does not even mention *Taxi Driver* except in the listed categories for nominations. Incredibly, it merely records that 1976 was dominated by three movies – *Network*, *Rocky* and *All the President's Men* – and makes no reference to the fourth, *Taxi Driver*, which received a nomination for Best Film alongside those movies. In box office terms, of course – always the key to Hollywood adjudication – *Taxi Driver* was well beaten.

By the time that official history was written the connection between John Hinckley junior and *Taxi Driver* was well known and Ronald Reagan, actor of that parish and past Governor of California, counted a large section of the Hollywood hierarchy among his most powerful supporters and campaign financiers. Even so, the antagonistic messages that surrounded the movie were wafting around Hollywood back then, at the time of the Awards ceremony.

It was one of the reasons that De Niro himself did not pay much regard to the event. He did not even turn up to hear his name called among the Best Actor nominees, along with Sylvester Stallone, who came in from nowhere as the star of his own screenplay for the first of the *Rocky* series; Giancarlo Giannini for his role in the Italian-made *Seven Beauties*; and Peter Finch and William Holden, both appearing in that year's most successful movie, Sidney Lumet's *Network*. Stallone, who was also nominated for Best Screenplay, did not get either, though the reception and hype for *Rocky* were enormous – so perhaps it was no surprise when it won Best Picture. The personal accolades were reserved largely for the stars of *Network*, and made more poignant by the recent death of Peter Finch, whose widow came to receive his posthumous Oscar. Jodie Foster also lost out to *Network*'s Beatrice Straight, while the Oscar for Best Music Score went to *The Omen*.

And so, while the rest of the world was hailing *Taxi Driver* as a masterpiece, it was effectively shunned by Hollywood. But by then it was history for De Niro: one for the album, that would be taken out, dusted down and shown time and time again in the future, with far greater regularity and attention than some of the big-budget turkeys still being let loose on an unsuspecting public by the major studios. De Niro had moved on, knowing that his prediction that *Taxi Driver* would be viewed 'fifty years from now' was probably correct, although he had not foreseen the role of John Hinckley junior.

When that incident occurred both he and Scorsese were shocked and upset, and took the media's allegations about the effects of the movie very personally. Both refused to discuss it whenever challenged, and Scorsese even stopped working for a time. De Niro still avoids the subject to this day, though Scorsese is rather more forthcoming. 'Movies don't kill people,' he pleaded. 'People kill people. I do not regret having made *Taxi Driver*. Nor do I believe it was an irresponsible act – quite the reverse. Bob and I are at one on this.'

At the time of its release, *Taxi Driver* brought De Niro immense pride and a feeling of security that he had never had before. It seemed a firm fact, now, that his acting career would not be that of a mere journeyman. He was a major star, and Diahnne Abbott liked hearing that description of her lover. But as far as De Niro was concerned, nothing would change. New York was their home, although the increasing calls from Hollywood meant they would have to spend more time there. Otherwise he was as anonymous as ever, except to those familiar with his sudden appearance in the bars and restaurants he frequented within a mile or so of the place where he was born, and where no one except the occasional stray autograph hunter troubled him. Out in Manhattan and greater New York he was nobody, and that's the way he liked it.

7

A Tycoon of Sorts

So was he just an East Side punk who played type, or a man of innate talent? The argument was already simmering, and De Niro did not even know it. Big, bustling Hollywood producer Sam Spiegel opted for the former phrase, his own creation. Director Elia Kazan took the opposite view. So what was going on?

In spite of De Niro's busy acting life over the previous two or three years, Hollywood until now had remained a distant place. Eventually he would have to be there on a regular basis, but not without some reluctance. Hollywood spelled excess, back-biting, bitchiness beyond measure, gossip columns, paparazzi and all those other consequences of fame that he could, if he so wished (and he so wished), avoid in New York. To De Niro, this kind of fame was a dubious status which he viewed more as a burden than as an incentive.

However, there was no better summing up of the importance of De Niro's current position than to let the eye wander down the names of the *supporting* cast for his next movie, over whom he would receive star billing: Robert Mitchum, Jack Nicholson, Tony Curtis, Donald Pleasence, Ray Milland, Dana Andrews, Jeff Corey and Anjelica Huston. Behind the cameras were Sam Spiegel and Elia Kazan, with a screenplay by Harold Pinter from a story by F. Scott Fitzgerald. It was a veritable star-studded galaxy – or as Louis B. Mayer, one of the thinly veiled characters in this story, would say 'more stars than in heaven' – and if achievement were to be measured by the company he kept on this picture, De Niro seemed destined to be a true king of Hollywood.

He and Diahnne packed up their necessary belongings, along with Diahnne's four cats and transported themselves across country to become temporary residents in Tinseltown. Home at first was a suite in a hotel which did not allow pets, so they sneaked them in through the back door. After a few days they were reported to the management by a chambermaid, fed up with cleaning up the mess. He and Diahnne were out at the time. When they returned, they found that the cats had been put out into the garden and their hotel suite locked. They were asked to leave immediately, though not before De Niro had spoken his mind. After this they rented a minor mansion in Bel-Air, which was much more in keeping with the role in which he was now about to immerse himself. Vastly different from Travis Bickle, this was a quiet, gentle genius, the young mogul in *The Last Tycoon*, Fitzgerald's unfinished tale of old Hollywood based partly upon the life of one of its legends, Irving G. Thalberg, with a few autobiographical elements tossed in.

There was a certain irony to all of this which was perhaps lost on those who did not know De Niro's personal feelings about fame and making movies. Thalberg, former production head of MGM, was himself a rebel and often in conflict with his superiors, notably Louis B. Mayer. The prolific 1930s' screenwriter Charles MacArthur (*The Front Page*, *Barbary Coast*, *Crime Without Passion*, *Wuthering Heights*, and many others) said of him: 'He's too good to last. The lamb doesn't lie down with the lion for long. . . . Entertainment is his God . . . and he is content to serve him without billing like a priest at an altar.' Although very autocratic and with no time for creative people – represented in his scene with Donald Pleasence, who played a script-writer – Thalberg was probably the nearest among the Hollywood executives of the 1930s to the modernistic film-makers of the 1970s. He did not, however, survive to see the fall of the dream or the studio system with which he was himself so often in conflict. This boy wonder, a studio chief at the age of twenty-one, worked sixteen-hour days for twelve years and burned himself out. He died of a heart attack at the age of thirty-seven.

Thalberg's ideals and dedication bore certain similarities to descriptions of De Niro, except that one was a mogul while the other an actor. Thalberg, always camera-shy and uneasy in crowded rooms and parties, remained modestly anonymous by keeping his name off the credits. His aims were reputedly high: 'I believe that although the motion picture may not live forever as a work of art, except in a few instances, it will be the most efficient way of showing posterity how we live.'

If, as Jack Nicholson maintains, a bit of the character that an actor plays remains inside him for ever, this is the one which may be predominantly identified as remaining with De Niro. Already he was being described by journalists whose advances he had rejected as a mysterious, almost mythical figure – parallel comments to what had been written about the mogul he was about to re-create. 'On a clear day,' wrote the comedy playwright George F. Kaufman, 'you can see Thalberg.' It was a statement easily comparable with some of the headlines applied to the actor who would play the role based upon him, such as 'De Niro is . . . a black hole' in *Newsweek* or 'De Niro: elusive to the core' in *USA Today*.

The character of Thalberg, merged with droplets of Fitzgerald's own complexities, provided a fascinating characterization in *The Last Tycoon* in the shape of Monroe Stahr. This could have been glory time for De Niro, but there was a problem. He was chosen by Elia Kazan as a young, modern actor who had the vibrancy of a Thalberg-style character. De Niro was a product and star of the 'new' Hollywood – the group of people who did not view that town as being the centre of the universe. Fitzgerald's searing portrait attacked the system that was a precursor to the young bloods of the new age, and 'old' Hollywood, in which his story is set, finally came crashing down in the late 1950s. *The Last Tycoon* might well have been a suitable subject for the younger generation of film-makers as they enjoyed the new-found freedom of expression which emerged with the rise of the independents and the relaxing of censorship controls in the early 1970s. There was every opportunity to build upon Fitzgerald's portrait and turn it towards the biting realism evident in many of the recent pictures turned out by the non-Hollywood brigade. But in the event the movie lay in the hands of what might be termed the left-overs from the old system – veteran producer Sam Spiegel, then seventy-five.

True, Spiegel had long been associated with classic material. His name had appeared on the credits of a number of major movies since the forties, among them *The Stranger*, *Tales of Manhattan*, *The African Queen*, *On the Waterfront*, *The Bridge on the River Kwai* and *Lawrence of Arabia*. He was a grandiose showman who constantly talked about money, threw lavish Hollywood parties at which everyone who was anyone would be present – and then counted paper clips.

He also wanted to populate *The Last Tycoon* with stars associated with that bygone era. The result would be that, in a peculiar way, they were a parody of themselves, especially Tony Curtis and, to a lesser degree, Robert Mitchum. De Niro, along with Jack Nicholson who appeared in a brief sequence as a union organizer, carried the banner for modernity. The freer spirit of the 1970s should have been the launch-pad for a vibrant, critical and even nostalgic look at the past. But it wasn't.

The background to this journey is almost as intriguing and complex as some of the nuances in the Fitzgerald novel. Spiegel, who had reputedly put $5.5 million of his own money into the production, was intent on making it a big, plush, 'old Hollywood' production – perhaps his last – and the key, he believed, lay in the writing of the screenplay.

He hired Harold Pinter, the British dramatist whose highly personal idiom so confused London critics that at first they were extremely hostile to his work. Later he became a leading light among British writers, praised as a superb verbal acrobat. He had found wider fame and acclaim with his film scripts, notably *The Servant*, *The Caretaker*, *The Pumpkin Eater*, *The Birthday Party* and *The Go-Between*. Spiegel sought him out because he knew that the main hurdle in presenting *The Last Tycoon* was to find a writer who could achieve the near-impossible task of transferring Fitzgerald's words to the screen.

Producer Robert Evans had had a similar problem, when he was production head of Paramount, with his 1974 remake of *The Great Gatsby* with Robert Redford and Mia Farrow. The screenplay by Francis Ford Coppola went through a dozen rewrites and still did not do the author justice, although it had considerably more pace than Pinter's slow narrative.

Spiegel was convinced that F. Scott Fitzgerald and Monroe Stahr were in the safe hands of British 'literary royalty', as Kazan sardonically described Pinter. Kazan came as close as anyone could to saying that he believed Pinter's eventual screenplay was dull and boring, without actually using those words in public print. Privately, he had several shouting matches with Spiegel, especially over the central love scenes. It was this area with which Coppola had experienced similar difficulty in *The Great Gatsby*, in the female character played by Mia Farrow. Fitzgerald's vision of his women in both novels showed them as perfection, with hidden complexities to their characters which were almost impossible to portray on screen.

Much work had already been done on the script before Kazan was hired. Pinter had been working in consultation with Spiegel and Mike Nichols, with whom De Niro had had his recent run-in. By then, said Kazan, the concrete had set hard and Spiegel was treating Pinter's script as holy writ. He seemed dedicated to saving this eminent writer from the attacks of an ebullient director, and the long, tedious script conferences usually ended up with nothing more than a comma or semi-colon being changed. In desperation Kazan wrote to Pinter three times, asking for amendments to the love scenes and suggesting other alterations to tighten up long passages of dialogue. 'Pinter never replied or commented on them, and absolutely nothing was done to make it interesting,' Kazan recalled. He suspected that Spiegel, to whom he gave the letters, never passed them on.

Kazan resolved to shut off his objections and proceed 'as best I could'.

Monroe Stahr is the young genius mogul of the fictional International World Studios, who is sick and haunted by the untimely death of his wife, the Hollywood star Minna Davis. Then, by chance, he sees a girl, an equally mysterious young Englishwoman called Kathleen Moore (played by Ingrid Boulting), whom he sets out to woo – thus the central love story about which Kazan was so concerned. Around that are strung all the machinations, conflicts and skulduggery of a working Hollywood studio of the 1930s which Fitzgerald both loved and hated, and made his vilification of it the theme of *The Last Tycoon*.

De Niro was Kazan's choice for the role of Stahr: 'I told Sam to forget any notion of using Dustin Hoffman (who was, incidentally Mike Nichols's preference) or Jack Nicholson (Sam's) for the role of Irving Thalberg [*sic*] and that we make the film with De Niro. I knew little about Bobby. I was playing a hunch.' On Kazan's hunch rode Spiegel's millions.

From De Niro's point of view, the chance of working with Kazan was a dream come true. A long-time mentor of all those who studied at the Method schools of New York, Kazan was essential study for any modern actor. He had, after all, directed Brando's two most alluring early screen performances, *A Streetcar Named Desire* and *On the Waterfront*. His most prolific period was in the Brando/Clift/Dean era of the fifties, when Method films burst on to the screen. In the previous fifteen years, however, he had made a mere five films, of which only one had been a commercial success. Kazan had revived his professional relationship with Monty Clift in *Wild River* in 1961, but by then Clift was already in serious personal decline and the movie disappeared without trace. Critics were asking if he had lost it long before Spiegel signed him for *The Last Tycoon* – especially after his last effort, a disastrous 1969 screen version of his own novel *The Arrangement*.

So there was an old-time Hollywood producer aged seventy-five, hiring a one-time directorial ace aged sixty-six attempting to recapture past glories, hiring a thrusting young Brando/Clift/Dean admirer who had never taken on anything resembling the role. All three were working with a screenplay produced by a famous writer trapped by his own mystical structures and eccentricities, in an attempt to make a comprehensible movie out of the unfinished work of an alcoholic genius. Added to that were several side-issues, not least of which was the suitability of Ingrid Boulting – Spiegel, it would appear, had omitted to ascertain whether or not she was an actress.

In fact, Ingrid was a fashion model whose name had been mentioned to him across the dinner table while he was visiting Britain for a meeting with Pinter and to search for his leading lady. Spiegel forced her upon Kazan, who came to like her, but her inclusion in the cast was forcefully opposed by Pinter. Spiegel, meanwhile, adopted a stance in the middle, allowing Kazan to become her sponsor – thus if she was a failure it would be Kazan who would take the blame, not him. As it turned out, *The Last Tycoon* was her first and last major movie.

While Kazan and Pinter had reservations about Boulting, Spiegel had reservations about De Niro. Spiegel telephoned Kazan repeatedly. He said he thought De Niro was 'common' and had no poise or grace. He was also angry over De Niro's expenses, complaining to Kazan that he was always asking if Spiegel would 'pay for this, that and the other'. 'He's a petty larceny punk!' Spiegel shouted. Kazan recalled, 'There were two Sam Spiegels: the cultured, generous, intelligent, charming dinner companion and "Big Sam", the Spiegel a director rubs up against in the stress of production.' Regardless of Spiegel's criticism, Kazan continued to have faith in his casting of De Niro, whom he described as one of the select band of actors he had directed who actually worked hard at their trade.

Old hands like Tony Curtis and Robert Mitchum stood back in amazement as De Niro even asked if they could rehearse on Sundays during preliminary line work with Kazan. Even more incredible to those older stars was the way De Niro monopolized the director, discussing, interpreting and analysing his character almost line by line. Kazan assessed this as the 'rare thoughtfulness' of an actor who was seriously interested in producing a perfect characterization. To others on the set, it might have indicated a man who lacked confidence. In

85

fact, De Niro was heavily into the part before filming began. He wore the kind of clothes that Monroe Stahr would have worn in the thirties, and ambled around the studio lot as if he owned it. He also lost 42 pounds in the space of little more than a month to get that look of the sick and slender mogul who in the script weighed a mere 120 pounds.

After three weeks of rehearsals, they began filming. Spiegel turned up at the soundstage to wish them luck and to see his eighteen-year-old girlfriend, who had a walk-on part. Kazan whispered, 'Do me a favour . . . try to persuade her to give up acting.' Spiegel stayed on to watch De Niro and once again made his objections known. 'He still has that petty larceny look,' he told Kazan, 'especially when he smiles. He has no nobility.' Later he told Kazan, 'There is no director in the world except you who could have influenced me in taking a chance on Bobby De Niro. I have five and a half million dollars of my own money invested in this fucking movie . . . it's riding on this boy who's spoiling fast and is so wilful and arrogant. I am thinking of replacing him.'

For a time it seemed a serious possibility that De Niro would be fired, but Kazan persisted with his expressions of confidence and diverted Spiegel with further attempts to alter the script. It failed. They had an enormous row over the telephone, ending with Spiegel slamming down the receiver. 'It was,' Kazan recalled, 'in moments like that I had to remind myself this was the man who made *Lawrence of Arabia* – what courage! – and *The Bridge on the River Kwai*, and how, except for him, *On the Waterfront* might not have been made.'

As filming proceeded, Spiegel kept returning to the same topic: De Niro had no power, was monotonous and lacking in humanity – which, as everyone who had seen the movie will know, was not an inaccurate assessment. De Niro was underplaying the role according to the old Stella Adler adage: 'Never give 100 per cent. Let it rest at 80 per cent.' He seemed to have assessed his character and then taken two paces back. There was never any impact, never a forceful moment in the film that made him come through as a character to hold the audience's interest. This was also a flaw of the screenplay, because the lines seldom provided the opportunity for such scenes – and there was no question on this movie of De Niro improvising the lines as he did with Scorsese. Everyone who saw *The Last Tycoon* had their own particular dislike, but most also just wanted to get up and physically shake all concerned to try to put some life into them.

Halfway through the filming Kazan was seriously worried about the scenes with Ingrid Boulting, who, he felt, was soft and unconvincing. Spiegel disagreed and continued to blame De Niro. Kazan then claimed it was Pinter's fault for not having written strong enough love scenes in the first place. One other matter badly affected Kazan's attention. His mother had terminal cancer, and died towards the end of filming. There was then a temporary truce between Spiegel and Kazan, but very soon they were screaming at each other again. Given this unsatisfactory mess everyone was glad when the final scenes approached in early January 1976. But even to the last Kazan was complaining that the screenplay had left him in the lurch, and without a proper ending. He had to make one up, he said, with De Niro walking slowly into a dark unused soundstage.

No one on that shoot could be sure what kind of picture he had made. For once De Niro looked at the daily rushes, though not on a regular basis. It was at that point impossible to say whether it was good, bad or indifferent. Kazan took the temperature from a man who instinctively knew success from failure. He asked cameraman Vic Kemper to telephone and tell him what he thought of the film. Kemper did not call back, and Kazan feared the worst.

He flew to New York to begin the editing process. Spiegel, despite all his earlier misgivings about De Niro, was in ebullient and confident mood and thought – or was kidding himself so that he did not worry about his five and a half million – that they had a winner. When Kazan had completed his cut, they gave Pinter a preview. Each congratulated the other and said it was a fine film. Kazan recalled, 'I wrote in my diary that day: "The picture hangs together, the performances are good, outstanding in the case of Ingrid and Bobby De Niro, and the film has class, beauty, humanity, subtlety and even emotional power." It was the only supremely favourable notice we were to receive.' Dark clouds were moving across the sky. The promotion people at Paramount raised 'severe doubts' about the commercial viability of the film – 'the "kids" wouldn't go for it' and the 'kids' were the backbone of paying customers. Sam Spiegel got the message. He now admitted that there should have been more drama, more sex and more conflict in accord with 'the modern-day idiom'. It was at that moment that the producer agreed he should have demanded more of Pinter.

There were several private screenings to test opinion. Sam sent for David Lean, the double Oscar-winning British director who had worked for him on *The Bridge on the River Kwai* and *Lawrence of*

Arabia, and whose many other successful films such as *Dr Zhivago* and *Ryan's Daughter* made him one of Britain's few directorial legends. Lean came out of the screening in a very quiet manner. De Niro had sat in the row behind him; it was his first look at the film, and he left soon afterwards without voicing any reaction. Lean, meanwhile, told Spiegel that he did not like De Niro's performance, and said De Niro was no leading man.

'There you are,' said Sam to Kazan. 'I told you. He's just an East Side punk.'

So all except Kazan were blaming De Niro until, after another private screening, someone else said it was Ingrid Boulting who was weak, and that the picture failed because of her.

Eventually, Spiegel and Kazan would admit to themselves that they, not the actors, should carry the burden of guilt. They had talked to each other, but neither had listened. They argued from day one, but neither did anything to resolve the other's fears and both knew enough about the business to realize that, if either had serious reservations about a particular aspect, it was worth putting right. That was never done. The result was a half-hearted movie that never went anywhere and flopped at the box office.

To this day, when *The Last Tycoon* is mentioned among movie buffs there is always a debate. The discussion rests always on whether De Niro mishandled the role, or whether Kazan/Spiegel mishandled the movie; whether De Niro was the wrong choice, or whether his co-star, the untried Ingrid Boulting, was wrong. It was a combination of all those factors plus the wafting, anchorless meandering of Harold Pinter's screenplay, pointing always towards the built-in difficulty, if not impossibility, of filming Fitzgerald.

Two decades later, the movie is still being shown on television where the perception is always different. Time has not improved it but, long after the heat of the moment has passed, when the money has been counted and the spilled milk cried over, a movie can be seen in a different light. For me *The Last Tycoon* remains a very watchable armchair movie, among De Niro's most curious but intriguing performances. It is always irritating, too, because you know it could have been so much better.

De Niro's was the only performance of real merit, but even so it was a monosyllabic, toneless character that the script gave him to play. 'I never thought he quite got to grips with it,' Donald Pleasence told me, continuing:

I think it could have had a greater dimension, but I appreciate the difficulties he was working under. Fitzgerald is notoriously difficult, and it was something completely new to him. I found De Niro a very studious, hard-working man but, apart from our scene together, I barely saw him. He kept himself very much to himself. I remarked upon the fact that he was just as you might imagine Irving Thalberg to be in real life. I had no basis for saying that; but that's how it seemed at the time.

Years later, Elia Kazan reflected that there were individual scenes which were good, it had tender and amusing moments, and scene by scene the film flowed. But there was nothing to compel the audience to see it. De Niro came to pretty much the same conclusion. For a time he suffered personally for the critics roundly trashed the movie, although several gave his performance limited praise.

As to the director who had chosen him and defended his work in the face of dire opposition, it was the end of the line. When Elia Kazan filmed the last scene of De Niro walking into the distance, he knew it was the end of his own career. He had already decided, as he neared the end of making of *The Last Tycoon*, never to work in films again. And he never did.

8

Songs and Lovers

The undercurrents of personal relationships in the movie business are an ongoing saga that keeps the gossip columnists in business. De Niro's next film, which would explore some of the darker elements arising from the pressures that his chosen profession puts on people's private lives, came at a particularly pertinent time in his life – and, for that matter, in that of his friend Martin Scorsese. Both were soon to experience the joys of fatherhood and both, for quite different reasons, were involved in deeply personal developments concerning their respective partners at the very time when they were delving into the life-meets-art complexities of showbiz and matrimony. For one it would lead to marriage, and for the other divorce.

The happier of these two events took place as De Niro began work on *New York, New York,* and it came as a complete surprise to those of his associates who were not even aware that he and Diahnne were living together. There was some speculation that the apparent secrecy might be because of their different ethnic backgrounds, but from De Niro's point of view this was a non-starter. 'Black?' said his friend Harvey Keitel. 'I doubt that De Niro even noticed.'

That may well have been true, and it was certainly in line with the Brandoesque, politically correct stance that De Niro adopted on many issues of social consequence. However, some people noted a further similarity between De Niro and Brando in their choice of female companions. Brando had been involved in a string of obsessive relationships with exotic-looking women beginning with his first wife, Anna Kashfi, who claimed Indian birth, through to various other wives and girlfriends of Mexican, Caribbean or South Seas origin. De Niro too would be involved with a number of high-profile women of Afro descent. There would be some speculation about those liaisons, but as to any motive only De Niro could put such speculation to rest. But discussion about this aspect of his life has always been strictly off limits, guaranteed to make him clam up and head for the nearest exit. Typically, his marriage to Diahnne was designed as a quiet, non-media event.

It took place after he had finished filming *The Last Tycoon*, in June 1976. The select band of guests was typical De Niro, comprising only those with whom he had worked and who had been good to him on his way to this very satisfactory point in his life. Listed in chronological order, they were: Sally Kirkland, Shelley Winters, Brian De Palma, John Hancock, Julie Bovasso, Martin and Julia Scorsese, Harvey Keitel, Paul Schrader, Elia Kazan and Sam Spiegel. As Schrader said: 'It was a curious line-up of people. Significantly, every one of them had helped De Niro to become a different person.'

The non-denominational ceremony was held at New York's Ethical Culture Society, and he also formally adopted Diahnne's daughter Drina, then eight, whom he adored. Not long afterwards came more news: Diahnne was expecting his child. While in Rome earlier that year for some final sound dubbing for the English version of *Novecento* he and Diahnne had stayed at the Hotel Raphael, a charming, ivy-covered building in a quiet corner behind the Piazza Navona. It was there, they worked out later, that the child must have been conceived, and when their son was born, in 1977, they named him Raphael.

These personal affairs in order, he moved rapidly on to his next movie, which would return him to a New York theme. It would be his third collaboration with Martin Scorsese, whose wife Julia was also expecting their first child – though by the time the picture was over she would be threatening divorce as well, accusing him of becoming too close to his star, Liza Minnelli. The Scorsese–De Niro movies all tended to be rather familial gatherings, and in this instance there were some unfortunate side-issues yet to be thrown in.

De Niro and Minnelli looked, on the face of it, an interesting screen partnership, a blending of the dark, edgy characterizations for which the actor was best known, with the aura of glitz and showbiz that surrounded the singer. Minnelli herself was in need of a movie revival. Following her scorching performance in *Cabaret*, for which she won an Oscar, her last two movies, *Lucky Lady* with Burt Reynolds and *A Matter of Time* with Ingrid Bergman, directed by her father Vincente, had been severely punished by the critics. From her point of view, joining the De Niro–Scorsese unit held much promise, with both currently riding high in the afterglow of *Taxi Driver*.

Scorsese brought them together after months of negotiation and bartering for *New York, New York*, which in spite of its title would be shot entirely on soundstage 29 at MGM Studios. This was where those great musical extravaganzas of the Golden Age had been filmed and where Liza's mother, Judy Garland, had been one of their top stars. In fact, when Liza arrived at the studios she discovered she had been allotted Judy's former dressing room, though had her mother been alive she might not have been so positive and enthusiastic about Liza playing at MGM or having her old room. 'Those bastards, those lousy, fucking bastards!' were her last words when she walked out of it twenty-seven years earlier, having been unceremoniously fired by Louis B. Mayer.

De Niro too was faced with curious reflections from the past. He found himself, appropriately for the man who has become known as the male version of Greta Garbo, in the dressing room once occupied by the actress who had been his father's obsession – though any similarity between his and Liza's quarters ended there. Her room was warm and well furnished, filled with flowers and telegrams from well-wishers, bright lights and comfortable furniture. His was sparsely furnished and drab, containing only his script, a few telephone messages and a tape deck with some jazz recordings.

Minnelli had not met De Niro until shortly before they started filming. Like everyone who knows the name but can never remember the most forgettable face ever possessed by a famous movie star, she asked, 'Is he the one who wore the suit all the time?'

'No,' replied Scorsese, 'that was Harvey Keitel.'

So they gathered in Hollywood, where De Niro and his wife returned to the sprawling Bel-Air mansion which they had rented while he was filming *The Last Tycoon*. Once again the pre-production preparation was meticulous as he sank himself into the role of a jazz musician. For both himself and Scorsese *New York, New York* represented a new departure, and there was some surprise in the trade press that they had turned to what was being billed as an upbeat, modern musical. However, anyone who had followed the work of these two men would hardly have been expecting anything conventional in the genre. The music was merely the backdrop to a deeper exploration of relationships, in which the dark chasms of the De Niro role would be offset against the anticipated ebullience of Liza Minnelli's character.

The film has a superb opening on VJ-Day 1945, as thousands of people fill Times Square. De Niro tosses his military uniform out of

92

his hotel window and puts on white slacks and a shirt emblazoned with the Statue of Liberty. Then he sets off to join the fun at a victory ball at the Starlight Terrace of the Waldorf Astoria, where he is blatantly in search of female company and has a stock of chat-up lines to achieve this aim. That night they weren't working, and certainly not on Francine Evans (Liza Minnelli). He falls into a chair beside her; she says the seat is taken and he responds with the sharp dialogue that peppers the script: 'I know it's taken but I'm going to sit here and I'm going to think out another angle.'

This prelude to the romance is set against a spectacular opening sequence with a cast of hundreds, meticulously clothed to the last 1940s' detail and jitterbugging to a re-creation of the Tommy Dorsey Orchestra. In terms of time and expense, the scene was extravagant but essential.

Jimmy leaves the hall and goes home alone that night, but with the help of coincidence and persuasion he begins an affair with Francine – though the attraction of this typical De Niro weirdo to Minnelli's delightful 'sweet kid' is never really explained. Eventually they marry. The film really revolves around their respective careers, he as a jazz musician and she as a band singer, until she is whisked away to Hollywood and becomes a star. In between, they fight a lot, make up, he drinks a lot, they have a child, they fight again and he gets violent before their final separation when she takes up the offer that leads her to fame and fortune.

He too, becomes successful and has his own club with a classy black singer played by Diahnne Abbott, who gives a faultless rendition of 'Honeysuckle Rose'. Jimmy and Francine meet again at the Waldorf, exactly ten years after their first encounter in 1945, and by then she is the star attraction. Seeing Jimmy in the audience, she belts out the now famous song without which no Minnelli stage performance is complete: 'New York, New York', which in the film Jimmy had written for her when they were struggling.

In old-style musicals this would have been the cue for a reunion. But when Jimmy goes backstage afterwards to explore a possible reconciliation the gulf between them remains and Francine has no intention of picking up where they left off. Jimmy accepts the situation and they part, accepting that they have reached their own particular goals in life without each other.

Relationships were supposedly the underlying key to the film, and Scorsese himself underscored the fact that personal matters crept into its making. 'We see things in the character that relate to ourselves,' Scorsese explained.

> The picture was about that period in your life when you're about to make it; you know you're talented, you know you're this, you know you're that, but you just don't quite make it, not for another four or five years . . . and people who are crazily in love with each other can't live with each other. And in *New York, New York*, Jimmy Doyle freaks while his wife [Liza] is pregnant. Both our own wives were pregnant while we were shooting, and we talked about it a lot.

That was one element of the like-for-like explorations of the character De Niro would portray. Another lay in the musical side of Jimmy Doyle, for which the actor's obsessive dedication to correctness and believability drove his coach, jazz saxophonist George Auld (formerly with Benny Goodman and Artie Shaw), to the point of acrimony. De Niro made it plain that he did not want to be identified as an actor mimicking a jazz musician – he wanted to *be* that musician in every respect, right down to learning to play the tenor saxophone. He said afterwards,

> It's my job as an actor to create the feeling that I'm the one doing the playing. I've seen too many movies where the actor is so obviously merely moving his fingers up and down the keys while the music is going in the opposite direction. So I learned to play the same material that George recorded, and though I can't read music I wanted to make sure I could synchronize what he was playing.

Auld had mixed feelings about this quest for perfection. 'He was just relentless in his preparation,' says this affable, outgoing man who enjoyed the social side of his work as much as the playing. 'I have never seen anyone with such a talent for absorbing the music and the tuition. He must have listened to thousands of records, watched dozens of tapes of jazzmen at work, but he took it to such extreme lengths that it became a real turn-off as far as I was concerned.'

Auld said De Niro's intensity reminded him of Benny Goodman, who was not the best liked of men among his colleagues. 'I used to call De Niro "Mumbles",' Auld recalls. 'He never laughed or joked about what we were doing. It was deadly serious. He asked me ten million questions a day, and my wife said she expected him one night to get in bed with us. It was a robot in there, always seeking, always searching. He mastered all the externals – the musician slang, the movements. But not the inside stuff – playing from the heart.'

Auld's views merely repeated those of many who have worked with De Niro. His absorption in the role showed in his constant attention to detail and his customary long, deep on-set conferences with Scorsese. On this picture, however, he was not the only one to demand the director's time and advice. Similar attention was sought by Minnelli, with whom Scorsese was also ensconced for long periods. Actors in costume, slouching around the set, would raise their eyes to heaven as Scorsese disappeared into his private quarters with either De Niro or Minnelli. The director himself was prompted by the mounting aggravation to comment, 'Look, the real stuff between me and Bob is private. Bob talks to me in private. He needs a lot of time. We both need a lot of time.'

That now well-known fact was confirmed by De Niro's stand-in Jon Cutler, who had also worked with him on *Bang the Drum Slowly*. 'Bob is unapproachable when he is working. He doesn't want to be bothered . . . he hates to break character, even at night or weekends. I have no problem with that, except when I try to take too much of his time on set. But that's the way he works.'

Sometimes, however, the reverse happened. De Niro needed the assistance of other actors to achieve his celebrated non-verbal reaction to a given situation: at such moments his facial or physical expressions spoke louder than any words and his silences were such that most other actors would be scared to attempt them. To achieve this, he often needed surprises from the actors themselves, just as he himself often shocked his fellow actors with unscripted, out-of-shot actions – such as the time he lay in the grave of the dead gangster in *Bloody Mama*. Cutler, therefore, often found himself having to use off-camera shock tactics to give De Niro the cue for a reaction.

This is itself created a problem for Liza Minnelli, who was completely unused to such acting techniques. Her leading men of recent times, such as Michael York on *Cabaret* and Burt Reynolds and Gene Hackman on *Lucky Lady* had borne no comparison to the quiet quirkiness of De Niro, and that was evident in some of her own facial expressions.

Although she claimed to be a 'listening actor' who would keep right on with her lines regardless of what was going on around her, it was not always possible to do so without flinching. She has a rare kind of natural reaction – probably best seen in Marilyn Monroe in her better movies – in which her wide eyes and oval mouth reflect an innate, almost uncontrollable response to surprises. These were quite apparent in *New York, New York*, due partially to De Niro's delivery and partially to the setting of the movie.

Minnelli also has the ability to drop into character, putting her whole self into the portrayal – the opposite of De Niro's style. In *Cabaret* she not only captured the style of the period, but actually lived it and sang it. She did much the same in *New York, New York*, and in this respect there was an unfortunate abrasiveness in some of her scenes with De Niro, who stood out as a product of modern cinema while all around him were people of the forties and fifties.

There was evident conflict in producing a musical for the 1970s based upon times past. Scorsese reckoned his intentions were always to transpose the musical concept that was a throw-back to the days of the dream-factory productions into a drama of broken relationships: to mould nostalgia together with a modern social phenomenon. It was a point that the critics would take up when the film was released in 1977. They saw it as one of the more confusing aspects of the film, although it would subsequently be shown merely to represent attitudes ahead of their time, even in 1977. As the focus on marriage and fidelity turned into a more determinedly profound issue of the 1980s, *New York, New York* was seen as a precursor to the debate.

To achieve this effect the streetwise dialogue of De Niro's character was oddly out of sync with the period, as was some of the music he was purportedly playing. Even Minnelli's songs were redubbed to aid the illusion and create a pastiche complete with phoney backdrops and clichéd floating signposts of yesteryear to denote the passing of time.

The on-set discussions between the principals was apparently fast and furious, and the six-month shoot dragged on well beyond its completion date. Changes were being made almost daily, and Minnelli herself admitted: 'They came from everyone's imagination and enthusiasm. After a while we were all running around with tape recorders so that we wouldn't lose our ideas.'

This, according to Scorsese, was a 'fun' shoot, but it was also potentially a producer's nightmare. Undercurrents were also developing which threatened the progress of filming and attracted some untoward

In the movie that made Robert
De Niro an international star:
The Godfather Part II, for which he
won an Oscar for best actor.
(*Paramount Pictures*)

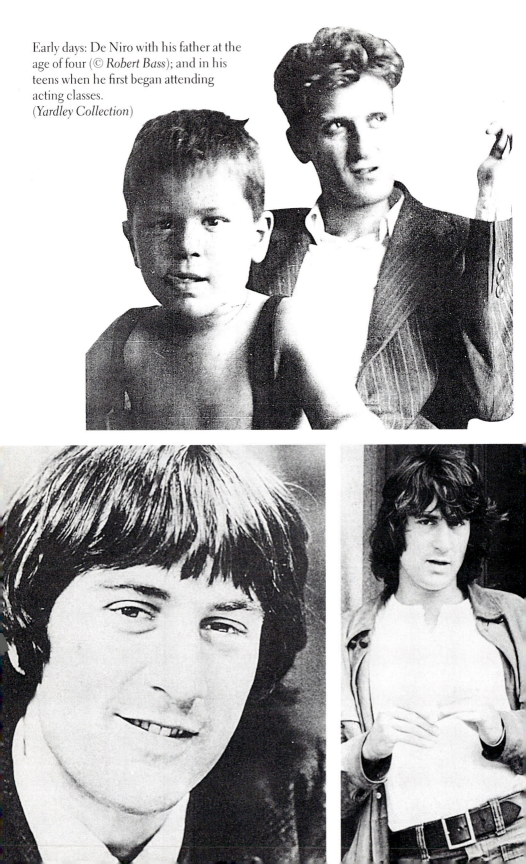

Early days: De Niro with his father at the age of four (© *Robert Bass*); and in his teens when he first began attending acting classes. (*Yardley Collection*)

Early roles that helped
launch De Niro. (*Above*) In
Bang the Drum Slowly with
Michael Moriarty and
Heather Macrae (*ANJA
Films*); and (*below*) with his
supporter and surrogate
'Jewish momma', Shelley
Winters, in *Bloody Mama*.
(*AIP Pictures*)

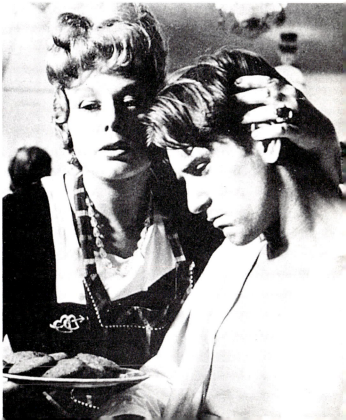

The leer that launched a thousand other faces. In *Bang the Drum Slowly*, De Niro established a style and stance reminiscent of Dean and Brando that made him a model for 1970s' youth and brought accolades from the critics. (*Yardley Collection*)

(*Below*) De Niro and
Martin Scorsese pictured
on the set of one of their
most important films,
Taxi Driver. (*Left and
bottom*) Two of the
movie's most menacing
scenes. (*Italo-Judeo*)

Overt sex is remarkably absent from De Niro's repertoire, though his screen partnerships with actresses have always been complicated and intense. In *The Last Tycoon* with Ingrid Boulting (*top left, Yardley Collection*) he was cool and shy; with Lisa Minnelli in *New York, New York* (*bottom left, Chartoff–Winkler Productions*) he was selfish and violent. His favourite actress is the like-minded Meryl Streep who made her screen debut with him in *The Deer Hunter* (*above, EMI Films*); later they collaborated in *Falling in Love*. (*Right, Yardley Collection*)

The now famous De Niro metamorphosis was at its most astonishing in *Raging Bull*, in which he played boxing champ Jake La Motta. For most of the movie he was fighting fit and could go ten rounds with anyone; then production was halted for four months while he put on 65lbs to appear as La Motta, the bloated has-been. (*United Artists*) publicity on a set which had already seen a good deal of media attention because of its high-profile visitors including Minnelli's father, Vincente, who dropped by the set regularly and offered some fatherly advice. Others included Jack Nicholson, Sylvester Stallone and Bernardo Bertolucci. 'We are so enthusiastic we just keep on going until the early hours, no matter what time we started the previous morning,' Liza told visiting writers. But with a flurry of journalistic interest on events at soundstage 29, some darker stories and gossip began to emerge. Costume designer Theadora Van Runkle recalled, 'People still tell horror stories about the filming of *New York, New York*. We would get our first call at 7 a.m. and often they wouldn't get their first shot in until after dark. The crew were treated like peasants . . . totally ignored. Meanwhile, Marty and Liza would be closeted in her trailer. Going over the script, presumably.'

Scorsese's and De Niro's wives were often present, Diahnne Abbott because she had a small role, Julia Cameron Scorsese because she was increasingly worried about her husband's behaviour, a fear made worse now that she was in the later stages of pregnancy. She was afraid that her husband had fallen deeply in love with Minnelli.

Filming ended eight weeks past the production deadline and over budget. The atmosphere among the producers, the distributing studio and the media was sufficient to stir up that well-known pre-release situation known in the trade as bad-mouthing. In other words, the picture was being dismissed before anyone had even seen it. This difficulty was only exacerbated when Scorsese delivered his final cut version to United Artists: it ran to four hours and twenty-nine minutes, and studio executives held up their hands in horror. They knew, as did Scorsese, that it was virtually impossible to market a picture of that length, because most cinemas wanted to run a feature movie twice nightly. It was a rerun of the scenario De Niro had experienced when he made *Novecento*, which Bertolucci had only just managed to get into the US cinemas after months of wrangling, editing, redubbing, cutting and pasting.

The space for artistry in the cinema remains severely limited, and with an $8–$10 million budget – plenty in 1977 – plus that much again for post-production and launch costs at stake, it was virtually non-existent. So Scorsese was ordered back to the cutting room to reduce his creation by half. He returned, eyes bloodshot and shirt tear-stained, with a 142-minute version. United Artists were still not satisfied and ordered him to cut the film's musical centre-fold, Liza's eleven-minute spectacular entitled 'Happy Endings'. 'Out!' said United Artists, and Liza cried.

The scene, a mini-film within a film of Francine's rise to stardom, was considered a high-point, and many fans agreed when the movie was re-released four years later as the studio attempted to recoup some heavy losses. But by then the damage had been done. Scorsese was a fool unto himself in many respects. He knew the rules: showing twice-nightly. There was simply no getting away from it unless the film had staggering, once-in-a-lifetime potential, and *New York, New York* could not boast such qualities.

Although later it would take on the dubious title of 'cult movie', its biggest downfall at the time was a laborious plot and far too much downbeat dialogue between the unhappy couple caught by those familiar vagaries of a showbiz marriage: insecurity, success, drink, excess, their child. De Niro was admittedly not entirely satisfied with his own performance, and felt afterwards that he had given too much time to perfecting his musical proficiency and not enough to other aspects of the role. Scorsese had promised a movie that explored showbiz (if not all) relationships, in the final version but the deep-down implications are never really investigated. There are lots of gaps, and we can only assume they were left on the cutting room floor.

New York, New York is not a particularly pleasant film unless the viewer has a certain combination of reasons for watching it: admiration of Scorsese's technique, De Niro's inspirational talent and Minnelli's irrepressible, knock 'em dead delivery. Still, although it was a commercial flop which fell well short of costs on its opening release in the USA, it gradually gathered a reputation. It is today regularly on television, had a long life in video retail and rental stores and eventually crept to break-even point.

For those who were present at the time, however, there remained a feeling that it could have been so much better. That was a view shared by Minnelli, though she would never say such a thing in public. De Niro confirmed it by being low-key about his own performance, which is the only clue he gives to his feelings about any particular project.

Meanwhile, as their movie made its uncomfortable way towards the cinema screens, the relationships which Scorsese spoke of exploring in his movie were being mirrored to some extent in real life. Paul Schrader, author of *Taxi Driver*, had decided that 'unlike Warren Beatty, who procrastinates and hates to act, De Niro is only at ease in front of the camera'. This unease had been amply demonstrated to his fellow artists throughout the making of *New York, New York*, and was further evidenced at a post-production party that De Niro and Diahnne held at their temporary Bel-Air home in the early spring of 1977. While the guests were arriving De Niro was out of sight somewhere, still toying with the saxophone and mastering at last a full rendition of 'Misty'.

The partygoers, ten in all, trooped in for cocktails and De Niro entered almost unnoticed. He may have been the host, but he certainly did not intend to be the centre of attraction. He stood back, letting others do the talking while Diahnne fluttered like a butterfly among the guests who included Scorsese, Brian De Palma and actor Peter Boyle, who had appeared in a lesser role in *Taxi Driver*. They were all good friends and they expected no more than they got from De Niro: background noises and general accord to other people's lead in conversations.

Silences can be awkward, and sometimes guests say or do silly things to keep a difficult party moving along. On this occasion, as they all went into the dining room Boyle dropped his trousers and mooned the De Niros' roast turkey. Everyone cheered. De Niro merely stuttered a few 'Yeah . . . hey, heys', looked at his feet, scratched his nose and began carving the insulted bird. He remained, all evening, the onlooker, sitting next to his wife on the sofa, nodding and speaking only very occasionally.

'Fun?' jazzman Georgie Auld exclaimed when asked to recall a funny anecdote about De Niro from the three months he worked with him. 'Fun? Working with Robert De Niro, being with Robert De Niro, was about as much fun as the clap.'

9

The Hunter and the Hunted

There was a certain clamouring developing among the media to get to Robert De Niro. All the big glossies were sounding him out for interviews, and in July 1977 *Time* magazine extravagantly described him as 'the hottest actor working in films today'. This totally disregarded the likes of Jack Nicholson, Al Pacino, Dustin Hoffman and Robert Redford, who might have felt that they better deserved such a title – certainly in terms of box-office appeal. *Time* used the description in highlighting the curious difference between those stars and De Niro. Any one of them would have been instantly recognized and mobbed had they turned up in a city amid a cluster of college students, but not so with De Niro.

In that respect he once told a story against himself. The incident happened when he went to the Cannes Film Festival, where a crowd of stars and Hollywood VIPs were taking centre stage prior to the showing of one of his films. 'There was this media guy talking to a PR guy,' he recalled, 'and one said to the other, "No sign of De Niro." And I was standing right next to them.' The same thing happened when he was filming his next movie, *The Deer Hunter*. He made his way through the crowd of students in the lobby of the Holiday Inn, Pittsburgh, during their break from a workshop session – and not one recognized him. True, De Niro was sporting a beard at the time, but most cinemagoers would have easily seen through that on, say, Redford or Nicholson.

In De Niro's case, what his fellow actors had been saying about him for some years was undoubtedly proved that day in the Holiday Inn – that he possessed the unnerving ability to fine-tune his screen characters while blurring his own, that he was interested not in his career but in the challenge of a particular role. He did not need to be a recluse and incidentally was not, despite what the magazines said. Unlike most of his colleagues who went on publicity jaunts, he just did not talk to the media.

He fuelled the continuing mystique by refusing point-blank to give anything other than a surface-depth interview relating specifically to whatever movie he was currently appearing in, usually limiting his disclosures to the preparation work and his view of the characterization he aimed to achieve. Occasionally he would open up briefly, though in a vague, faltering manner, about his acting techniques, which he described as a mixture of anarchy and discipline. Even less frequently he brooded on feeling guilty about success. But that was it.

More and more, he treated potential interviewers as if they were bailiffs, and those established topics in Hollywood 'star' profiles – childhood, parents, background, hobbies, schooldays and so on – continued to be taboo. His increasing status in the league table of power did not mellow his resolve in that regard; it merely strengthened it. Those who came calling after *Taxi Driver* and *New York, New York* found no change in the much-reported situation. De Niro was not talking.

It was reiterated time and again, often amusingly so as demonstrated in the summer of 1977 when *Playboy* made one of many attempts to get De Niro to open his heart to its readers, an invitation which many regarded as the ultimate accolade. Los Angeles-based writer Joseph Block finally penetrated the ring of steel, and a few exchanges from his tape-recorded transcript show just how tenacious De Niro had become in warding off unwanted questions:

> *Block*: You have sprung into superstardom status. Can you tell us what trials and tribulations you have had to overcome?
> *De Niro*: No.
> *Block*: Don't you ever talk?
> *De Niro*: Yes . . . no. . . .
> *Block*: What was your childhood like? What kind of kid were you. . . . Spoiled? Underprivileged?
> *De Niro*: I don't know.
> *Block*: What do you do in your spare time?
> *De Niro*: I golf . . . I play tennis, you know. I'm a typical New Yorker. . . . I. . . . No, I don't do anything, I sleep. No, I'm only kidding. . . . I spend time with my wife and family and that's it. We're working so hard we have no leisure time.

Block: What does this do to your head?

De Niro: I'm spending about $600 a week talking to an analyst about that. So I'd rather not talk about that now. No, I'm not really seeing one . . . but I don't know how to answer that question.

Exasperated interviewer: Okay, we give up . . . let's get back to the movies. . . .

By now the media and even Hollywood itself had come to regard De Niro's comments with a cautious, jaundiced eye. Was this man for real? Or was it all just another act to preserve the mystique which he had created for himself? No one could really tell.

When he had finished *New York, New York*, the only news the press got from him was that he would be taking a year off to devote to his wife and family, although in reality that plan was already being superseded by approaches for him to join another controversial project, which would become *The Deer Hunter*. For a brief while, however, it looked as if he might settle to the kind of Hollywood lifestyle that he had always said he would not be drawn into – flash cars, mansions and swimming pools. The accepted route of everyone around him in the business involved the horrors of Tinseltown itself, where so many fine actors had lost their youth, their simplicity and their freshness somewhere between the clauses of a million-dollar contract. If there had been a theme to De Niro's career in his discussions with his friends in recent months, it was the fear that he would lose the demonic, uncompromising stance that had propelled him so far, and the greatest threat to that possibility was to lose himself in the quagmire of Hollywood excess, conformity and run-of-the-mill movies.

So was the radical New York actor really thinking of assuming the trappings of a star? Diahnne certainly liked the sunny life and enjoyed the pace better than New York. They became regulars at the Los Angeles nightspots. Although they had recently acquired an elegant brownstone house back in a leafy street in Greenwich Village, it had been a mark of success which harked back to De Niro's past. Their own mansion in Beverly Hills represented something else: the future. The question was not so much how De Niro would fit into it, but whether he would do so at all.

He had originally planned to build a place for his family in the fashionable Brentwood district of Los Angeles. Then, however, he decided they could not wait that long and bought a sprawling contemporary ranch house, surrounded by shrubberies and with glorious views over the Pacific and the hills. There were two swimming pools, a sauna and even a guest house in the grounds. He immediately set about having it refurbished, but even so it was the kind of property which was a familiar landmark in the careers of superstars – the one that said: 'I've made it.' Thus the man who had been seen to shun virtually every other convention expected of a film star was displaying a slight chink in his armour, one which revealed that this stern, obsessive and methodical non-participant did indeed perhaps possess some of the aspirations and acquisitive traits that normally lived at the glamour end of the market.

Meanwhile there was a slight altercation going on with the landlord of their rented house in Bel-Air, who made noises about suing De Niro for $10,000. He reckoned that Diahnne's cats had soiled the rooms, clawed the furniture and caused an unsightly mess.

Even as he and his family moved into their new home in the early summer of 1977, De Niro's plans to take time off had evaporated. By June he was already working with director Michael Cimino on preparations for *The Deer Hunter*. It was a movie whose life began with a slow burn, so slow that it was almost extinguished. But gradually it became one of the most memorable films of the 1970s, and the one that had the most impact on the subject of the Vietnam War.

For Cimino, who had come to life again after a four-year break since making *Thunderbolt and Lightfoot* with Clint Eastwood and Jeff Bridges, this was a very personal project. As with his last film, he had co-written the outline for *The Deer Hunter*, although at the time when he was hawking the idea around Hollywood it was no more than that – an expanded idea. Cimino wanted to home in on a different angle, taking the war to the heart of the people. He wanted to demonstrate the views and effects of Vietnam on a tight-knit community of steel workers in Clairton, Pennsylvania, which would be achieved by following three of the community's sons who were drafted. Cimino would show the three men living a nightmarish existence in a Viet Cong prison camp, and the film included scenes of terrible violence. When the three men return to their community one has lost his mind, another his legs and the third his self-respect. Life back in Clairton is never the same again.

Hollywood believed that America was still in too great a state of shock after Vietnam to receive such a movie, a view borne out by the poor reaction to the handful of Vietnam movies already on the circuit.

Studio after studio turned down *The Deer Hunter*, and the finance was eventually raised from an unexpected source. Two British producers, Barry Spikings and Michael Deeley (responsible for *The Italian Job*, *Murphy's War* and *The Man Who Fell to Earth*, among others), who had never tackled anything quite like this story, took it to Deeley's erstwhile employer, the British music and entertainment conglomerate EMI, and persuaded them to part with a budget of $7.5 million 'on a hunch'. It was one of the few major movies to be financed by British money, and incidentally the most successful. It appealed because the reaction to the Vietnam War had been analysed far more objectively in the British press, which could distance itself from the loss of life which had affected every town and city across the United States. As yet, no mainstream film-maker had dared to address some of the issues which had been critically dissected in the foreign press until Cimino came in with his astounding and dramatic exploration of these themes.

De Niro himself was never an overtly political voice, unlike those well-known liberals Jack Nicholson, Michael Douglas and Robert Redford, whose anti-war stance was well known, as would be their later dedication to the cause of the Democrats. Later, when speaking about the movie, he did venture a fairly flat comment that he thought the war was wrong and that he did not respect the decisions of those in authority. In fact *The Deer Hunter* was never intended as a politically motivated piece, but was aimed at examining aesthetics in local communities at the heart of American society.

Cimino's deal with EMI rested, as ever, upon securing the services of the right leading man. He had a shortlist of names headed by Robert De Niro and, to attract his interest, he sent the actor a photograph of a hunter with a deer tied over the hood of a white Cadillac, with steel mills in the background. 'It was such a great shot,' De Niro admitted in a press launch for the film, 'that I called him immediately and we talked. I met Cimino a few times and went with him to look at the locations in America. I was curious about him and his motivations for this story, and it was a way of getting to know him.'

Once they had talked, De Niro became engrossed by the project and joined in pre-production planning, involving himself with virtually every aspect from ideas for the script to suitable locations. They travelled the country for six weeks, clocking up a staggering 150,000 miles as they pulled together ideas and characters to populate the film. In the steelmaking region which provides the hub of the film they met dozens of blue-collar workers who became models for the characters and situations that would explode with such controversial reality in *The Deer Hunter*.

Cimino's story began in 1968 and then travelled through three stages to create for the audience the experiences of men drawn from everyday American life and thrown into a horrific war which they believed did not concern them. But it was not an overtly anti-war film. It was about many things, from male bonding to mindless patriotism. The plot of the movie was simple – so simple that it was possible for Cimino to condense it to a few paragraphs in his 'spiel' to the EMI producers over dinner. The description was as dramatic as it was succinct: in sharp, short sentences, he outlined the set-up.

The movie opens in the dark, satanic steel mills, enlivened by the spectacular fireworks of molten metal. Here, in the town of Clairton, Pennsylvania, descendants of the original Slavic immigrants continue the old family-led traditions. The men, fathers and sons, generation after generation, work in the mills, while the women marry young and produce the next generation.

The camera moves down, focusing on a group of friends at work, and follows their lives before, during and after the war. De Niro's Michael Vronsky is the central figure. They are all to be discovered in the opening sequences at work, sweating profusely in their asbestos suits in the sweltering heat of the blast furnace where showers of metal fly high and provide a dramatic backdrop.

There is hefty male bonding here, especially the camaraderie of Michael (De Niro) and his buddies Stan (John Cazale), Steven (John Savage), Nick (Christopher Walken) and Axel (Chuck Aspergren, a real-life steelworker) in this vision of American life. These are hard-working men in the industrial heartland where its youngest are being drafted for Vietnam, an obscure, faraway place about which they have little care or understanding. All they know is that good Americans are being killed, and they cannot figure out the political reasoning – nor, perhaps, do they consider that political regimes of the native countries of their immigrant ancestors support the other side.

Cimino says he wants to show the ordinariness of their lives by introducing the principal characters as they gather for Steven's wedding, which is a ritual of Russian Orthodoxy Americanized by the rented tuxedos reminiscent of the opening sequence of *The Godfather*. Everyone who is going to get drunk does so, and the rest eat the food and dance till they drop.

Next, Cimino demonstrates that ordinary men from this community can be wild, boozy and brutal, as the four friends go to the mountains to shoot deer, a scene which would be shot 10,000 feet up on Mount Baker in Washington State, another of the locations scouted by De Niro and Cimino on their travels. The interlude ends with the crack of rifle fire and an immediate scene shift across the world to South-east Asia, where a massive wall of sound puts the three characters and the audience in the centre of the Vietnam War.

Michael, Nick and Steven are eventually captured and tortured by the Viet Cong in a remote prison. There is brutality and extreme violence, so convincing that some people will be brought to the very edge of their seats while others will barely be able to watch; some won't, and will run from the cinema. The three are held with others in bamboo cages partially submerged in a rat-infested swamp, and are let out only during their captors' playtime. Did this really happen? audiences will ask. Cimino wants to convince them that it did, and he will do so in the most controversial manner. . . .

He now comes to the most nail-bitingly horrific and realistic scene of all time as the men are forced to play Russian roulette, passing the gun with one bullet in the chamber around a table while their captors bet among themselves on which one will blow his brains out. Michael, Steve and Nick watch in horror as they wait their turn, sunk up to their necks in an aquatic cell.

Cimino pictures the scene in the most graphic and dramatic fashion: the three watch the enforced suicide of the first victim. The bullet goes in and a stream of blood spurts forward. He falls to the ground, and his still smoking skull head is kicked by a Viet Cong guard. Steve breaks down. The guards scream at him and Michael is repeatedly slapped in the face. De Niro will play that scene for real – real slaps, real pain. This scene is the one that Cimino knows will be controversial. These will be some of the most tense and emotive scenes ever seen in a motion picture, which in the event even the actors will have great difficulty sustaining without breaking down. Even De Niro, always deep in character, will find it one of the most difficult sequences of his life, unmatched before and since.

Cimino knows they will accuse him of gratuitous violence. Audiences will be physically sick with horror; grown men will cry, and some will even rush out of the cinema. This scene, this film will shock America and tell them what it was really like for their boys in Vietnam.

And then, at the height of this intensity, Cimino breaks it with wild release. When Michael's turn comes round, he knows that the bullet must be in the next chamber. He manages instead to shoot one of the guards, and in the mayhem that follows makes his escape. Michael leads his friends through the jungle, one of them crippled from the waist down, the other in severe mental disarray. Yet more thrills will keep the audience in suspense as a US helicopter appears and hoists Nick aboard. Then, just as Michael and Steven are almost at the chopper's doors, they fall back into the water and have to be abandoned. But through more incredible twists and turns, they make it to Saigon. In the third episode the film switches back to Clairton, Pennsylvania, to the homecoming and a remarkable ending to the movie in which they all end up singing 'God Bless America'.

The making of *The Deer Hunter* had more than its share of offscreen drama too. De Niro put himself into the centre of the imagined hub of home town activity six weeks before filming began. He virtually lived with the steelworkers, drank with them in the local bars, played pool, visited their homes, studied their accents and even changed his New York driving licence for a Pennsylvania one. He took out a Pennsylvanian gun licence to get the feel of the hunting episode, became completely at one with the surroundings and made copious notes. He did everything apart from working shifts at the steelworks – he tried to, but the bosses refused: they only let him visit and watch.

He was already 'in character', amply demonstrated by the fact that, throughout his visits, not a single person recognized him as Robert De Niro. He introduced himself as Bob and became 'one of them'. When the filming was ready to begin Cimino moved his crew to locations in Pennsylvania, West Virginia and Ohio and obtained permission from US Steel to film the dramatic, spectacular opening sequence in its Central Blast Furnace in Cleveland, Ohio. For that few minutes of film, EMI had to take out an additional $5 million insurance cover for the actors and crew.

A real-life drama developed during the making of *The Deer Hunter*. It centred on one of its stars, John Cazale, who not long before had been diagnosed as suffering from bone cancer and given at best a year to live. Cazale was best remembered for his role as Fredo Corleone, assassinated on the orders of his own brother Michael in *The Godfather*. He had also appeared in Coppola's *The Conversation* and in Sidney Lumet's *Dog Day Afternoon*. When Cimino, on De Niro's suggestion, offered him the role of Stan in *The Deer Hunter* he was already very sick.

Meryl Streep, who was living with Cazale, took a minor role in the picture so that she could be with him. She was offered the part of the bride's attendant in the opening sequences, where De Niro's character takes a shine to her. In the original screenplay the role was negligible. Cimino explained the set-up and suggested that Streep should write her own lines, which she did. He was so impressed that he extended her part, and she went on to win an Oscar nomination as Best Supporting Actress. It also brought her to the attention of Hollywood. Up to that point she had appeared in only one film, a bit part in Fred Zinnemann's *Julia*, which starred Jane Fonda.

For her lover John Cazale, the chance of them working together meant a great deal. However, the day before filming began an executive from EMI contacted Cimino and said that the standard medical had revealed Cazale's condition; he would therefore have to be replaced, because they could not get him insured. Cimino recalled:

> Shooting had already been delayed and both John and Meryl wondered if it would ever work out for them. I bluntly told the company we were going to start shooting the movie and they responded by saying that, unless I got rid of John, they would shut down the picture. The only alternative, they said, was to write another script which excluded John's character completely. I said, 'Go-ahead and shut the picture down', and slammed down the phone.

Finally, EMI relented and Cazale stayed and completed his role without a hitch. Sadly, however, he died before the film was released and he never saw the finished product, but it remains to this day a lasting memorial of him for Meryl Streep.

After filming the opening sequences in Pennsylvania Cimino moved his cast and crew to Thailand for location filming in terrain as close as possible to that of Vietnam. More drama followed. First, the monsoon rains were the worst in living memory and the production was marooned in north central Thailand. Next there was a revolution and a military-led group seized power in Thailand. EMI, faced with the prospect of having a hundred crew and actors stranded 10,000 miles from home, contacted the new government through the British Foreign Office and were given assurances that they would be safe. In fact the next day a large contingent of Royal Thai Police turned up at the location site beside the River Kwai and remained on guard until filming had finished.

De Niro, meantime, was discussing one of the most dangerous stunts in the picture, in which he and John Savage had to hang on to the bottom side of a helicopter 30 feet above the icy waters of the Kwai. In the film, a US helicopter attempts to rescue the three buddies. With one aboard, Michael and Nick are clinging to the undercarriage as it ascends in the air. But Nick falls off into the river, and Michael drops down into the water to save him. The stunt team had worked out the details but it became apparent that, with such close shooting, the stunt men could be recognized. So De Niro and Savage insisted on doing it themselves, in spite of warnings of the danger from the professionals.

Stunt chief Buddy Van Horn took them through the procedures and taught them how to take their falls, and the helicopter took off with the two actors hanging on to its undercarriage. The stunt was rehearsed and performed fifteen times before they got it right, and the next time it almost killed them. For once, De Niro was willing to talk about the experience. He recounted:

> The helicopter pilot didn't want to go too low because there were rocks on either side of us and a narrow passage where the water rushed through. We were coming in at the bridge when suddenly the two runners snagged under the steel cables that held the bridge. What the pilot did not know was that he had lifted the whole bridge with him, with me and John hanging underneath. . . .

John Savage shouted a warning to the pilot, but he did not hear. Down below, Cimino was screaming and waving his arms, fearing that the helicopter would crash and they would all be killed. The helicopter swung to one side, De Niro yelled, 'Drop!', and he and Savage fell into the muddy river. Motorboats positioned nearby quickly pulled them out of the water. They had come within a second or two of disaster, and in fact the whole episode of filming that sequence gave the trio of actors so many duckings and mudbaths that it was a wonder they all escaped without pneumonia or some tropical disease.

And so it was that Cimino achieved his vivid drama, bringing to life those mind's-eye scenic portraits that he had verbally drawn for the EMI producers at the outset with a dramatic intensity which was achieved at great risk to everyone involved. To the other actors, De Niro was the hero of the piece long before filming was completed. During their pre-launch interview Meryl Streep, Christopher Walken and John Savage all made a point of mentioning his generosity as an actor. Most of all, Cimino himself had much to be thankful for, and the elegance of De Niro's final scenes undoubtedly saved him from more severe critical reaction.

The crew, the actors and the producers knew very well that they had a winner. In spite of the traumas which had drained them all, everything had worked. Cimino's direction had been entirely tuned to the kind of debates that De Niro liked – which, coincidentally, also fitted the other leading men, not least because of the great psychological build-up required for many of the scenes. The memorable photography of Vilmos Zsigmond provided the broadest canvas for the sharp editing of Peter Zinner, which in turn provided easy movement of the film through the massive changes of sound and scenery.

But of course there would be controversy. They all knew that, too. *The Deer Hunter* was rushed into the cinemas in December 1978 to qualify for that year's awards, and it chalked up its first major success when the New York critics voted it Best Motion Picture of the Year. The reviews were abundant, profound and effusive – though not all complimentary – and De Niro was almost universally applauded for an outstanding performance. He was not only the absolute pivotal figure on whom the success of the movie hung; it was a riveting personal triumph, a performance which he himself later identified as the best he had ever given. His line-up of characters to date presented a remarkable diversity which stretched his powers of immersion to the limit and showed a range and depth which very few of his contemporaries could match; truly he was a man of many faces. He had also become the actor's actor, the ultimate in character creation which, as indicated earlier, meant that his place in the star rating system by which all Hollywood success is measured was never high.

In fact, there were critics who in their attack on the film itself took side-swipes at De Niro. Tom Buckley, who had reported from Vietnam for the *New York Times* and knew the background from personal experience, wrote in *Harper's* magazine that in *The Deer Hunter* Cimino had turned the truth inside out. 'The North Vietnamese and the Vietcong become the murderers and the torturers and the Americans their gallant victims,' he said. As for De Niro, Buckley reckoned that at approaching forty he looked too old to play a draftee, and far from seeming Slavic, as the film intended, he remained what he was in real life, the Italian-American he had played in virtually all of his films. Buckley did, however, concede that De Niro was a powerful screen actor whose presence gave the film whatever life it possesses.

The negative view of *The Deer Hunter* followed the euphoria after its release, when the liberal press began looking closer, examining the implications of Cimino's statement – if such it was – on the heroism of the American troops against the terrors that the politicians in their wisdom had assigned them. Soon it would be branded a racist movie that, as Buckley had said, presented situations which were far from accurate or factual. The most controversial scene, the Russian roulette sequence, was roundly criticized, and many Vietnam veterans came forth to say they had never heard of the North Vietnamese using such torture. Some even reduced the comparison to a modern-day film of cowboys and Indians, in which the Vietnamese were the Indians.

Perhaps it was only to be expected that, when *The Deer Hunter* was shown at the Berlin Film Festival, the Soviet Union, four other Eastern Bloc countries and Cuba packed up and went home, saying that the film was an insult to the people of Vietnam. Cimino continued to insist that it was not a political film, merely one about the horrors of war.

But the two are inseparable, and the row rumbled around the globe for months. It was bound to, even when viewed today the film's impact is no less emotive or tense, though some of the wind has gone from its sails. A stream of movies on Vietnam followed, notably those in the Oliver Stone trilogy which began with *Platoon*. These did much to redress the balance with equal controversy, and the debate about *The Deer Hunter* subsided.

Buried amid the controversy were more tender moments in *The Deer Hunter* which struck a chord for De Niro himself. He found his scenes with Meryl Streep enthralling. This was because, apart from his quirky screen romance with Liza Minnelli in *New York, New York*, relationships with attractive women had been a rare event in his films so far. His love scenes were sparse, and sexual situations of the kind which had fallen to his male contemporaries had been non-existent.

Working with Streep gave him the impetus to seek another film in which they could appear together. Apart from their friendship, which had developed up to and beyond the death of John Cazale, De Niro and Streep possessed a very similar attitude to their craft and out of it was born a mutual attraction. Coming as it did so early in her career,

The Deer Hunter came to mean a lot to her. But instead of seeking to project herself as a screen beauty she was content to adopt a plain Jane look as Linda, the part for which she also wrote the lines. De Niro, noted for his shyness in the presence of colleagues, quickly saw in her a female De Niro. 'Women who are very beautiful often let their beauty inhibit them,' he told Michael Cimino. 'They tend to have no character. When a woman is beautiful and has that extra edge – like Meryl – it's nice.'

Streep was also unusually forthcoming about the experience of having worked with De Niro: 'When you look into his eyes, it's like looking into the fathomless deep. In my scenes with him I felt the unreality of the set and the cameras and all those things that want to interfere. Bobby's eyes were like – oh! I just felt enveloped in their gaze. Huge emotions right under the surface.'

Other awards were showered upon *The Deer Hunter* in a year of stiff competition from outstanding work such as Warren Beatty's production of *Heaven Can Wait*, Hal Ashby's more politically motivated post-Vietnam film *Coming Home*, starring Jane Fonda and Jon Voight, and Alan Parker's *Midnight Express*. In the final analysis, *The Deer Hunter* found itself pitted against Beatty's sentimental comedy *Heaven Can Wait*: both received nine Oscar nominations. Beatty and De Niro were lined up in the Best Actor category, but Jon Voight won it and Jane Fonda secured the Oscar for Best Actress to make it a double for *Coming Home*. But *The Deer Hunter* won Oscars for Best Picture, Best Director (Cimino), Best Supporting Actor (Christopher Walken in his first major attention-winning role), Best Film Editing (Peter Zinner) and Best Sound.

The official history of the Academy Awards gave scant attention to De Niro in this outstanding movie and once again gave the impression that he and the Hollywood establishment were not walking the same path. Even if De Niro had won the Oscar for Best Actor, he would not have been there to receive it – he did not turn up for the 1979 Oscar night celebrations. One of his friends suggested that, still painfully shy of such gatherings, he had suffered an attack of nerves and did not want to attend. What was more likely was that by then Robert De Niro was already another character, changing his physical features considerably while working on his next film, once more with Martin Scorsese.

10

In and Out of Character

Diahnne Abbott was fed up to the back teeth and her marriage was on the brink of collapse. She hadn't spent more than a few days with her husband in months and for most of that time he was someone else, not Bobby De Niro. Almost without a break he took a bath, towelled away the remnants of Michael and began sliding into the skin of another man who stood at the opposite end of the spectrum to the hero of *The Deer Hunter*.

The new De Niro character was a much less attractive figure, a self-confessed creep who beats his wives, bullies his brother, falls in with the Mafia and whose life story reads like a manual on how to become a great success and then drop into the gutter in three easy moves. It was the type of character Robert Redford would not even consider playing and Burt Reynolds couldn't.

It may sound as if the record is stuck in a groove but it must be said again, because it is part of the continual process of De Niro's renewal and reinvention after each picture. The protean quality of his work was beyond doubt. It was no longer possible or even necessary to compare him to past icons who had carried the mantle of rebellion. He had moved on and away from the mould of Brando and Dean in which he had been cast, for want of comparison, in his early films. De Niro had developed into something else entirely. As Elia Kazan had adroitly speculated, he found his fulfilment in becoming other people.

Picture after picture had shown him getting more strongly and more deeply into authentic role-playing as opposed to mere acting. Brando, said Kazan, was a happily arrogant free spirit and remained so, ever rebellious against the over-ordering of life and a man whose persona overshadowed his roles. Dean had been the sad, sulky figure of parental

113

rebellion and died before he could show any other direction to his work. But De Niro was not rebelling against anything, except perhaps Hollywood itself. He was a law unto himself and possessed a power that did not even begin to flirt with star charisma. His ability and need went far beyond that and were most evident in his personal portrayal of the dark side of the American dream which was consistent in one absolute fact: he was always entirely believable as that character, able to drain himself of any personal identity. Even modern contemporary greats such as Jack Nicholson always possessed a twinkle in the eye that said, 'Hi, kids . . . it's me, Jack. Are you enjoying it?'

Sean Connery, still fighting thirty years on to subjugate James Bond, put his finger on the button years later when he worked with De Niro, albeit briefly, on *The Untouchables*. 'Many actors send signals to the audience when they are playing nasty characters, saying, "I'm not really like this." De Niro never did. He is always that character.' Some were even comparing him with Olivier. To British purists this may have seemed an outrageous statement, and probably was, but there were distinct similarities which were best exemplified by comparing his work to Olivier's performance in *The Entertainer*.

That De Niro had performed some remarkable chameleon acts in the past was beyond doubt. What happened next remains the most extraordinary physical and mental transformation of his career, the like of which had never been achieved by any screen actor before or since. And as he moved to this latest submersion of his total self he went obsessively over the top in a very personal way; it cost him his marriage.

Even as he completed *The Deer Hunter*, emotionally drained and baggy-eye tired, he was already absorbing the mean streaks of one of the most unattractive anti-heroes ever brought to the screen – the real-life former boxer Jake La Motta, whose story he had persuaded Martin Scorsese to turn into a film called *Raging Bull*. In an interview for *American Film* De Niro admitted: 'There was something about [La Motta's] story – a strong thrust, a portrait of a direct man without complications. Something at the centre of it was very good for me. I felt I could evolve into the character. If you're lucky, you make good choices that will work. As Stella Adler used to say, "Your talent lies in your choice." ' There are few actors in Hollywood, even today, who would take such a risk and test their relationship with their audiences by playing such an unmitigated slob of a character. Recent comparisons might include Michael Douglas in *Falling Down* in 1993, but

114

by then Douglas had a considerably higher popular profile than De Niro and was therefore taking less of a risk – and therein lies a major difference that built up between De Niro and his contemporaries. It is particularly interesting to lay his CV alongside that of Douglas, who simply could not break into mainstream movies as an actor – even though he had won an Oscar for his production of *One Flew Over the Cuckoo's Nest* in 1976 – at a time when De Niro was being acclaimed as the greatest screen presence since Brando. It would take Douglas another six years or more to become a major star, but when he did his popular appeal, measured by box-office returns, swamped De Niro's: overnight he was able to command fees that were three or four times what De Niro was earning.

To De Niro, money and career never seemed to be an over-riding consideration, and in that respect he and Douglas, or he and Nicholson for that matter, cannot be compared. There was a curious truth in the fact that he was never quite the big star that people believed, and certainly not the financial attraction to producers. His appeal tended to rest with urban cinema-goers looking for more challenging, thought-provoking entertainment than was being turned out by mainstream Hollywood producers. De Niro's classics to date came out of a gallery of characters with lives intricately woven into social matters which were sometimes too heavy, perhaps even too close to home, for the mass market. This had caused some pressures on the home front. He was a star, but he wasn't. He wanted the acclaim, but not the fame. He wanted the comforts of life which were derived from financial security, but shunned the glamour. Diahnne, on the other hand, enjoyed the Hollywood lifestyle and had ambitions of conducting their lives on a much higher social plane.

By and large, their social lives had involved the same fairly small group of friends who had been around almost from the beginning of their relationship. Their participation in the social whirl had been minimal. His refusal to attend the Academy Award celebration night in April 1979 was a typical example. Glittering Hollywood nights simply did not appeal to him, whereas Diahnne would have happily become more involved in the 'star' life. They had many rows about his reluctance to take a more active part in that side of his business, which she maintained could be achieved while still maintaining the measure of privacy that they had achieved in their personal lives.

The pressure on the marriage from that standpoint, and from the fact that he had hardly been home in the previous six or eight months, were merely heightened as he began preparing for the role of Jake La Motta. This work took him deep into the character of the man he was playing, and for some time he virtually shut out the rest of his personal world as he took in the details of the boxer's life. The result was that in the spring of 1979 he and Diahnne separated, although, as so often in De Niro's life, it was a stuttering, inconclusive kind of separation. He did not want to let go, and friends said that he remained devoted to Diahnne and the family. Yet it came to the point where she just could not live with him. So he moved into the Chateau Marmont and returned to the lifestyle of a single man, even though they did not get divorced for several years and maintained a kind of open-ended relationship which included family outings and holidays.

The curiosity of this arrangement remained a matter for themselves, and neither gave the slightest clue to the gossip writers scurrying around trying to get the low-down on the De Niro marriage. Friends of the couple said that, while agreeing with the principle of privacy, Diahnne felt almost caged by the lengths to which De Niro took his seclusion. She wanted to be part of the Hollywood life. He did not.

There was also no doubt that the intensity of De Niro's role-playing took some living with. Actors are not always able to shake off their character when they go home at night. One of the most spectacular examples was Jack Nicholson's portrayal of McMurphy, the mental hospital patient in *One Flew Over the Cuckoo's Nest*. They were filming for eleven weeks on location at a mental institution in Oregon, and Anjelica Huston, Jack's long-time partner, had joined him for the duration. However, she found him increasingly difficult to live with. Nicholson explained, 'Usually, I don't have much difficulty slipping in and out of character, but in Oregon it was different. I was so deep in the role that it became harder and harder to create separation between reality and make-believe. . . .' Gradually, Anjelica began to get worried and challenged him. 'Can't you snap out of this? You're acting crazy – you're evil.' But Jack just could not break character, so Anjelica packed her bags and flew back to Los Angeles, complaining to producer Michael Douglas: 'I can't tell whether he's sane or not. I'll see you all when you come back to the real world.' Later, Douglas took the trouble to apologize to her and said that Jack had really got into the part – which, he added, would also guarantee that the movie would be 'a smash'. It was.

Diahnne Abbott lived with this kind of situation all the time, day in and day out, when De Niro was working. The making of the Jake

La Motta story, which had been his obsession since 1977, was typical. The extremes of his role-playing cut across every aspect of his life, mental and physical, in an all-consuming way in which familiar surroundings and people were virtually shut out while De Niro psyched himself up for the performance, a process which could take months. His personality during this time could, said one of his close friends, turn 'ugly'. His temper would flare up and his colourful language would flow unrestrained.

His separation at the time was kept typically under wraps. He went back to the brownstone house in Greenwich Village while Diahnne and the family remained in Hollywood, although they would all follow him back to Manhattan before long. When he returned to Los Angeles for filming he would check into the Chateau Marmont. In this way they could stay friends, seeing each other when they felt like it and not suffering recriminations about other friendships.

At the time of their separation he had begun a secret affair with the black model Toukie (born Doris) Smith. A typical New Yorker, busily involved in the social life of the fashion and art world, she was the younger sister and business partner of fashion designer Willi Smith who would die of AIDS in April 1987, leaving her the main beneficiary of his very considerable estate. In the late 1970s they were the rage of the New York fashion scene: Willi was the inventor of the outrageous and outsize 'street couture', which had a major influence on later fashions for young people, while *Esquire* magazine dubbed Toukie 'a cyclone of dizzy charm'.

She met De Niro at a party in 1978 and, after his split from Diahnne in 1979, he and Toukie were seen together so often in New York that their close group of friends considered them a couple. They never lived together, however, and the relationship certainly did not preclude friendships and dalliances elsewhere, at least on his part. This was quite apparent when another black beauty, singer Helena Springs, entered his life at a time when he needed occasional social relief while working on *Raging Bull* – or, more accurately, he entered her life..

Helena Springs was then twenty and came from Los Angeles, although her parents originated in the Mid-West. The product of a broken home, she had barely seen her mother in her childhood and had been brought up by her father and grandmother. She was a talented singer and in her teens entered the music business, first attempting her own shot at stardom and later working as a busy support vocalist and backing singer for many famous names in pop.

At twenty, she was already worldly-wise. She had been backing singer for Bob Dylan, with whom she claimed a brief affair. She was with him at a concert in Germany and then went round the world. She had appeared on two tracks of Eric Clapton's 1979 album *Backless*, went on tour with David Bowie, and later became backing singer to Bette Midler and Elton John, travelling the globe with major pop stars of the 1970s and 1980s.

Her meeting with De Niro, however, did not take place at some showbiz party. It was typically unconventional, a street pick-up one afternoon as she was driving her little car down Wilshire Boulevard in Los Angeles. When she stopped at some traffic lights, a sports car being revved up by a man with sleeked-back hair and wearing a loud Hawaian shirt pulled up alongside her. When she drove away he followed, overtaking and then dropping back.

At the next set of lights he wound down the window and said, 'Excuse me . . . hello.'

At the time she did not recognize him as Robert De Niro, so she made no response and drove off. According to Helena, he followed her again. Just under the bypass at Santa Monica Boulevard she stopped again at some lights, where he pulled up a few inches away and called out: 'Sorry if I scared you.'

She now realized who he was and had a conversation with him. By coincidence she had met Diahnne some time earlier when she had gone backstage after a Bob Dylan show at the Universal Amphitheater, and again at a party after the Los Angeles premiere of the Martin Scorsese rock documentary *Last Waltz*.

De Niro was surprised but undaunted by this information and continued to chat, mentioning that he and his wife were now legally separated. He told Helena he was staying at the Chateau Marmont while working on his latest film, and asked for her telephone number. He called her late the following night and arranged to meet at her house.

Shortly afterwards, he arrived at her door in a rented Mercedes. They drove off down Sunset Boulevard to buy some wine at a local liquor store and returned for what Helena described as developing into a night of incredible, passionate lovemaking. It was the first of many such meetings and his affair with Helena would span many years, ending with an explosive 1992 courtroom drama.

In the late 1970s and beyond, Helena was happy to be De Niro's occasional lover in a scenario which he described as 'You are Shelley

Winters to my Montgomery Clift.' Helena apparently took this reference as a romantic compliment, perhaps not realizing that in A *Place in the Sun* Shelley Winters played Monty Clift's rather common and troublesome fiancée who gets pregnant and is accidentally disposed of when the Clift character has the chance of marrying a wealthy young socialite. So it would seem that even in lovemaking De Niro was role-playing and when Helena later became pregnant and contemplated suicide the whole affair came perilously close to the fictional scene he had been acting out.

But those dramas in this intermittent relationship which spanned fourteen years lay well into the future. At the time, however, De Niro had immersed himself in a new character, Jake La Motta.

De Niro's involvement with *Raging Bull* actually dated back to the time when he and Scorsese had first worked together on *Mean Streets*. While travelling to take in the atmosphere of Sicily for *The Godfather Part II* De Niro had read the autobiography of Jake La Motta, the Bronx-born fighter who became world middleweight champion in 1949 and then went into spectacular, seedy decline. This uncompromising, risky and often brutal story so intrigued him that he gave it to Scorsese and together, more than five years later, they began to pull it together as a movie. It was a story that would take De Niro's immersion tactics to almost horrific lengths.

In the space of four months he became two characters. First he was the fighting-fit boxer with thick neck and bulging pectorals from a thousand training rounds with sparring partners; then he turned himself into a drunken, ageing has-been, which required him to increase his weight by an incredible 60 pounds. The new movie also possessed that other ingredient which had become a seemingly essential part of De Niro–Scorsese collaborations – it was largely based in their own patch, New York.

On De Niro's recommendation Scorsese persuaded his old film-school chum Mardik Martin, who had co-written the screenplay for *Mean Streets* with him, to produce an outline based upon La Motta's life story. Then, in 1977, Paul Schrader, who had written *Taxi Driver*, produced a second draft which De Niro and Scorsese both liked. The upshot was that, after *New York, New York* was completed Schrader and Scorsese took themselves off to a Caribbean hideaway and wrote a final draft which went to their good friend, producer Irwin Winkler. It was Winkler who had produced *New York, New York*, which he had sandwiched between producing the first two *Rocky* movies with

Sylvester Stallone, the first of which had won Winkler and his partner Robert Chartoff an Oscar for Best Picture. Now that public interest in the boxing genre had been aroused *Raging Bull* seemed a very likely prospect, especially with the award-winning combination of Schrader, Scorsese and De Niro so keenly involved. With that package, Winkler and Chartoff went in to bat to arrange finance with United Artists.

The key to the film, as discussed and analysed by Scorsese and De Niro to the point where they knew the story inside out, was to be found in a sentence right at the beginning of Jake La Motta's book: 'Now sometimes at night when I think back, I feel like I'm looking at an old black and white movie of myself. Why it should be in black and white I don't know, but it is. Not a good movie, either, with gaps in it, a string of poorly lit sequences, some of them with no beginning and some with no end.'

The sentence came from La Motta's ghost-writers, but even so it gave Scorsese an immediate vision of shooting the film in black and white which, in that age of the spectacular, would cause flutters in the corridors of Hollywood power. De Niro himself was intrigued from another standpoint. The autobiography was a jerky narrative which spun through incidents of the boxer's life in the manner that the opening sentence signified, and provided the reader not so much with a chronological record of events but more with a transcription of his state of mind at various points in his life.

La Motta was born and raised in the streets of the other Little Italy of New York, the slum district of the Bronx where Italian immigrants had gathered at the turn of the century and which became the heart-land of Mafia gangsters – far more so than the Little Italy which edged De Niro's own birthplace in Greenwich Village. The street-fighting kid became the epitome of the American dream, boxing his way to fame and great fortune and fighting men whom no one else would take on. In ten years he rose to become middleweight champion of the world, a title which he took from Marcel Cerdan and then lost a year later to Sugar Ray Robinson. He earned hundreds of thousands of dollars, though much of it was taken by managers and hangers-on. The rest he spent on fast living, fast cars and fast women. He was courted by the Mafia to fix fights and, as his career began to dive in the 1950s, he was widely trashed by famous sports writers. The public humiliation became final when he was sentenced to six months on the Florida chain gang for allowing a fourteen-year-old girl to offer sexual services from his bar in Miami. In later years, as an overweight, heavy-drinking has-been, he became a nightclub bouncer and then a stand-up comic in a strip club. In all, the story of Jake La Motta provided De Niro and Scorsese with an abundance of themes to explore in depth. It enabled them to present a film that was far from the familiar saga of one sportsman's decline and fall into the abyss of excess, and belonged instead in the realm of significant psychological and biographical study.

For the preparation ritual La Motta was hired as a consultant and Sylvester Stallone's trainer came on board to help get De Niro fighting fit. They trained daily at New York's Gramercy Gym, and Jake recalled, 'I guess in the first six months we boxed a thousand rounds, a half-hour straight every day. Bobby wouldn't train unless we wore headgear and mouthpieces because he knew he was starting to get through my defences. We both ended up with black eyes and my upper teeth caps were busted, which cost United Artists $4000 to get them redone.' By the time they were ready to film, he ranked De Niro 'in the first top twenty middleweights, I swear'.

The physical changes were already taking place. His neck had added a couple of inches through muscular expansion and he had added pounds of protein-induced muscle to his normally slender body. But by then the psychological changes were also apparent. To those who had watched the transformation from the outset it had been an eerie progression until finally he had become Jake La Motta.

This was borne out when De Niro went to Florida to seek out Vicki, the second of Jake's three wives, and their daughter Stephanie, who both agreed to help by giving him their impressions of the boxer and their turbulent life together. Vicki, who had been just fifteen when she became involved with Jake, dug out old home movies of the couple and their three children which had been taken during the early years of her marriage. A curious thing happened as De Niro and Vicki, by then almost fifty but still an attractive woman, talked and went year by year through her ex-husband's life. 'Bobby was so much like Jake that I just wanted to go to bed with him,' she recalled. 'How could I not? An affair seemed the most normal thing to do. But Bob wanted things to be business-like. I should have just attacked him or something.'

Further testimony of De Niro's resurrection of Jake La Motta came from actress Cathy Moriarty, then a sixteen-year-old unknown spotted in a disco by the similarly unfamous Joe Pesci, who was to play Jake's manager brother Joey. Scorsese, De Niro and casting director Cis

Corman had been searching for months for a girl to play Vicki, and Pesci was sure he had found her. Cathy had no previous acting experience but she had a remarkable sophisticated beauty and, more important, a gravelly Bronx accent which was exactly what they were looking for – although it took months for Scorsese and De Niro, who were calling all the shots together, to make up their minds. 'I went to read for them for about three months, almost on a daily basis,' Moriarty recalled. She continued:

> It was like taking private acting lessons. They never once said that I had the part or anything, and I knew they were seeing other actresses too. But I was just happy to be learning about acting from two of the best people in the business. I just kept on going, reading with Bobby and taking Marty's instructions. Before long, I learned how to find and hold the character I was playing . . . it was easy, because Bobby was Jake all the time. And so I'd be Vicki. Since he felt it so much I was able to feel it too.

There was also a good deal of improvisation, especially after Cathy was eventually signed for the role. They would describe a scene to her and then provoke her into reacting. In one scene, in which La Motta thinks she has been flirting, Scorsese says they were just going to run through it with the cameras rolling when De Niro slapped her hard. 'I was so shocked,' said Moriarty, 'that I just stood there hardly knowing what to do, and then I reacted and they said that was exactly how Vicki would have reacted. I did feel intimidated, but I think that's the way they wanted me to feel.'

The search for realism was, as ever, a prime consideration and this went on and on and on as Scorsese filmed the fight sequence – which in fact took up less than fifteen minutes of the film itself. But for a three-month period they shot sequence after sequence, first in an auditorium in Los Angeles and then on a soundstage. Most were filmed with an overhead camera, and had been worked out in advance so that they were virtually editing as they went along. There were no crowd scenes like those which punctuated *Rocky*, but surreal shots that conveyed something much deeper than a mere boxing match, so that the audience was given clues as to the feelings of the boxer himself.

Having completed those early scenes where La Motta is the hero and champion the picture was shut down for four months to allow

122

De Niro time to move into the next phase of the characterization: La Motta as the bloated, red-faced, over-the-hill nightclub performer. It was to be the most critically controversial part of De Niro's performance and physical alteration, in which he put on that immense amount of weight. 'It was Bobby's idea,' Scorsese admitted. 'When he suggested it I thought it was great, but I knew he was setting himself a tremendous challenge.'

De Niro took off for Italy as soon as Scorsese had finished with him, and during the late summer he began eating himself through all the restaurants he had visited on his earlier travels. 'If there is one thing that Bob knows about,' Donald Sutherland confirmed, 'it's food. He can identify a particular ingredient in a pasta sauce by just a minute taste. He knows them all. And he can cook them, too.' And so, sitting in front of mountains of his favourite pasta dishes, he began a four-month eating binge. By the time he had finished he was unrecognizable even to his friends. The muscle which he had built up in the previous six months turned to fat, and he had increased his weight from 150 to 215 pounds. He became obsessed with the bathroom scales, checking his weight increase daily. He reckoned it was fun at the beginning and said that putting on weight was very easy. He would get up at 6.30 in the morning and eat breakfast at seven in order to be able to digest the food he would take at lunchtime, and then relax in the afternoon to prepare for a three-course dinner with wine at 8 p.m. 'By the time I had gained fifty pounds it was hard to tie my shoe,' De Niro admitted in an interview, going on:

I couldn't bend, my thighs were rubbing against each other, I was getting rashes and my heels were starting to hurt. I was very uncomfortable with the weight. But we gave ourselves a deadline when we were going to shoot again, whatever the weight was. By then I was getting blood pressure, and the doctor who was monitoring my health wasn't too happy because my breathing sounded strange. My daughter got so she was terribly embarrassed for her friends to see me. I looked like an animal.

And then came one of the most poignant sequences in the picture, which De Niro and Scorsese invented and De Niro used to arouse the audience's sympathy for a man whose unappealing nature had made them squirm and whose decline is pathetic. It came in the nightclub act, where La Motta is supposed to give dramatic readings

123

from Shakespeare, Tennessee Williams and Chayevsky to intersperse his anecdotes about his career. Scorsese put a direct focus on De Niro as, interpreting La Motta, he researches the famous scene from *On the Waterfront* in which Terry (Marlon Brando) tells Charley (Rod Steiger) that he threw a fight only because Charley told him to, so that he would get a shot at the title – just as La Motta had thrown a fight for what he claimed were similar reasons. And so La Motta recites those famous lines: 'I coulda been a contender, Charley, instead of a bum which is what I yam!' It was an interesting performance on De Niro's part, and one suspects that he used it as his own answer to those who have likened his work to Brando: 'This is Robert De Niro talking. Not Jake La Motta. Not Brando. Take it or leave it.'

But unlike Elia Kazan's *On the Waterfront*, which had a sentimental Hollywood ending, *Raging Bull* faded uncompromisingly with no uplifting final scene, leaving with the central character reciting the words of Terry Malloy as spoken by Brando almost thirty years earlier. It was a classic piece of cinema and, although everyone has a favourite De Niro film, even a favourite scene, this performance probably ranks as one of the most intriguing for most of his admirers.

The word 'admirers' is used deliberately in this context because De Niro remains an acquired taste whose work cannot be put to a mass audience with the assured guarantee of universal acclaim. *Raging Bull* was no exception: although it did reasonably well at the box office, much of it could be attributed to the enormous publicity which surrounded the film over De Niro's physical change. There were those, myself among them, who take issue with the technique of an almost grotesque use of the 'external' props, as Stella Adler described them. The external prop in this case was his own body.

In doing so, De Niro demonstrated how he personally has utilized and improvised upon techniques of Method acting since Brando's sensational breakthrough. His own references to Stella Adler during a magazine interview about the film showed that her teachings were still well to the fore in his mind, and that using her instructions had taken the Stanislavski notion of becoming a character so literally and completely that finally there was no space between De Niro himself and the character he plays.

Pauline Kael, the redoubtable film critic of the *New Yorker*, made a good point when she complained: '. . . he put on so much weight that he seems to have sunk in the fat with hardly a trace of himself left. What De Niro does in this picture isn't acting, exactly. I'm not sure what it is. Though it may at some level be pleasurable. He has so little expressive spark that what I found myself thinking wasn't about La Motta or the movie but the metamorphosis of De Niro.'

It was a very astute comment which made Kael, normally an ardent fan of De Niro, stand pretty much alone among the New York critics. De Niro had reached a point at which self-immersion in a real-life character had been taken so far that it was not acting but imitating – as evidenced by the fact that La Motta's wife felt compelled to jump into bed with De Niro. He obviously realized that the point might be taken up when he admitted in a *Sight and Sound* interview: 'I just can't fake acting and maybe the first rule is to fake it – but not for me. I want the experience. I want to deal with all the facts of a character. . . .'

It was the odd one out among his gallery of characters because this was the one that he did not create but adopted, and for months beforehand he had entered into the role as if he was going into an hypnotic trance. Having said that, *Raging Bull* was another terrific film that garnered some lavish critical praise; it also made a profit, even though it came nowhere near the success of Stallone's *Rocky* which went for the jugular of popular appeal. Perhaps, in a way, *Raging Bull* confused many potential customers in that it was never intended as a boxing film but as a drama.

The Hollywood establishment was also still half-hearted about De Niro and Scorsese. Although the film received eight Academy Award nominations it eventually won only two Oscars – De Niro triumphantly for Best Actor and Thelma Schoonmaker for her editing. However, the two new talents were recognized virtually at their first outing. Joe Pesci, who would shadow De Niro in his future career, won an Academy nomination for Best Supporting Actor, while the total newcomer Cathy Moriarty – who, it will be recalled, had never acted in her life before her personal tuition from De Niro and Scorsese – was nominated for Best Supporting Actress. There was talk that she had a bright future ahead, and comparisons were being made with Meryl Streep who shot to fame after her first major screen appearance with De Niro in *The Deer Hunter*. Sadly, however, Cathy made only one more movie before being seriously injured in a car smash and did not work again until the late 1980s.

De Niro, meanwhile, was basking in the knowledge that he had made another movie of enduring quality, though he was left in a state of depression and anti-climax. In retrospect, it can be seen as a point at which an imaginary dotted line might be drawn under his list of movies, indicating that this was the time when he reached a peak. That is not to say that he did not make good films afterwards – he did, of course – but no future performance could better those of his first decade, when even in alleged failures like *New York, New York* De Niro had considerable merit.

11

Money and Myths

Helena Springs welcomed Robert De Niro into her bed the night after he had received his Oscar for *Raging Bull*. He was still quivering from the night before. The assembled galaxy of superstars had witnessed one of the most uncomfortable, stumbling acceptance speeches in the history of the Oscars, in which he thanked his mother and father for having him and his grandparents for having them. As one commentator described it, he sounded like James Dean doing an impression of Marlon Brando, though perhaps he might be excused for his nerves.

The previous day Ronald Reagan had been shot by John Hinckley junior, which brought up the sensitive issue of De Niro's movie *Taxi Driver* which the gunman claimed had influenced him. Hinckley, it was discovered, had also been trailing De Niro's co-star Jodie Foster and had bombarded her with love letters. Foster was said to be shocked and frightened, and De Niro refused point-blank to discuss the matter.

He arrived at Helena's house still in a depressed state. She, as ever, was on hand to smooth his brow. Whatever she initially hoped for from her association with the star might well have influenced her continued acceptance of his arrival at her door whenever it suited him. She may have fantasized about a more permanent arrangement, perhaps even of becoming his wife once he and Diahnne had divorced. Very soon, however, Helena would get the message. A year or more after their first meeting when De Niro had virtually crash-landed on her car, it was fairly clear that she had become his flight of fancy – literally.

She continued to settle for these occasional encounters, hoping that the situation might change, and it suited her at the time because she was still a busy singer and her trips to Europe with Bowie and others meant that she was not always around when De Niro came looking for her. It was around this time, too, that she discovered she was pregnant. She decided not to tell him and had an abortion.

Much later, De Niro more or less confirmed that their meetings were a matter of sexual convenience. He somewhat cruelly denied that he had ever 'formed a relationship' with her, and stated that the only arrangement that existed was one of sleeping together on periodic occasions over the course of three or four years. If he was in Los Angeles making a movie, he would call her. If she was in New York, she might call him. She, according to De Niro, was never his girlfriend and he never considered himself to be her boyfriend, whatever Helena herself may have thought – and quite obviously she had a far different view of their relationship from the one he did.

He would say that he did not love her and that marriage was never discussed. Helena believed differently. He may never have discussed marriage with her, but their meetings were passionate and regular enough for her to consider that she was something more than a passing fancy, available whenever he chose to call.

De Niro, however, said the liaisons were purely for pleasurable purposes by two grown-ups. At the time he had a girlfriend in New York and Helena knew that. But in spite of his somewhat clinical approach to their occasional sleeping arrangements she felt that she was more than just a woman of convenience to him, and that in a way she was in competition with the girl in New York.

De Niro himself had told her that he was seeing the now high-profile show model Toukie Smith and then, when the occasion arose, he would return to Diahnne to play the father to his children. If these arrangements had been public knowledge, his love life might have seemed as contorted as some of his screen characterizations. Helena herself would say that at times he seemed to be acting out a role even in their lovemaking, which she described as ranging from sensational to almost cruel depending on his mood and temper.

Unlike Helena, the girl in the Hollywood wings who believed she meant something to him, Toukie Smith and De Niro did have 'a relationship' which was ongoing and long-lasting. Their affair was one of those topics that De Niro refused to discuss in the few media interviews he gave in New York and London to promote *Raging Bull*, and as far as the media were concerned Helena Springs was as yet an unknown presence in his life.

As ever, De Niro kept his mouth firmly shut on matters personal and from the early eighties he pulled down the shutters almost entirely.

Most requests for interviews were refused, to the chagrin of studio publicists and showbusiness columnists. He made an extremely rare television appearance in Britain to promote *Raging Bull*, virtually being frogmarched by studio publicists to appear with chat show host Michael Parkinson, veteran of a thousand interviews with everyone who was anyone in the international film world. De Niro was one of the most difficult subjects he had had to deal with; he seemed disinterested and disorientated, and answered in monosyllables that gave absolutely nothing away. His small circle of friends remained similarly tight-lipped, and attempted to excuse his retiring behaviour by explaining his particular discomfort at talking about himself, especially after he had spent months working on a picture in which he had drained himself of personal vitality in order to bring the character he was playing to the surface.

Actor Barry Primus, who had known him from the early days and appeared in *New York, New York*, would tell of his need to relax after the gruelling effort that almost all of his movies had entailed. He travelled widely, often to Paris, Rome and London. There was a small island in the Caribbean that he and Scorsese visited just to get away. 'As a friend, I have to say that he is the best, loyal and sweet,' said Primus. 'He never forgets birthdays, and loves those family rituals. Even though he wasn't with Diahnne, the family was still important. He was in touch with his children constantly.'

These were matters which De Niro did not wish to discuss, because to answer questions on one aspect of his life invariably led to questions about other areas. And so he might be 'tricked' – a word he used often about the media – into revealing that there were three characters within his own personality: the devoted family man and friend; the publicity-shy dedicated actor; and the secretive seeker of manly pleasures achieved by his penchant for exotic, dusky-skinned companions.

This predilection might have caused problems in past times, as he pointed out in what was probably his one and only comment ever on the subject of his girlfriends:

I never thought it took particular courage to marry someone
who isn't white. When I married Diahnne, no one said anything
about it. There was no warning, as there was to Sammy Davis
junior when he wanted to marry Kim Novak and was warned
off. If someone thought about it at all, nothing was ever said

to me . . . and that's just as well. Because I would not have
listened anyway.

Helena Springs would eventually form her own opinions about De
Niro's quest for relationships with women of Afro origins, which
involved some of the most desirable women of her colour. It was, she
would say, a combination of bravado and sexual attraction, coupled
with a signal of his rejection of social conventions – though the latter
aspect, which may have been socially noteworthy in the early 1970s,
undoubtedly became less important as the years rolled by. Even if it
was, it would not have mattered to De Niro. He had still managed to
keep a moat between himself and the Hollywood hierarchy. He
remained his own man and continued to shun the advances of the
major studios. He plotted his own course, selecting roles that he
wanted to play and rejecting the rest regardless of the money.

It must also be added that the Hollywood power brokers and studio
heads were not at one in their assessment of De Niro's ability, since
they viewed talent largely from the standpoint of the dollar sign. A list
of De Niro's movies which had received critical acclaim unmatched in
its consistency and controversiality by his contemporaries was not
enough to inspire confidence among the people who signed the
cheques. By 1981, only two of the movies in which he had played
the lead – *Taxi Driver* and *The Deer Hunter* – had made any serious
money, and even then the figures from the box office paled to insig-
nificance against the likes of Sylvester Stallone's *Rocky*, Jack Nicholson's *The Shining*, Dustin Hoffman's *Kramer v Kramer* or Harrison
Ford's *The Empire Strikes Back* and *Raiders of the Lost Ark*. All these
movies were aimed at commerciality, but each had merit in its own
particular genre.

There are plenty of reasons why one group of film-makers can be
expected to make money, but another is accepted as being surprising
if it does. De Niro believed the difference was that his movies would
be around for years, and that was more important than the money.
When questioned in his *Playboy* interview about *Raging Bull*, which,
in spite of the publicity build-up, lost money on the American circuit
and was not a commercial success overseas either, he replied:

'I did not expect it would be. We just did the movie the way
we wanted to do it and that was it. Of course, you always
want people to see it and hope that it will be okay, but it's more

important to do movies that have meaning and will have some relevance in 50 years time from now. I'd rather be part of a movie like that than of a movie that's not gonna be around. Certain types of films – I won't even say which ones – you know the ones – are recognized for other things. . . .'

'*Rocky* sorts of movies?'

'You said it. I'm not gonna say it.'

There was an arrogance in De Niro's attitude here. He holds back from naming names. Sylvester Stallone is his friend and many believe that Stallone could not act his way out of a paper bag, as the saying goes. But he has made hugely successful films and his earnings dwarf those of De Niro. De Niro treated commercialism with disdain and by the sheer process of his selection of material shied away from any project that was in danger of making money, although it was necessary for himself to keep making money – and, incidentally, he had put his fees up to match his fame. But there was room for everyone and, although *Rocky* appealed to the masses far more than the expletive-filled rantings of the ultimate anti-hero in *Raging Bull*, the cinema would be a lesser place without the likes of the De Niro–Scorsese partnership, concentrating on improvisation and experimentation. There always has to be a place for those who try to produce and direct non-formulaic movies.

Like him or hate him, De Niro had proved he could offer a range that few could match, and fewer still would even want to try. Money was a greater God to most of his contemporaries, and they would do nothing that would jeopardize their huge pay-days. A string of failures represents a far greater threat to those who are part of the conventional Hollywood star system, which De Niro continued to avoid. He started from a low base and, despite upping his rates, maintained a salary level that was far below some of the mad, mad fees being paid out as the 1980s rolled in. Naturally, though, as he won greater status as an actor money began to play an increasing role in De Niro's personal life. He had taken advantage of the higher lifestyle, the travel and all the other conveniences of modern living that his success had brought him, and it was quite noticeable that as he acquired more he spent more. As the years passed money gradually became another of his obsessions.

The irony of this was that he was at the brink of a period of scrutiny in regard to his box-office appeal. The years ahead, throughout the

1980s, would involve him in a succession of productions which were financial disasters – five in a row between 1981 and 1984 – as he relentlessly chose screenplays and scripts with which he could pursue his exploration of the human condition.

We can see it at a glance: in the figures below, the rentals amount is the portion (roughly half) that the film companies receive from cinema box-office takings for the US domestic market only, and excludes foreign takings. Similarly the cost excludes marketing, which can run into millions. The general rule of thumb is that a successful film should more or less earn back its cost in domestic rentals, which in the case of this group was a distant target.

True Confessions took $5.09 million in rentals and cost $12 million to make, excluding marketing costs.

The King of Comedy took $1.2 million and cost $19 million.

Once Upon a Time in America took $2.5 million and cost $30 million.

Falling in Love took $5.7 million and cost $12 million.

The Mission took $8.3 million and cost $24.5 million.

These daunting profit and loss accounts by which Hollywood judges its participants all lay in the immediate future. De Niro would see his fortunes and bankability fluctuate wildly, yet as ever most of the films he made were beautifully crafted and acted, not just by himself but with the aid of some of America's finest.

The sad fact was that they possessed no mass appeal whatsoever. It is often argued within the business that a film, whatever its pedigree, is made to draw audiences into the cinemas and make money, and if that simple criterion is not met then it is a failure. Conversely it is argued that film-making should be operated on a broad accounting basis which accommodates the artistic as well as the spectacular. Today, in the high-finance age of money men, powerful agents looking after the interests of their clients and multi-national conglomerates involved in the production of virtually all movies coming out of Hollywood, in theory no producer sets out on a project without being deadly earnest about making money.

De Niro's character in *The Last Tycoon* was based upon Irving Thalberg, one of the few Hollywood executives who fought to maintain a policy of making a movie for the sake of getting it made, regardless of financial success. His biggest arguments at MGM with Louis B. Mayer used to be over financing films that were unlikely to show a profit, offsetting their costs with other more successful productions. That policy virtually died with Thalberg himself, officially at least, but a good many accidents still happen and Hollywood is awash with horror stories of massive failures, the most quoted example being *Heaven's Gate* which bankrupted United Artists.

Ironically, it was often independent producers who in the 1970s and beyond begged the money for films which were of questionable financial outcome. It was fortunate that De Niro's collaborators included two of the most prolific – the Irwin Winkler–Robert Chartoff partnership, which produced his next movie, *True Confessions*, the first of this sequence of financial bombs. As noted earlier, Winkler and Chartoff stood on both sides of the art v. populism divide. They had been responsible for such varied fare as *Rocky I, II, III, IV* and *V*; *They Shoot Horses, Don't They?*; *The Right Stuff*; *Comes a Horseman*; *New York, New York*; *Raging Bull*; *Round Midnight*; *Guilty by Suspicion*; and *Goodfellas*, as well as several notable commercial flops.

In De Niro's case, there would be a combination of reasons why his films did not find the mythical pot of gold. Meanwhile, some of those on the other side of the track, turning out popular movies, expressed wonder that De Niro could continue to receive such glowing praise while all around him was financial mayhem. However, one interesting fact which is missing from any profile of De Niro is a list of projects which he turned down and which went on to be major hits – a list which most stars such as Beatty, Nicholson, Hoffman and Pacino are able to recite. De Niro's presence in a project, as Irwin Winkler said he well knew, was never a guarantee that the film would make money because he was not a top-drawer box-office attraction. As far as De Niro was concerned it did not matter that much, although in reality it did. Sooner or later, the day of reckoning has to arrive. For De Niro the theme of money, the crisis of capitalism v. art or social wellbeing, had already become a recurring theme in his work. Eventually he would be called to account in his personal life, too.

The phenomenon of wealth or power justifying the actions of others, be they politicians, businessmen, city fathers or even gangsters, is present in almost every film he had made to date and the central character, his role creation, was either a victim or that power. It is possible to track this theme through his work as if he is either deliberately or subconsciously injecting an autobiographical element into his acting by the selection of those scripts which most appealed. He seemed to choose material which provided him with the opportunity of drawing a character which reflected the plight of his mother and his father, people of great talent whom life passed by and gave them nothing. This was especially apparent in *True Confessions*, which actually turned out to be a very watchable film, was highly praised, selected in Britain as the *Daily Telegraph's* best American film of 1981, but did not stay long in the cinemas and is rarely seen on television.

It revolves around an interesting counterplay between two brothers, one a police detective who is honest as the day is long and the other an over-ambitious Roman Catholic priest who possesses less fastidious principles. The story came from the novel of the same title by John Gregory Dunne, which itself was based upon a horrific murder in Los Angeles in 1948, when a call girl with aspirations of becoming a movie star was kidnapped, tortured and then murdered. Her body was cut in half and dumped. It became known as the Black Dahlia murder, because the victim had been last seen wearing a black dress. The killer was never found and the murder remains unsolved.

The screenplay which Dunne himself wrote began with a scene in which De Niro's character, Monsignor Desmond Spellacy, is reunited with his brother Tom, a Los Angeles detective played by Robert Duvall, whom he has not seen for years. Both men are bitter and uncomfortable. Desmond is dying of cancer, living out his days as pastor of a small, dilapidated church in southern California to which he was banished after a scandal years ago, revealed by Tom.

Tom comes to visit him, knowing that his brother does not have long to live. Their meeting is difficult after so many years, and there are long silences which become unfortunate punctuation for this film. In flashback sequences the action switches to the 1940s, to the time of the murder. The two brothers are contrasted immediately, Desmond in full regalia conducting a nuptial mass at his fine church while Tom is in another part of the city investigating a seedy murder in which a prostitute has been sawn in two and dumped on waste ground. The evidence points to a local business tycoon called Jack Amsterdam, played by the ebullient Charles Durning, who in turn is named by Desmond as Catholic Layman of the Year for his services and donations to the Church.

Desmond has made his name raising funds for the Church, has

become more of an accountant than a priest and is aiming for the top on commercial rather than religious principles. Slowly, Tom discovers that his brother has links with both Amsterdam and the murder victim. The tycoon is arrested, and his brother's career is in ruins.

After the excess of *Raging Bull* De Niro felt he needed a contrast. There could have been no other script around at that time which offered a character so absolutely opposed to Jake La Motta and which jogged along, so laid back and low-key, coolly manoeuvring its way through the intricacies of police and city politics and Church finances, with undercurrents reminiscent of Polanski's *Chinatown*, though nowhere near as good.

De Niro's portrayal set the mood of the picture. After the gut-spilling, free-range action of his performances in *The Deer Hunter* and *Raging Bull* he reverted to the eloquent, bottled-up interpretation that he had used as Irving Thalberg in *The Last Tycoon*, in spite of the fact that one of the main criticisms of this performance had been that he was far too inactive and flaccid. The same could be said about his characterization of the priest. As Pauline Kael noted in the *New Yorker*, De Niro seemed to have gone back into a trance, unable to solve the puzzle that he brought to *The Last Tycoon*, which was how to act without doing anything. Fortunately Duvall, though often similar to De Niro in holding back, had considerably more bite and grittiness that lifted the scenes in which they were together and quite often left De Niro looking over-economical with his actions – deliberately so undoubtedly, yet lifeless.

De Niro's creation of the character had not been without his usual deep and lengthy preparation. He studied the liturgy of the Catholic Mass and learned it in the original Latin, as required for the flashbacks to the 1940s. He worked day and night with the film's religious adviser, Father Henry Fehren, who taught De Niro the correct pronunciations, the symbolism and the meanings of Catholic dogma. Fehren, like Jake La Motta who reckoned he could have become a boxer, said De Niro became the most authentic priest ever to appear on screen, and could have fooled any Church assembly into believing he was a true man of the cloth.

This in turn brings us back to the original point about the success or failure of a particular film. What was the point of *True Confessions* in De Niro's mind? To entertain the public who pay to go to see his movies and by and large expect to be entertained? Or to provide another canvas for his body of work, to be viewed later, like an artist's collection, when movie buffs and critics could analyse and pontificate about the meanings and nuances, the quality and substance of his films? He answered the question himself when he said, 'There is nothing more ironic or contradictory than life itself. What I try to do is make things as clear and authentic as possible. Technique is concrete. I don't want people years from now to say: "Remember De Niro? He had style." Affectation and style . . . that's all bullshit.'

There was by then adequate proof that he intended to conform to that edict, and it won him respect. It even recalled, in a way, his father's adamant refusal to let anyone who did not truthfully appreciate his work buy one of his paintings – regardless of the fact that at the time he might not have had the price of his next meal. His son seemed to go by a similar rule of thumb, but he also had the resources to ensure that his work was, by and large, untainted by the power of wealth – the requirements and expectations of Hollywood. There was abundant evidence for this thinking on De Niro's part, but it is still difficult to be certain that he really went that deep – that although he had become the man of a thousand faces, ranging from languid to explosively brutal characters, it was actually within the man himself to be all of those things. The one human trait that he had now shown was humour, and that would be covered, after a fashion, in his next film, *The King of Comedy*. It also became the biggest financial disaster of both his and Scorsese's careers.

12

Comedy Without Laughter

The year of 1982 was a bad one for Robert De Niro. It brought with it tragedies and complexities that would live with him for a long time afterwards and attracted unwanted publicity about his private life. Then his friend John Belushi, of *Blues Brothers* fame, died of a drugs overdose, and in the hugely sensational media event which followed De Niro was drawn in on the periphery. The drugs story was particularly damaging, both for him and others named through association with Belushi. It came at a time when President Reagan had just announced his war on drugs and organized crime as the Italian Mafia flooded the USA with high-grade heroin and as the South American cartels were on the brink of unloading cocaine by the ton on to unsuspecting US city streets at knock-down prices.

Wine, women and drugs. There was nothing new in that in Hollywood. The only thing that had changed, and was changing almost daily, was the extent of it and the availability of cocaine in particular. Few movie lots were free of pushers. No swingers' party was complete without a dish of Quaaludes and a few lines of white powder sniffed up eager noses through rolled-up dollar bills or fashionable solid silver implements. Terms like 'gone for a blow' replaced 'out to lunch', though the meaning was the same. It became a popular pastime among those in the know to track the dialogue of certain movie stars in their films to discover nasal tones and watch for glazed eyes, indicating that they had been snorting some stuff before going on camera. As Pauline Kael wrote of one famous star – not De Niro: 'He plays the role like the before half of a Dristan commercial, with nasal passages blocked. Why, I don't know, and I don't care to ask.' Another wrote that he had a 'peculiar nasal voice and a fogged manner', which was as close as he could possibly come to saying that the man sounded as if he was stoned on cocaine.

So celebrities, as ever, were a target, and any connection with drugs and other excesses became front-page news on the dubious notion that here were our self-appointed icons whose potential for influencing ordinary people was so great that they ought to know better. No, nothing had changed except that drugs connections were highly damaging and the old adage about no publicity could be bad publicity was being proved seriously adrift.

Later on it became popular for stars afflicted by these addictions and excesses to revive that adage and turn it to their advantage. Many who had been recent residents of therapeutic institutions came out, as part of their treatment, to confess their sins, tell all and explain how they had only survived through the love and support of their families and fans. Carrie Fisher, another good friend of Belushi and De Niro, even turned her story into a best-selling novel and movie, *Postcards from the Edge*, and Elizabeth Taylor did the same with a get-well book entitled *Elizabeth Takes Off*.

At the start of this depressing period, however, such confessions were nowhere in sight because the participants were having a high old time; drugs death scares, like that of Belushi, did nothing to stem the flow. De Niro's involvement in the Belushi affair put him directly in the spotlight under headlines such as: 'Actors to face police quiz over Belushi death.' He was dragged in purely because of their joint presence at the Chateau Marmont. The two most famous names mentioned were himself and Robin Williams, both of whom had been in Belushi's room the night before he was found dead.

De Niro and Belushi had been friends for a long time and admired each other's work. Both had been in Hollywood in recent months, working on separate projects. They often went out together, dashing out late at night to the private club On the Rox which is reserved for celebrities – a place where they can eat and drink with their friends without being pestered by fans and autograph hunters. Another popular haunt for De Niro and Belushi was the Playboy Mansion, a Polynesian-style social club for the stars set in six acres of lush gardens on Charing Cross Road. Hugh Hefner's personally approved members – almost entirely made up of showbusiness people and the literati – could arrive at any time. Meals being served continuously, started with champagne breakfasts from 6.30 onwards to the last sitting for supper at 2 a.m. The pools, exotic saunas, games room and theatre provided the stars with relaxing interludes from the pressures of their high-powered lives, so they say.

Belushi, like De Niro, hated the Hollywood social order and never stayed in Los Angeles longer than he needed. Along with Billy Crystal, Chevvy Chase and others he had become famous through the satirical comedy television programme *Saturday Night Live*, and swept to cult fame in *The Blues Brothers*, even though it had been panned by the critics. His other films, like Steven Spielberg's *1941* and the comedy *Neighbours* with Dan Ackroyd, had both failed to live up to expectations, and it was at these times that Belushi was most vulnerable to his drug habits. He snorted copious amounts of cocaine, which he called Hitler's Drug because it made him feel powerful. He also flirted with heroin and various pills.

Belushi knew De Niro from New York, and lived a couple of blocks from where De Niro was born. He used to call him Bobby D., and was especially intrigued by De Niro's portrayal of Jake La Motta imitating Brando's speech from *On the Waterfront* at the end of *Raging Bull*. Belushi had seen the movie countless times and could recite Brando's lines by heart. He used the same speech as a comedy routine, along with an impression of Brando in *The Godfather* which he exaggerated into a hilarious skit.

During the spring and early summer of 1982 De Niro saw a lot of Belushi. By then, everyone knew of the comic's explosive personality and that Belushi was on a dangerous course, but no one – not his wife Judy, his managers, his partner Dan Ackroyd or his numerous other friends like Jack Nicholson and Robin Williams – could stop him.

On the night of 5 March Robin Williams had been doing a stand-up routine at the Comedy Store on Sunset Boulevard, which he did free of charge quite often to keep in practice. He was about to embark on a sixty-city tour. He took the 1.30 a.m. slot, completed his routine and came outside around 2.15. A car park attendant said Belushi and De Niro had been looking for him. Williams drove to On the Rox but it had closed, so he telephoned De Niro's suite at the Chateau Marmont and they arranged to meet in Belushi's room. Williams drove his silver BMW the few blocks to the Marmont and went to Belushi's room, where he discovered he was not alone. A 'tough and scary' woman was there with him; and Williams felt very uncomfortable and left soon afterwards. When he got home he told his wife about her, and said he had never seen Belushi with such a 'crusty' woman. De Niro obviously felt the same. He went to Belushi's room around 3 a.m., glared at the woman, whose name was Cathy Smith, and then left. At 11 a.m., when Belushi had failed to turn up for an appointment with his agent and producer, he was discovered dead in his hotel bedroom. An autopsy revealed an overdose of heroin and cocaine. Cathy Smith, a self-confessed former dealer in both drugs and herself a heroin addict, fled to Canada the following day.

When De Niro learned the news later that afternoon he retired to his suite at the Marmont and sat making telephone calls, one after the other. He kept out of sight for several days as the press horde were camped outside the building, along with crowds of morbid fans and voyeurs, all craning to get a glimpse of the comings and goings at the death scene.

It was later in the investigation that De Niro, Williams and others found themselves in the headlines. Cathy Smith was the subject of an article in the *National Enquirer* in which she admitted being present when Belushi injected himself with his lethal cocktail of drugs. Although the inquest recorded a verdict of accidental death, a Federal Grand Jury was called to investigate his death and asked De Niro and Williams to appear before them to tell what they knew.

Williams did so on the basis of a prior agreement that he would not be questioned about his own previous drug use – which, incidentally, he ended after the shock of Belushi's death. De Niro fought hard to keep out of it, but could not. It was, however, eventually agreed with the Los Angeles. District Attorney's Office that he could give his evidence over the telephone, amplified to be heard by the Grand Jury; he thus became one of the very few people to whom such a facility has been afforded in US legal history. The issue might well have rested there, as far as De Niro was concerned, but for one other development.

John Belushi's wife Judy was unhappy with the verdict and the police investigation and contacted Bob Woodward, the famed *Washington Post* journalist who, with Carl Bernstein, exposed the Watergate scandal. She asked him if he would consider looking into her husband's death. Woodward flew to New York to meet her, and agreed. The upshot of the meeting was his best-selling book entitled *Wired: The Short Life and Fast Times of John Belushi*.

Judy Belushi got in touch with many of Belushi's friends and asked them to co-operate with Woodward; had she not done so, the noise of slamming front doors would have been resounding around Beverly Hills. Many did co-operate, including Carrie Fisher, Jack Nicholson,

Robin Williams, Dan Ackroyd and Chevvy Chase. Robert De Niro refused point-blank. However, when the book came out De Niro and Williams were both mentioned as having been in Belushi's room on the night before he died, and it was claimed that both had snorted a little cocaine with him. Many of those who had agreed to be interviewed turned on Woodward. Nicholson described him as 'a ghoul . . . an exploiter of emotionally disturbed widows'. De Niro said he refused to give it the recognition of even commenting, stating that he had never read it and did not intend to. Woodward had struck a nerve – many nerves in fact – in a well-researched and fact-studded work that gave early indications of the undercurrent of drug use in Hollywood.

Running concurrent with the Belushi drama was another personal matter. At the beginning of the year Helena Springs, whom he had continued to visit on an irregular basis since their first meeting in 1979, told him she was expecting a baby and asserted that he was the father. He would later privately relate that at the time he was busy working on *The King of Comedy*, and 'I was naturally shocked and confused and frankly I could not deal with this news.'

According to her account of events which followed, De Niro was furious and told her to have an abortion. He told her that he could not let anything interfere with his work nor his life in New York. He did not want Toukie Smith, whom he referred to as 'my girlfriend', to hear about it, and certainly he did not want his own family to know. De Niro would admit later that they had 'disagreed' over what she should do, but Helena insisted she was going to have the baby, with or without him at her side. He said he 'could not deal with the situation at that particular time in my life'. Helena explained:

I'd already made up my mind. I did not want to have another abortion. He became very animated, thrust his finger towards my face and yelled, 'I can't be involved with this. You're just trying to steal my money.' I told him that was ridiculous, and as far as I was concerned he need not be involved. I wanted the baby and, if he did not want to be around, then that was fine. I'd manage on my own.

When the row died down, and De Niro could see she was determined to have the baby, Helena said he agreed to help her financially in the latter stages of pregnancy and immediately afterwards. She said

141

that in all he gave her around $35,000, always in cash. Helena claims that De Niro himself chose the name of Nina for their daughter.

He, meanwhile, remained 'confused', although he did discuss the question of the child's name. He described it as a scene from a bad movie.

There is no question that Helena believed he was the father. De Niro maintained contact for some months up to and immediately after the birth but then, he said, 'we went our separate ways'. He was not present at the birth of the child in July 1982 and maintains that he was unaware that Helena had registered her daughter's name as Nina De Niro.

There was a further confrontation between them in the autumn of 1982 and then De Niro severed contact between them, saying he was 'seriously embarrassed' by what had happened. They did not see each other again for almost two years. For the time being Helena did not pursue the issue of De Niro's angry rejection of her and her child and got on with her life and career. But if De Niro ever believed in his 'confusion' that Helena Springs had gone from his life, he could not have been more wrong. It would all blow up again before long.

The irony of all this was that his attempts to keep his private life and other associations under wraps and firmly away from public gaze came at exactly the same time that he was working on *The King of Comedy*, a film which had as its theme the pressures and dangers of celebrity status. De Niro had once again joined forces with Martin Scorsese for what was another adventure to the dark side of the moon, fishing out those human characteristics that are least attractive and have the ability to make an audience squirm as they witness them. At times *The King of Comedy* comes close to being scary, not in a horrific way but in the realization that you are watching a person who is severely deranged and yet who, in the end, is turned into a hero in spite of his dangerous and criminal actions.

On this occasion De Niro created a most unlikeable portrait of a seriously dysfunctional would-be comedian in a story that represented an enormous departure for both himself and his director. Paul Zimmerman's original screenplay has Rupert Pupkin, the wannabe comic who is embarrassingly lousy and half sharp, pursuing the true King of Comedy, the famous comedian Jerry Langford (played by Jerry Lewis) in an attempt to get on his show. When all else fails he kidnaps Langford with the help of a similarly unstable accomplice and holds him to ransom, threatening to kill his victim unless the producers agree to give him, Pupkin, a spot on the show. He gets the spot, does his TV show, gets arrested, goes to jail, gets a book and film deal and becomes a celebrity himself – a particularly silly ending but, when you think about it, not out of sync with what happens today.

In the main, however, it is a one-line gag that is drawn out to the full 108 minutes with all the fun of having a wisdom tooth pulled. It hurt. This was a painful, frustrating movie in which audiences must have been expecting an imminent happening which never came. It wound its way onwards, like a dentist's drill striking a nerve every so often, becoming more repellent as each minute passed. De Niro's was an edgy performance, creating a characterization with an uncomfortable menace which in the end was an absolute turn-off to American audiences. It may well have been that there were too many recognizable features for a world which has a fetish for celebrities, and which is also populated with an abundance of lunatics who would do anything to achieve Warhol's fifteen minutes of fame in the hope that it would turn into a lifetime.

Scorsese and Zimmerman both hyped up the story in advance and in the wake of filming the movie. 'I can identify with Pupkin,' Scorsese claimed. 'I remember I used to go any place, do anything to get into a situation to talk up my projects.' He seemed to be speaking for De Niro as well when he added that he could also identify with the Langford character in facing the problems of being a celebrity, especially in its effect on personal relationships. 'The final line for me, at the time, was that if I had to make a choice between work and a relationship, the personal relationship would go by the wayside,' he said, a statement which could readily be confirmed by a cursory examination of the recent past of both himself and his star. The fact that De Niro's estranged wife Diahnne was invited to read for a role in the film, and was cast as Pupkin's girlfriend Rita, provided further evidence for what Scorsese was saying about the complications and the pressures upon celebrity relationships.

Diahnne's role, and that of Jerry Lewis and the fourth leading member of the cast, Pupkin's accomplice Sandra Bernhard, were all difficult roles which were performed with quality acting. De Niro actually wanted Meryl Streep for the part that Bernhard took, but after reading the script and talking to Scorsese she decided against it. She did not like the look of the movie at all.

The same went for Johnny Carson, the real-life comedy chat show host whom Scorsese wanted for the Langford role. Carson declined partly through fear of inspiring a real-life kidnap attempt and partly because he could not imagine himself participating in a scenario whereby it might need forty takes to get a scene shot, when in real life he did it in one.

Although second choices, Jerry Lewis and Bernhard provided the exact characterizations that Scorsese was seeking. They and the rest are jostled along in the semi-action but somehow are always left hanging mid-scene, as if Scorsese had pulled the pay-off line – which he had. He did not want people to laugh, despite the fact that audiences were itching to do so. He gave them nothing to laugh at, no point of release from the tension as the characters, for separate and different reasons, were unable to solve their particular hang-ups. For the first half of the picture the audience would have found it embarrassing to laugh at a man who was so evidently a nut-case in need of treatment, and in the second half it was equally impossible to laugh at a man at the centre of a criminal plot in which he was threatening death to his bound and gagged victim.

It was full of the usual De Niro quirks and displayed the customary pre-production homework. He spent weeks watching stand-up comics – for which his friendship with John Belushi and Robin Williams was a bonus. Then, when he had found the character, he retained it from the moment filming began to the moment Scorsese called a wrap. Jerry Lewis, who has eight Best Director awards, mostly from Europe, sitting on his mantelpiece from the days of his own comedy films, actually felt quite slighted when he invited De Niro home to dinner one night.

De Niro said he did not think that would be a good idea, and walked away without further explanation. It was left to Scorsese to explain that when 'Bobby is in character he does not think it wise to soften the intensity he's built in the relationship between the two characters by forming a friendship'.

'What?' Lewis replied.

It was explained again. De Niro does not mix with the rest of the cast while he is in character. Period.

Lewis had another opportunity to witness this intensity when De Niro thought that there was not enough fire between them in an angry scene. De Niro leaned over and whispered an anti-Semitic remark to Lewis who immediately exploded, and Scorsese got his shot. 'I had to bust your balls,' De Niro explained.

There was, however, no animosity between them. De Niro was as much in awe of Lewis's outstanding, word-perfect performance as Lewis was of watching De Niro work. 'I have never witnessed anything quite like it,' Lewis said. 'It goes by numbers, almost. In take one, he's getting into it; by take ten you're watching magic; by take fifteen you're seeing genius. He was also very helpful to the other actors, and does odd and superstitious character aids, like wearing a watch like mine so that he could transfer some of my own humour.'

Lewis was a mainstay of the film. His superb treatment and timing were recognized by the British Academy, who awarded him the accolade of Best Supporting Actor. *The King of Comedy* was also chosen as opening film for the 1983 Cannes Film Festival, and the British Critics' Circle voted it the best film of the year. Lewis was, however, neglected by his colleagues in the American Academy which had been expected at least to give him a nomination for Best Supporting Actor. Hollywood was continuing to demonstrate a pretty obvious indifference to the work of Scorsese and De Niro – though it would deny that there was any such feeling against the two New Yorkers who only rode into Los Angeles when they wanted something, like money for a film or a soundstage.

Hollywood, like the critics and the audiences, was demonstrably unsettled by this movie and by De Niro's performance in particular. He produced another distillation of human complexities in a portrayal of Pupkin that was as flamboyant as it was chilling, and provided one more remarkable addition to his array of characters. It is a film that is memorable for the discomfort it causes but not one that could be ignored. As with pretty well all of the De Niro–Scorsese collaborations it was very easy to take extreme stances – for people to say they either hated or loved it. Many influential critics praised it to the hilt and said it ranked among their best work together.

Audiences, however, did not follow the lead of the critics and stayed away in droves. Perhaps in the end it was De Niro's brilliance that wrecked the film, by making Pupkin so immediately like a person you know and detest and avoid like the plague – which is what cinemagoers eventually did.

So once more there has to be an examination of the motives for making a movie which so obviously jangled the nerves of its viewers in an irritating rather than a pleasurable way. Entertainment? It wasn't that either. An audience that has been entertained leaves the cinema with a feeling of satisfaction, whether it is from the standpoint of being cheered, shocked or horrified. *The King of Comedy* produced annoyance, and a character remembered only for that dubious effect. It was also more than an annoyance to 20th Century-Fox that $20 million went down the pan.

13

Once Upon a Time . . .

If *The King of Comedy* was a Van Gogh of its day, a masterpiece without an audience, *Once Upon a Time in America*, De Niro's next work, might be considered a masterpiece which was vandalized before anyone had a chance to see it. Director Sergio Leone, and De Niro himself to some extent since he collaborated throughout on the picture, must bear some of the responsibility. But at the end of the day it was once again the gulf between artistic merit and commercial dogma that ultimately torpedoed the success of this most outstanding of films.

Leone, the Italian director who came to the fore on the strength of his savage spaghetti westerns, had contracted with Warner Bros to deliver a finished film of two hours and forty-five minutes and ended up with an epic lasting four hours twenty-five minutes. Warner Bros ordered massive surgery to overcome the traditional resistance of American cinema chains and the mass audiences to lengthy features, just as Bertolucci had suffered with *Novecento*. The result was farcical and American audiences who were shown the cut version – as opposed to the more enlightened European cinemas who mostly saw the original – were left wondering what it was all about. The whole structure, which was the key to the telling of the story, was decimated and both De Niro and Leone were shattered by the result.

Leone may be perhaps excused for accepting the time constraints on what he knew was going to be an epic. He had been nurturing the project for a dozen or more years, and at times it seemed that he would never bring it to the screen. So when the chance came he was ready to accept any conditions, especially as he would be awarded a substantial budget.

The saga went back to the time when Leone was at the height of his fame with *A Fistful of Dollars*, which turned television cowboy Clint Eastwood into a world star. Then came *A Few Dollars More* and *The Good, the Bad and the Ugly*. In 1969 he completed his first epic, *Once Upon a Time in the West*, the long, violent and beautifully made western which marked his first collaboration with an American studio. It starred Henry Fonda, Jason Robards, Charles Bronson and a cast of dozens in a credit list that reeled for twelve minutes.

Soon afterwards he came across a little-known *Godfather*-style novel called *The Hoods* by retired Jewish gangster Harry Grey, a long and rambling tale spanning almost fifty years from the era of Prohibition. From that book he conceived his first draft screenplay for what would be the follow-up to his epic western, to be entitled *Once Upon a Time in America*.

Many false starts and broken promises later he was contacted by the young Israeli-born producer Arnon Milchan, whose work had included *The Medusa Touch* with Richard Burton and an epic mini-series for television called *Masada*, starring Peter O'Toole. (Coincidentally, at the time Milchan was about to begin work as producer of the very expensive Scorsese–De Niro project *The King of Comedy*, for which he naturally had great hopes.)

Milchan arranged for Leone to fly to New York. Before long he had secured a deal with Ladd Productions and Warner Bros for the distribution, a budget in the region of $25 million, and De Niro named in the lead role. Expecting *The King of Comedy* to be a major hit, all seemed in place for a blockbuster. Initial photography began long before De Niro had completed his work with Scorsese, and as soon as Scorsese did release him he went straight into the role. Reportedly guaranteed his first fee ever to exceed $3 million, De Niro would work on the film intermittently for almost a year, including location filming in New York, Toronto, Rome and Venice.

What Leone had honed from the book was a huge tapestry of gangster life in De Niro's most familiar and favoured location of New York, where six of his movies and most of his own life had been set. It tells the story of four gangsters who have a special bond between them spanning five decades, which was set up during their childhood when they swore allegiance to each other and decided to pool half their profits from crime. The story is told by way of flashbacks and memories through the De Niro character, an old man recalling his life. It is filled with symbolism, such as ticking clocks and a constantly ringing telephone to denote the conscience of the man, and with complex interconnected scenes and relationships of the kind that De Niro enjoys being involved in. It also required absolute concentration on the part of audiences and had to be watched in one sitting to keep track of all the movement and characters in a narrative spanning fifty years. In fact it is impossible to do justice to this screenplay with a brief précis: the subcurrents of the plot, all the nuances that Leone built with the six co-writers who were employed at one stage or another on the mammoth writing task, were vital to an understanding of the finished work.

Sure enough, the filming of the movie rambled on out of control and, like Bertolucci with *Novecento*, Leone shot far too much footage even to be accommodated in two movies. The budget too had been blown apart, running eventually in excess of $3 million – and more than that by the time post-production and launch costs had been added in. If there is a criticism to be made it is of the director's own lack of self-discipline, of filming take after take, often egged on by De Niro's own insistence on perfection.

It was finally brought to the screen in July 1984, sixteen years after the director had first had the idea. The première showing of the director's cut was to be in front of a packed audience at a charity event for which the admission price was set at $35. Even so, the queue stretched around the block, and a minor riot broke out when the doors were closed and the remaining customers turned away. On that basis, the movie seemed a likely winner.

The audience sat back as the titles rolled and were confronted immediately with one of the most violent scenes of the film, where the girlfriend of the De Niro character, known as Noodles, is discovered in a bedroom being threatened by four gangsters.

'Where's he hiding?' one of them calls out.

'I don't know. Honest. I've been looking for him since yesterday.'

'Lying bitch.' One of the gangsters strikes her across the face and breaks her nose and with such force that she is sent hurtling across the bed.

Another fits a silencer to his gun, and fires. Blood spurts out of her breasts but she is still alive, squirming in agony. He fires again, until she is dead.

The scene stunned the audience, and for the next four hours they remained stunned by scene upon scene of dramatic, overwhelming blood-letting, countered by others of sheer poetry and tenderness and some marvellous, often beautiful cinematography. At the end, the audience sat silent for a moment or two, still stunned, then gave Leone a standing ovation. It still seemed that the movie would be a blockbuster.

At that point, however, Warner Bros stepped in with the knife. There were already rumbles of protest from the Jewish community, and the Israeli government had even discussed the possibility of launching an international protest at the 'terrible slight' against their race perpetrated by Leone and De Niro. Various feminist movements were also gathering arms to protest at the shocking violence against women and the cold-blooded rape scenes.

Fearing a major backlash, and already worried about the length, Warners ordered producer Arnon Milchan to cut the film to 140 minutes, on top of twelve major scenes which Leone himself had already taken out. In the middle of the furore Leone suffered a heart attack, but continued to battle to save his movie. The US distributors remained adamant, however, and so the cuts were made. The result was not only an insult to the director and the actors, it also showed contempt for the audience. 'I felt very bitter,' said Leone, 'very bitter indeed.'

Many of the carefully contrived and constructed situations were hacked away: the constantly ringing telephone only rang once, and people who had been introduced in earlier cut scenes wandered in and out of the action without the audience knowing who they were. Important relationships, built up over the course of the longer version, were truncated to a meaningless degree. A lot of the famous Leone emptiness and beauty in his camera work was slashed. De Niro walked into a room and disappeared through a secret passage which he discovered in an earlier scene which had now been cut . . . and so on.

The work was turned into a mockery of its former self, an incoherent mess, and the critics were right in drawing attention to this form of commercial censorship. Fortunately, De Niro's reputation did not suffer too greatly. He was the saviour of the shortened version, giving the film a dimension that would otherwise have been lost. In France, where cinema audiences are more used to longer films, they showed it in its entirety and both audiences and reviewers responded with lavish praise. This inspired the British distributors, Thorn-EMI, to show a three-hour forty-minute print. But by then the damage had been done, and there was still some residual backlash.

Even at the Cannes Film Festival De Niro was collared by a woman member of the audience, an American as it happened, who screamed at him: 'It is blatant, gratuitous violence! As a woman, I feel deeply embarrassed to have witnessed it. I feel totally demoralized.' De Niro's face set like a mask. He said nothing but merely pushed himself through the crowd, pulling his white cap over his eyes as he drove off to his hotel at Cap d'Antibes. After that episode he took little part in efforts to promote the film.

The $30–40 million epic had become a financial disaster from which there could be no rescue. It took only $2.5 million in US rentals, which meant that, with the now recognized tragedy of *The King of Comedy*, producer Milchan had dropped something like $50 million on two pictures. If he and De Niro had been men of lesser talent both would have been laughed out of the business, in accord with the old Hollywood saying that you're only as good as your last picture. But they survived with their reputations virtually intact, and most people recognized that the débâcle was not entirely of their own making.

De Niro was strong enough to endure several more flops, as did Milchan who would later produce *Brazil*, *The Adventures of Baron Munchausen* and *Memoirs of the Invisible Man*. These failures at the box office were more than offset by *The War of The Roses*, with Michael Douglas, and the blockbuster *Pretty Woman*, with Richard Gere and Julia Roberts, which earned $450 million.

If there was any consolation in this increasingly familiar tale of Hollywood adventures for those of a less than populist bent, it lay in the fact that eventually the full-length version came out on cassette, to which it was eminently suited. It was the kind of movie that is appreciated more each time it is viewed, rather like a good book. The subtleties and the nuances become more striking, the narrative becomes less of an endurance and *Once Upon a Time in America* can be seen for what it was, decent but decimated.

Although De Niro's performance had been the film's salvation there was undoubtedly a hidden crisis of confidence, a hint that by continually playing characters afflicted by human aberration, diverse though they were, he was slowly but surely becoming a complete turn-off to the paying customers. Recent events in particular seemed to reflect a growing disenchantment, especially among the female members of audiences. None of his roles had been of an overtly sexual nature, and compared with some of his contemporaries he was positively low-key in that direction. Charm and star quality had never been part of his résumé. The heavy hand of Method acting from which he seldom veered had placed him for fifteen years in a kind of constant murky gloom, playing some of the cinema's most sordid, miserable and thoroughly unattractive characters virtually without a let-up.

Since they were all his own creation, it was not unexpected that some of those characteristics had lingered within his own psyche. That was certainly the image of him that was coming through the media, whose representatives he continued to avoid with steadfast resolution. Those who did manage to break down his door and get to the man for an on-the-record conversation that lasted more than a minute found it an uncomfortable experience. Victor Davis, for the *Daily Mail*, had achieved the almost impossible feat of having two sit-down chats with him, which was two more than most, and reported: 'At all times, he remains low-key. There's never a flamboyant gesture, never a Green Room actorish moment . . . and as director John Sturgess told me, he enters a room like a snake. But does he have presence? . . .'

De Niro's rule of thumb and immediate reaction to any approach by writers or television chat show hosts was: 'I don't do interviews.' Occasionally, perhaps when he had a particular point to make or wanted to answer a recent criticism, or when he was under pressure from a studio, he would select a writer by a tortuous process which usually involved a meeting to discuss a meeting. He did not bother with publicists or press agents, like other stars. He would suggest a meeting somewhere, probably in an inconspicuous back-street bar or café. If the writer got through the first stage he or she might then proceed to the next stage, at which De Niro would allow notes to be taken or the tape recorder to be running.

He had given virtually no interviews to speak of since 1977, and had clammed up completely in the wake of *Washington Post* reporter Bob Woodward's book on John Belushi. However in 1984, with *Once Upon a Time in America* doing so badly and his next film, *Falling in Love*, co-starring Meryl Streep, due out shortly, he came out of his shell briefly to talk up his image. For this occasion he selected Barbara Goldsmith to interview him for *Parade* magazine, which was ironically an insert of the *Washington Post*.

Goldsmith, a veteran of star interviews which had begun thirty years earlier with Clark Gable, had long ago deserted that particular line of work for more general writing. But she was intrigued by De Niro and sent him some of her recent work and essays with a request for an interview. Weeks passed with no response until one day she received a telephone call from one of De Niro's aides, warning her to wait by the telephone and adding that she might hear something to her advantage – but then again she might not. Apparently De Niro had noticed an article she had written for the *New York Times* about celebrity, and thought she understood the phenomenon of celebrity status in modern society. Soon after the first call he himself called personally, and said, 'Hi . . . this is Bob De Niro. Maybe we can talk . . . [long pause] maybe not.'

They met in a brightly lit restaurant. When Goldsmith waved so that he would recognize her he backed away momentarily and then made a gesture for her to stop in case they aroused attention. If he was recognized, no one showed it. De Niro made it clear from the outset that this wasn't going to be an interview. 'I thought we'd just meet and talk,' he told Goldsmith, 'about the possibility of an interview. I don't know if I want to talk about some things. I mean, what does it matter?'

Having got this far, Goldsmith wasn't going to give up that easily. She kept him talking until a teenage waiter arrived to take their order. De Niro was looking around him, behaving in a way that was not far off what might be expected of one of his film creations.

When the waiter had left, De Niro said, 'Do you think he recognized me?'

Goldsmith said she did not think so.

Later, he noticed two men and a woman who had moved to a nearby table. 'Do you think they are listening?' asked De Niro, putting his head down and furtively looking around as if he was surrounded by spies or potential assassins.

'I don't think so,' Goldsmith said reassuringly, but he wasn't satisfied and they moved to another table.

Slowly he began to open up, and the conversation was about his recent films. He said he thought the dialogue in *The King of Comedy* was brilliant. Then, as he spoke of his desire to make a comedy with Meryl Streep, he suddenly stopped when he noticed that Goldsmith was making notes.

'You writing this down?' he said gruffly. 'I mention Meryl and you whip out your paper. Is this an interview? We're still meeting. . . .'

Goldsmith persevered and got the conversation moving again. Then she asked him a perfectly normal question about how it was that he could play so many unsympathetic characters and yet people still liked Robert De Niro, the actor.

'Are you trying to trick me?' he asked.

'No. What do you mean?' Goldsmith replied.

'I think you are trying to get me to make a statement on that subject. I know what the answer is but it's for you to say . . . what we're dealing with here is a one-dimensional portrait . . .' and he rambled off into a lengthy explanation about why it was never possible to do a successful interview, ending mysteriously with the statement, 'Never complain, never explain – that's what I say.'

A waitress hovered close by for too long. De Niro cupped his hand to his face and said, 'That waitress keeps looking at us. I'm sure she knows who I am.'

If she did, she did not trouble him. And so it went on, in a state of virtual paranoia about doing or not doing an interview. But De Niro gradually warmed to his companion sufficiently for Goldsmith to know that a second meeting would not be necessary.

In fact they chatted for almost three hours, virtually unheard of by any known interviewer of Robert De Niro, although it must be said that at the end of it, when Goldsmith transcribed her notes, she discovered he had actually said very little. He refused to talk about people he worked with, didn't want to discuss Stella Adler in the same context as Lee Strasberg in case it would be seen that he was comparing one with the other, and throughout had difficulty expressing himself.

Goldsmith would note that De Niro recognized this shortcoming. It was not that he was inarticulate, but words were not his best means of expression. His form of expression was through his work and that, he said, was all an illusion.

At the end of her conversation, Goldsmith was paying the bill when she saw the waitress who had caused De Niro some temporary worry and asked, as a matter of interest, what she had been staring at. The girl replied that she wondered why Goldsmith was scribbling away in a notebook every time the man spoke.

Did she know it was Robert De Niro at the table?

'No?' the girl replied vacantly.

So much for all those fears. . . .

It was said that there was no connection between what must have been something of a concern about De Niro's image and the choice of his next film, which would bring him as close to a 'normal' person as he had ever been – or would ever be, for that matter – in any of his roles. It was his encounter with Meryl Streep, long awaited by both of them on a professional level. The film was talked up so that it would arrive with great expectations of an 1980s' version of the Trevor Howard and Celia Johnson classic *Brief Encounter*.

The ingredients were certainly all present, and the title of the piece, *Falling in Love*, had a special poignancy at a time when more conservative, less promiscuous values were returning, albeit temporarily, to society in the wake of the AIDS panic. This film was supposed to reflect the sea-change in the man-meets-woman scenario, and therefore suited De Niro, who has never been keen on appearing in overtly explicit bedroom scenes. Neither, for that matter, has his co-star. They had been itching to work with each other since *The Deer Hunter*.

De Niro and Streep were a mutual admiration society; the making of *Falling in Love* was one of the few occasions when he was chirpy and cheerful while making a picture, and he spent many off-duty hours with her. The character and storyline called for this kind of togetherness although they were also, as actors, inspired by each other because of their similarities in approach. Personally and professionally, too, Streep was as protective of her private life as De Niro.

She was also just as heavily in control of her career as De Niro, selecting the roles that suited her and not Hollywood in spite of the competitive nature at the top of the acting tree for female leads. She remained probably the most down-to-earth of the top women stars, and she worked at it – as demonstrated by her De Niro-style remark: 'You can't get spoiled if you do your own ironing.' Since *The Deer Hunter* she had appeared in roles which were meaty and substantial. In *Holocaust*, made for television in 1978, she gave one of her finest performances, followed by a string of award-winning appearances: *Kramer vs. Kramer*, in which she was superb and won her first Oscar, for Best Supporting Actress; *The French Lieutenant's Woman*, which won her a British Film Academy Oscar; *Sophie's Choice*, which won her an Oscar for Best Actress; and *Silkwood*, for which she received an Oscar nomination.

In other words, Streep was the closest there was to a female equivalent of De Niro in temperament and ability, which is probably why they hit it off so well. Far from flying sparks, however, they were both content to let the mood of the piece carry them along and, without great depth of characterization for either of them to explore, it was as natural an acting scenario as De Niro had ever been involved in.

He played the part of Frank Raftis, an average suburban male, an architect, who kisses his wife goodbye each morning and commutes to work on the 8.05. The best he could come up with to get into the

155

piece was to observe the work of real-life architects, but there would be only a few brief moments where this knowledge would be any use to him. After that he could have been any commuter setting off each morning for work, and in that respect De Niro had virtually no character to hide behind.

Streep is a fellow train passenger and, like the De Niro character, married to someone else. They see each other daily, but only meet when, just before Christmas and both carrying identically wrapped gifts, they collide and the parcels become muddled up. She takes home the present he bought for his wife while he takes the one she had bought for her husband. Subsequently they were said to be fascinated by the idea of an ordinary couple who have a brief encounter on their train, desperately want an affair but somehow never get to consummate their love.

What the part gave to De Niro, or at least so it was designed, was the power to demonstrate to female members of the audience that he did have another side to him which could be sexual, and that he was not entirely consumed by the squalid plots of films like *Mean Streets* or *Taxi Driver*. There are only two similarities to his previous films. The first was that his good buddy and co-star Harvey Keitel was cast as his work-mate. The second was that *Falling in Love* was set in New York and there were, as ever, demonstrations of his love for the city, seen through the lavish photography of British cinematographer Peter Suschitzky.

In that respect, too, Streep was in familiar territory. At the time she lived in a loft apartment in SoHo, not far from De Niro's own house. Before and during filming they often went back to her place and spent hours going over the script. 'We wanted something real, something awkward and crumpled,' said Streep. Between them, they probably achieved the best that could be achieved from a fairly low-key screenplay that never allowed them the final act, nor did it have the hand-wringing poignancy of *Brief Encounter*. Director Ulu Grosbard reckoned it was the personal chemistry between De Niro and Streep that brought the script to life. 'De Niro is not very articulate,' he admitted, 'which shows that intelligence and verbal facility do not go hand in hand. But there is a purity about him that he brings to his work. He is also a truly fine writer, going take after take, polishing, refining, going for the essence, for the Zen stroke, so to speak.'

Falling in Love showed a tender side of De Niro which Grosbard rightly claimed had never been seen before. Though the movie was classed as a fairly lightweight act on the part of both stars, a pleasant film that leaves the audiences happy, it must at some point have been considered to have rather more potential than it in fact possessed. It cost more than $12 million to make, even though there were no spectacular location scenes or hefty props to buy. Paramount would surely not have thrown that kind of money to the wind without the thought that *Falling in Love* might become a minor classic. It wasn't, and took a mere $5.8 million in US rentals. Once again a De Niro movie was showing a bottom line covered with red ink.

14

Mission Impossible

The change of pace continued, and this time there would be a change of scenery and a few surprises, too. Terry Gilliam, the controversial director of *Monty Python* fame, brought De Niro to London in 1984 to make *Brazil* at the behest of producer Arnon Milchan, who, straight from his financial worries with *The King of Comedy* and *Once Upon a Time in America*, was once again struggling to make the numbers add up although he had a reputation for putting creativity above profit.

He had agreed a distribution deal in the USA for *Brazil* with Universal Studios, who were looking for an American 'name' involvement in what was otherwise a line-up of British actors barely known in the USA. Bob Hoskins, who had just completed his pivotal role in Francis Ford's Coppola's *The Cotton Club*, was also signed for one of the peripheral characters which so helped keep this movie afloat, but at the time he was not big in the USA either.

The film itself was to be sold on the back of the *Monty Python* films, which did have a good following overseas. It was in the same mould. But Milchan really needed De Niro's inclusion to help justify a rather substantial budget of $15 million, of which Universal had provided $9 million. It is easy to imagine the queries from the money-men as to just how so much could be spent on a British-based movie of a somewhat eccentric nature – or, as Terry Gilliam himself described it, 'Walter Mitty meets Franz Kafka'.

Gilliam was apparently not pleased about being forced to take a star Yank on board, but laughingly accepted the situation by telling the media that De Niro had had to fight for his place in the movie – 'but that's another story'. It seemed an unlikely tale considering that De Niro, currently being billed as 'one of America's greatest actors', was making a mere cameo appearance as a plumber in circumstances which do not bear description other than to record that his name brought added weight.

The film, which owed much to George Orwell's *1984* as well as Aldous Huxley's *Brave New World*, was a supposed comedy, a disturbingly pessimistic view of the future via the familiar kaleidoscopic vision of Gilliam and company. Universal tried to make Gilliam cut the 160-minute picture by at least forty minutes, and to put in a new ending because the existing one was so depressing. Gilliam argued and fought back, and the movie was thus regarded by many at Universal as a boring misadventure – and a costly one at that.

De Niro's involvement was met with surprise by the critics, but did nothing to help recommend the film to audiences in the USA. There were enough Pythonesque jokes to please the intelligentsia, but it was too far out to whet the appetites of a mass audience. Box office rentals grossed a mere $4.3 million in the U.S. against an outlay of $15 million, excluding post-production costs, although compared to De Niro's previous two movies that might well have been considered a success.

To the money men, Milchan and De Niro might have begun to look somewhat accident-prone. De Niro himself was marginally perturbed by this, though it didn't stop him or Milchan from working and didn't seem to damage Gilliam's potential either. Before long, Gilliam and Milchan would embark on another hugely expensive project, *The Adventures of Baron Munchausen*, whose accountants had to send out for fresh supplies of red ink!

De Niro's trip to London that spring of 1984 had provided him with enough time to survey the scenery and local nightlife. He renewed his friendship with Bob Hoskins, whom he had met while Bob was in New York making *The Cotton Club*. Hoskins was seemingly surprised by De Niro's continued friendship, which went against the impression of him he had previously been given. He expressed his experience of De Niro's 'loyalty' as a friend in these terms. 'I was working on *The Cotton Club*, just finishing up, when he came to the set. He was a good friend of Coppola, of course, who was directing.' Hoskins said it was nearing Christmas and his wife and daughter had already gone back to England. He was desperate to finish the movie and get home in time for the festivities. 'When it looked as if I wasn't going to make it,' Hoskins recalled, 'De Niro came down to my hotel, knowing I was lonely and said "Listen, I'm going to have Christmas with my grannie. Do you want to join us? It'll be a quiet do, but it will be family."' Hoskins thanked him but declined, because he wanted to go home, but afterwards the friendship continued. 'He's a great guy to be with and he'll call me when he gets to London and say, "Can I come over for a meal?" Or we'll go off and get drunk together,' says Hoskins.

In London for the making of *Brazil*, De Niro took time to enjoy the nightlife. He was an occasional visitor to the nightclub Tramp, especially when there were friends in town such as Christopher Walken. He also spent two days trying to track down the whereabouts of a young black topless model whose photograph he saw in a newspaper. She turned out to be Gillian de Terville, then twenty-three, who lived with her mum, dad and eighteen-year-old brother in a three-up, two-down semi-detached in Sydenham in south London. She was cleaning her car one Sunday morning when her mother called out of the window, 'There's a phone call for you . . . says his name's Bob.'

Gillian went to the telephone, mystified. She could not call to mind anyone named Bob.

'Hi,' said the American-accented voice on the other end. 'We've never met, but this is Bob De Niro. Can I buy you dinner?' It took him five minutes to convince her that this was not a hoax. Finally she agreed to meet him, although she hesitated. 'I just did not feel like dropping everything and running off to have a meal with a man I had never met,' said Gillian. 'There are a lot of cranks around these days, and anyway I had a life which was very full and exciting. I reckoned he was also about twice my age.'

De Niro was staying in a London hotel at the time, and they arranged to meet for a drink in the bar. Even then, Gillian almost did not go. She had been working on a photographic shoot that day and she was tired. She called to cancel, but he talked her into going anyway. And so began a friendship which went on spasmodically for the next year or so while he was also seeing Toukie Smith, although she was quite often living in her Paris apartment.

While he remained in London De Niro occasionally called to collect Gillian in a cab, usually staying long enough to take a cup of tea with her parents and brother. When he returned to New York he arranged for her to visit him quite often. She stayed at his loft apartment in Greenwich Village, which she noted was hung with a mass of paintings, many of which were his father's, and a large round king-sized bed. 'A proper relationship developed between us,' said

160

Gillian, 'and it wasn't just a one-sided thing, where he was paying for everything and whirling me around. Sometimes he paid my air fare to New York, because obviously he has a lot of money.'

Gillian described De Niro as an 'old romantic' who used to hold her hand or put his arm around her whenever they went out. He was just beginning to grow a beard and long hair for his next film – with David Puttnam – which pleased him because, with the addition of dark glasses and a flat hat, he could walk around New York without being recognized. Gillian accompanied him to several parties in New York, including one given by Yoko Ono, and for many months she was a frequent visitor although he managed to keep her out of the limelight.

Gillian also witnessed the start of his immersion in a new character which she found interesting if a touch scary. This time he had been engaged by a British contingent and would be playing with another group of British actors, though entirely on location in Colombia. The marvellous Robert Bolt, screenwriter of *Lawrence of Arabia*, *Dr Zhivago* and *A Man for All Seasons*, had written the screenplay at the behest of the Italian producer Fernando Ghia, based upon a similar story he had read by an Austrian dramatist. Bolt's epic would be entitled *The Mission*. Ghia's co-producer was David Puttnam, then the great white hope of the British film industry and running Goldcrest Productions, although at the time he was already being eyeballed by Coca-Cola for a top job in Hollywood. As director they settled upon Roland Joffe, who had directed only one previous major movie, Puttnam's own production of the multiple award-winning *The Killing Fields*.

For observers of De Niro's work it was an interesting proposition which included a number of innovations. It was his first attempt at a period piece set outside the current century. He would, for the first time in his career, be working with a British director, on a screenplay by a man whose words were taken as fairly sacrosanct – quite the reverse of the modernistic work he was used to. Directors like Scorsese, De Palma and even Bertolucci had not only allowed De Niro great flexibility to improvise his lines as he went along, but actively encouraged it. Apart from his experience with Harold Pinter's screenplay for *The Last Tycoon*, the script had tended to be a mere starting point.

Additionally, he would be working alongside British actors such as Jeremy Irons and Ronald Pickup whose precision in the spoken word would represent a sharp contrast to De Niro's familiar Method-ized, New York inflection. By contrast Brando, who had admittedly made a bit of a hash of his English accent as Fletcher Christian in *Mutiny on the Bounty*, possessed a far greater vocal range than De Niro had ever attempted. For, as everyone now knew, the De Niro characterizations did not rest so much on voice change as on physical modification, although there would be ample scope for that here, too.

Robert Bolt's original screenplay of *The Mission* was set in the mid-eighteenth century, and in many respects could be compared to Bertolucci's *Novecento*. It was to South America and Catholicism what Italy and Communism had been to Bertolucci's film. Two central male figures would symbolize the issues. De Niro would be cast as Rodrigo Mendoza, an adventurer and fortune hunter who makes his living in the slave trade and typifies the imperialist plunderers who wanted to gather up the country's riches and slaves. On the opposite side is a Jesuit priest, Father Gabriel, played by Jeremy Irons; he represents the missionaries who want to protect the Indians and convert them to Christianity.

The two men come uneasily together when Mendoza kills his own brother in a fit of rage, and turns to religion and the priest to help him towards redemption. The Jesuits assign him an incredible task of penance, to climb a sheer cliff dragging behind him a net filled with heavy armour. And then, with his sin forced out of him, he becomes a missionary at a settlement run by Father Gabriel. As the film develops there is an inevitable confrontation between past and present when, in 1750, Spain and Portugal sign the Treaty of Madrid and the Indian lands are delivered to the Portuguese who, unlike the Spaniards, had not forsaken the slave trade.

The Portuguese governors order the closure of all missions. This is supported by a papal edict, to avoid trouble for the Church nearer home, in Portugal. The missionaries want to fight the closure, but Mendoza and Gabriel are at odds as to how it should be achieved. Mendoza returns to type and suggests a violent reaction, training the Indians for armed resistance, while Gabriel insists upon a religious response. In the end, neither of their solutions is effective and the film concludes in a profusion of battle scenes undercut by religious services.

Perhaps, before we go on, a word is necessary about the author, Robert Bolt. De Niro was intrigued by his work, as indeed was everyone who had witnessed Bolt's recent traumatic years. 'I think I've experienced a lot of anguish,' said Bolt soon after the movie was completed. That was something of an understatement.

His second marriage, to the actress Sarah Miles, was punctuated by her own troubles and scandals and ended in a highly publicized divorce in 1977. Three years later, he suffered a massive heart attack and stroke which left him partially paralysed and unable to speak, and with his memory partially impaired. He then married Ann Zane, former Marchioness of Queensberry, although they parted quite soon afterwards and were subsequently divorced. By then he had been approached by Ghia to write the screenplay of *The Mission*, which he embarked upon almost as a rehabilitation project, painfully tapping out his screenplay one-handed on his word processor and then turning it into a novel.

While the genius of his past work could not be expected, *The Mission* was still a remarkable piece of work under the circumstances, and displayed a continuation of his repeated theme of idealism versus pragmatism. 'I saw *The Mission* as a clash of temperament between Mendoza the fighter and Gabriel the committed pacifist,' said Bolt. 'I think Gabriel ultimately had the solution. If we do not turn away from the clash of cultures I think we have only fifty years to go, because one of these days one of the evil generals will let off a bomb and then it will be all over.'

The concept of human conflict always appealed to De Niro – it was a theme which he has toyed with repeatedly, as has Scorsese in his studies of Catholicism being out of step with real life. Even so, Puttnam and Joffe realized that their movie would represent such a major change of direction that he might not be interested. Puttnam's reputation was high after the success of *The Killing Fields* and the Oscar-winning *Chariots of Fire*, both of which had been built around lesser stars and virtual unknowns. But in this film he had to have a heavyweight to carry the $23 million budget and inject that necessary American presence into the cast list. Whether De Niro himself was the man to resolve that dilemma remained to be seen. He was not their first choice, as Joffe himself admitted:

Mendoza was a classical role and nobody had the balls and size to tackle it. The leading actor is your keystone, and if the director is the architect of a movie, then he has to choose the keystone very carefully because everything comes to rest on that in terms of performance. But I felt Bobby could rise to that. It was a very courageous step for him to take, and a proper one in terms of his career.

Joffe was already in Colombia setting up locations for the film when they contacted De Niro and invited him down to see for himself. He agreed and immediately became interested. Together, he and Joffe toured the regions around Santa Marta in Colombia and the walled city fort of Cartagena, built in the sixteenth century.

Joffe was apprehensive about De Niro's known penchant for improvisation, but they eventually agreed that Bolt's text was a fairly solid blueprint. In any event, it relied more upon De Niro's physical screen presence than on an oral one, and it was Jeremy Irons who would carry the bulk of the dialogue. Even so, it remained an area of difficulty as would be shown in the completed film: De Niro's contemporary style was never quite subdued sufficiently to dislodge memories of past performances, in spite of the historical settings and costume.

As usual with a movie shot in difficult locations, the filming of *The Mission* was one of those sagas from which everyone returned with a story to tell. To begin with, the logistics of bringing in an eighty-man film crew, with all their gear, cameras, lights, costumes, food and set-building materials, had to be planned with military precision. Virtually everything had to be imported, since Colombia had no major film company or suppliers of equipment; as a minor example, almost seven hundred wigs and hairpieces had to be flown in from Rome. Other things, however, could be provided locally.

A zoo of various creatures ranging from spiders to crocodiles, needed for various scenes, had to be assembled and maintained. A contingent of Indians had to be hired and drilled in their roles, for which they received a fee of $75,000 to be used for the benefit of the community.

Security problems were always to the fore, especially since the location of Gabriel's San Carlos mission was accidentally sited in the middle of a cocaine cartel route. That and the ever-present threat of bandits made the Colombian government mount a twenty-four-hour guard of machine gun-wielding troops around the location. Two of them were permanently assigned to De Niro and even stood outside his hotel bedroom after he had retired for the night. The weather was appalling, with torrential rain and unbearable humidity. Virtually everyone except De Niro went down with a particularly virulent form of dysentery. And so it went on.

As to the film itself, for once De Niro had remarkably few sources of research for his character and, since he had further restrictions imposed upon him by the rigid requirements of the script and the director, he had to do a great deal of imagining to create his character. Even so, the difference between the two male leads, himself and Jeremy Irons, was apparent. Comments which had become familiar in virtually every movie-making event in his career were uttered as if the speaker had discovered something new about De Niro. Joffe said of him, as others had:

> Bob is an extraordinary man. The approach of himself and Jeremy was totally different, but I had the greatest respect for him, and would give him time to discover where he was going. He would risk anything, do something in any order to allow a scene, and himself, to develop. It created instant difficulty, of course, because he and Jeremy were working in different directions. There was no answer to that, except to pray you get them to meet about halfway.

On set, De Niro was guarded and deep in his part. Like others who worked with him for the first time, Jeremy Irons judged him to be 'obsessed with his work' to the point that it took a long time to get to know him. Once past a certain point De Niro was warm and friendly, though, as Joffe admitted, he always seemed to be holding himself back. Irons and De Niro actually found they had much in common, and formed a relationship that endured long after the film was completed. 'It became easier when we discovered we could trust each other,' said Irons. 'It took us a little while to come together . . . but we did, eventually. I think Bob is a lovely man.'

As to the film itself, there was no question that it was a courageous effort all round, well intentioned and on the edge of genius – but it never quite got there. The photography was breathtaking and scenic shots through the Colombian mountains and valleys were spectacular. In that respect, Joffe did not waste a shot; there was interest in almost every frame. But in the jungles and the rain and the humidity of those difficult locations the heart of the picture went missing.

Joffe's direction seemed to lose its way, and towards the end slipped into confusion. Robert Bolt won a Golden Globe for his screenplay – a terrific adventure and a magnificent come-back on his part. Nevertheless his politics had by now mellowed and the film never achieved the potential impact of its political and social aspects. It rested more upon religious wellbeing to the point of piety.

De Niro did not come out of it too well, either. There were some very tense action sequences, but he remained awkwardly restrained in the scenes which rested on dialogue. Irons got the better of him in that respect. To De Niro fans, used to a streetwise performance which he had even achieved as the priest in *True Confessions*, this was not one they would relish with great enthusiasm.

The Mission would appeal to a particular audience and it found it in Cannes in May 1986, when the Film Festival awarded it the coveted Palme d'Or for Best Picture. The American Academy gave it seven nominations, including Best Picture and Best Director, though only one was converted to an Oscar, deservedly so for the photography of Chris Menges. This was acclaim indeed and another notch on David Puttnam's personal success graph.

Warner Bros, the US distributors, put it into a slow-burn release mode, opening in their most prestigious New York cinema and hoping to cash in on word-of-mouth recommendation. David Puttnam and Roland Joffe began their publicity round to talk up their film. At first, it seemed they were winning. Box-office receipts were encouraging, but then faded. Gross US takings of $17.2 million netted down into $8.3 million after the cinemas had taken their cut. Since the movie had cost $24.5 million before the marketing costs were added in, it was a commercial failure.

It was a fact, however, that continued low returns from his films had affected De Niro's bankability, and after *The Mission* there was a gap in his workload. He may have been ready for the rest after that gruelling work in the jungles of Colombia, but no actor likes an enforced lay-off – and that's exactly what his became. There were few offers or scripts attractive enough to bring him back to the screen, and in the two years after he finished work for Joffe he performed only two cameo roles.

His first full-length feature after *The Mission* was for British director Alan Parker, a former protégé of David Puttnam for whom he had directed the award-winning but controversial *Midnight Express*. He was making a movie called *Angel Heart* for a Hollywood studio. It was a modern Faustian tale of a private detective who steps into the world of satanism and voodoo, and eventually to hell itself, in pursuit of a missing person who has opted out of a pact with the devil. Mickey Rourke, the star, was at the time being written up as the 'new De

166

Niro'; now the old one had arrived to show him how it was done.

Angel Heart is a chilling tale with heavy blood-letting and notable for a scene involving Lisa Bonet, Bill Cosby's virginal television daughter, which caused a few palpitations at the ratings office, though today it would be passed without comment. De Niro was cast as Satan, with four longish scenes in the picture, and doubtless gave the director exactly the performance he was seeking. According to Alan Parker, on this occasion De Niro became obsessed with growing long fingernails for the part, in addition to a bushy beard. 'The physical thing is important to several actors,' said Parker. 'It gives them something to demonstrate their altered state.' He also thought De Niro was very courageous in risking his career on a cameo role of this nature. So did the critics, who were rightly beginning to inject a note of apprehension about De Niro's work, associated as he was with one more failure. *Angel Heart* statistics were no better than those for his last few: cost $18 million; gross US rentals $16.5 million. Cameo role or not, it was still logged as a De Niro failure by association.

He concluded the project in a state of depression, bemoaning to friends that nothing appealing was being offered to him. Weeks turned into months; for the first time for more than fifteen years he was actually without a project to work on, and nothing in sight.

It was this state of affairs that drew him back to his roots as an actor and led him to take an even greater risk with his professional life, by returning briefly to the stage. It was a risk because he would be placing himself in the hands of the fiercest critics in showbusiness and, as several of his friends would warn him, they could never be accused of being patronizing when a big star returned to the boards – not even a local boy made good, like De Niro.

The opportunity for stage work and a re-examination of himself occurred one day when he ran into Joe Papp, the then sixty-four-year-old director and producer and a driving force in the New York theatre. Papp, born in Brooklyn, had been around for years and ran a Shakespeare workshop from a church hall on the Lower East Side of New York way back in 1952. He became famous for giving free shows in Central Park which helped many now famous young actors, including Meryl Streep, to get started. In 1967 he formed his own Off-Broadway Public Theater dedicated to the work of new writers, and later became theatrical director of the Lincoln Center.

At the beginning of 1985 Papp was handed a new play by an unknown writer named Reinaldo Povod. Entitled *Cuba and His Teddy*

Bear, it was a gripping drama about a Lower East Side drug dealer and his teenage son. Papp sent the play to De Niro, and within a month New York audiences were amazed to discover that the star would be appearing nightly that spring for a limited eight-week run at Papp's Public Theater in downtown Manhattan, which, unlike London's West End which is awash with stars of stage, screen and television, is not particularly glamorous. The news brought an instant queue at the box office, and the play was sold out in no time.

De Niro's keenness to go back on stage had a lot to do with his unease at that particular time of his life and career when matters on both fronts were suddenly going awry. He had the desire, if not the need, to retrace his steps, go back to his roots and perhaps discover some guidance for the future.

The play itself was certainly reminiscent of past work that he and Scorsese might have settled upon for a movie: a gritty and realistic view of a father and son caught in the maelstrom of modern life. It was also set in his own back yard where, incidentally, the author Povod also grew up: he had based the play on his own experiences and his relationship with his Cuban-born father. Although he was nervous about meeting De Niro, his fears were soon quelled. 'He was just so ordinary, no affectation whatsoever. He changed my attitude towards people because he was more concerned about you than himself.'

Still sporting the beard from *Angel Heart*, and with longish hair which he tied back into a ponytail, De Niro began his work playing the father with some relish – at the Equity rate for the job, incidentally, and not at some inflated price just for being who he was.

Teddy, the son, was played by Ralph Macchio, better known for his appearances in *The Karate Kid I, II* and *III* and, later, *My Cousin Vinny*. De Niro was a hero, of course, and Ralph was also looking for a chance to do some 'real acting' away from Hollywood and the merchandising that went with the *Karate Kid* movies. 'Mr De Niro was great to me, and all of the cast. It wasn't the case of a big star just turning up and saying his lines, leaving the rest of us in awe of him. He just became one of us. He really seemed to be enjoying himself and his performances were stupendous. He came out different every night, as if he was treating it as a learning experience.'

Outside the theatre there was such demand for tickets that touts were making a killing every night. Joe Papp tried to offset this trade by hitching up a close-circuit television broadcast to a hall in an adjoining building, for which he sold tickets at $7 a head. But it was soon clear that audience demand would not be sated and Papp talked De Niro into moving the play on to Broadway. He agreed, and on 18 July Robert De Niro made his Broadway debut after almost twenty years in the business when he and Ralph Macchio opened at the Longacre Theatre. Opening night had the kind of excitement and appeal that is seldom seen at Broadway theatres, with crowds lining up behind police barricades at 7.30 to watch the stars arrive. The play ran until September, and De Niro concluded his 'back to basics' excursion in good spirits. When Hollywood called soon afterwards, he was revitalized and ready to puff himself up for one of the performances of his career, as Al Capone.

15

Big Al

While De Niro had been catching up with his past, the past had caught up with him. Helena Springs suddenly reappeared in his life. He had not spoken to her since they had parted in acrimony a few months after the birth of Helena's daughter, Nina. In the meantime she had moved to London to continue her career and in July 1984, when Nina was two, she married Anthony Lisandrello, a music company executive. They had remained in England ever since.

She and De Niro had passed like ships in the night once since then, when he was in London on film business and went to a nightclub. Their eyes met across a crowded room, but they did not speak. They saw each other again the following night. De Niro had gone to an Elton John concert at Wembley in which Helena was appearing as a backing singer. Afterwards he went backstage to the private bar and was talking to a group of stars who had turned up to see Elton when Helena walked in. According to Helena, he glared at her but showed no recognition, so she did not approach him. He left soon afterwards without speaking or attempting to enquire after Nina.

Then, in the autumn of 1985, Helena was in New York and made contact with De Niro through a mutual friend. She says he called her and they arranged to meet at his house, where they became reconciled and she stayed the night. They also agreed that De Niro should finally be introduced to the child the following day.

The meeting was arranged at the apartment of a friend, actor Barry Primus and his wife Julie. Helena left De Niro and Nina alone together for an hour or more. She said he was 'very sweet' to the child. They chatted and he bought her icecream. Afterwards, De Niro said he wanted to spend more time with Nina. Helena said it was difficult, because she now lived in London and he was in New York. 'We talked for a little longer and he said he would work something out,' Helena said. 'But he was still in a relationship with Toukie Smith and he did not want to upset that, because she was trying for a baby.'

De Niro's version of events was slightly different. He said he was 'embarrassed and uncomfortable' at his meeting with the child, but agreed to see her because he did not wish to be rude. He was also 'curious', he said, because at that time he could not deny the possibility that he was the child's father, even though he did not think she bore any physical resemblance to him. The meeting ended cordially, and Helena and Nina returned to London without any further decisions having been made about the future.

They spoke on the telephone occasionally but many months would pass before they met again, although Helena did say she had contacted De Niro for help with Nina's nursery school fees, but got no response. Whatever was going through De Niro's mind at the time, one thing had become clear to Helena: while on the one hand he wanted to have contact with Nina, he did not want their relationship to be stirred up in public, and so he was ignoring her. He was heavily involved with Toukie Smith; the British model Gillian de Terville was no more than a passing encounter. His claim that Toukie wanted a child was, according to mutual friends, borne out by the fact that De Niro and Diahnne Abbott were finally getting divorced, having been separated for almost ten years.

The friends surmised that this was being done by way of preparation for marrying Toukie, especially if she had a child by him. It was Diahnne Abbott's pregnancy which had originally inspired that marriage, as De Niro had long ago confided, so that their son Raphael would not suffer the stigma of having unmarried parents. But once Diahnne's baby was born the marriage lasted only a few months.

In spite of occasional dalliances elsewhere, De Niro and Toukie were still considered very much a couple. She was often with him when he travelled on location, and they took holidays together at their respective apartments in Paris and Rome. An impending divorce from Diahnne put the social gossips talking and suggested that a wedding was in the offing, although there was a question mark over their compatibility. De Niro, traditionally quiet at parties and social events, was now the immediate focus of attention when he walked into a room with Toukie on his arm. She was as eye-catching as ever, always attired in the sleekest, slinkiest, sexually enhancing dresses, often a brilliant red which was her favourite colour, while he, tousle-haired and plain, looked peculiarly out of place at her side.

Just as Diahnne had enjoyed socializing, Toukie too loved parties and seldom refused invitations to charity events, opening nights, benefits and all the other high-profile parties that De Niro is known to dislike. While he would attempt to slink in unnoticed, circling the periphery, her entrance was always spectacular and her voice carried across a crowded room. She would shriek with laughter or at the sight of a friend in some fantastic new dress. She was as outgoing and outspoken as he was retiring, and more often than not, when they were heading off to some kind of public do, they were not seen entering together.

It was De Niro's friendship with Bonnie Timmerman, casting director of the once top-rated television show *Miami Vice*, that secured Toukie's brief flirtation with acting. She was cast in a highly publicized episode with singer Sheena Easton at a time when the producers were attempting to revive the show's flagging appeal. Although she did not disgrace herself, Toukie did not take to acting and returned to New York to her other interest outside modelling – a gourmet catering company which she had founded, called Toukie's Taste.

In spite of their constant togetherness during the past seven years, they still maintained separate homes and separate lives which also mirrored their differing personalities. Hers was brightly decorated and modern. His was in an unbecoming block with a bank and a tool shop flanking the entrance; while the internal décor was a complex mixture, just what might be expected from a man whose acting displayed a gamut of emotions and obsessions. His furniture was large and comfortable, covered in richly textured fabrics. Paintings filled the walls. He had built a roof garden filled with exotic plants; there was also a gym, which he had equipped with the same eye for detail, where he could lose those extra pounds he occasionally put on for movies.

The stability of his personal life was as legendary among the socialites of New York as his loyalty to friends and associates, especially in their times of trouble or need. Equally, they knew that once he was on a project they would not hear from him for weeks, possibly months. In the autumn of 1985 he was preparing himself for a brief but important encounter with a larger-than-life character.

The immersion process was already taking up his thoughts. A new character to sink into had been presented to him, and he was going to give it the absolute De Niro treatment. It came to him by pure chance and forced him into making one of the most curious decisions of his life – to turn down the biggest fee he had ever been offered.

The story is one which British actor Bob Hoskins dined out on for months afterwards, and it dates back to the time when De Niro was appearing on Broadway. Brian De Palma and the rest of his chums came to see him on stage. At the time the director was casting for his big-budget movie *The Untouchables*, the biggest of his varied career. He had already filled the big slots, of course, with Kevin Costner as Eliot Ness, Sean Connery as Jim Malone and Andy Garcia as George Stone, but decided there and then that he wanted De Niro for the role of Al Capone.

Around the same time director Hector Babenco, fresh from *Kiss of the Spider Woman*, was casting his net for the leads in his own new big-budget assignment. *Ironweed* was the rather gloomy story of a couple of alcoholic drop-outs, and Meryl Streep was in the frame as the female lead. The money was huge. How much De Niro might have got is unclear, but he was wavering whether or not to do it.

De Palma, in the meantime, was left in limbo and decided to make a contingency plan. He contacted Bob Hoskins, who at the time happened to be in Los Angeles basking in the acclaim for his performance with Michael Caine in *Mona Lisa*, which had gone down very well in America. 'Brian was very straight,' Hoskins recalls:

> He said he really wanted Robert De Niro to play the role of Al Capone in his new movie, but there was a problem and he wasn't sure if he would do it. So he said, 'If De Niro won't come, will you do it?' He said it wasn't a massive part, just two weeks' work probably and the money was good, so I said yes. Anyway, a couple of weeks later he called, and said, 'Sorry, Bob . . . but I won't be needing you now.' So I said fine, I quite understand . . . and then a cheque for two hundred grand [$200,000] dropped through my letterbox. Although I'd told him he didn't owe me a penny, he paid me compensation. I couldn't believe it. It's the easiest money I ever earned.

So De Niro had turned down *Ironweed* for a lesser fee and a lesser role because, having weighed the two characters, he decided he fancied the part of Al Capone better. Jack Nicholson signed to do *Ironweed* with Streep and was paid $5 million. Although De Niro did not command such huge money, it would have been close.

The money aside, he probably made the right choice. Although Nicholson and Streep gave performances which at times matched anything they had ever done, *Ironweed* was too heavy for the audiences and, in spite of some decent notices, it collapsed on the cinema circuit. De Palma, on the other hand, was offering De Niro the chance to play Al Capone, which he had yearned to do. He did not do badly in terms of money for *The Untouchables*, either. His delay over making a decision had helped push up the pay packet to entice him in: and he reportedly signed on for a fee of $1.5 million, plus a percentage which gave him another $500,000 to do six scenes, shot quickly over a period of two weeks.

Up to the point of signing De Palma's producer Art Linson had never met De Niro, and when he finally came face to face with him to handle the contractual formalities he was shocked. De Niro was still in his Cuba mode for the Broadway play. After the meeting Linson telephoned De Palma in the early hours of the morning, terrified that they had made a big mistake. 'This guy turns up,' he shouted down the receiver, 'weighing about 150 pounds, ponytail and looking about thirty, weird and barely articulate. Capone was fat, forty and loud-mouthed. And we gave up Bob Hoskins for this guy? We're out of business.'

De Palma calmed him down and said the next time Linson saw Bob De Niro he wouldn't recognize him. He was right. De Niro flew briefly to Chicago, where the film was being shot on location, and then immediately took off for Italy for research and food. They told him in Chicago that all he needed lay in that city – a complete archive on Capone and plenty of fine restaurants. De Niro just winced, and disappeared.

When he returned five weeks later, he was indeed completely altered. While in Italy he had eaten his way through plates of pasta, potatoes and creamy desserts, washed down with litres of beer and full cream milk, and had managed to increase his weight by almost 30 pounds, just as he had done when he played Jake La Motta in *Raging Bull*. His face was rounded like a moon, and his body noticeably fatter. For added weight he borrowed a latex body suit which he wore when filming began. He had also spent fourteen hours in a barber's chair having his hair shorn of its ponytail and sculpted and greased back.

174

Another aspect of the preparation in Italy was to bone up on the Neapolitan accent. Unlike Don Corleone, who was Sicilian – a darker, more mysterious type with North African influence – Al Capone hailed from Naples, where not only was the speech different but the personality, too. He was loud and flamboyant. Next, De Niro studied hundreds of photographs of Capone and every piece of old newsreel he could lay his hands on. Then he had Armani research and design a complete wardrobe of suits and coats with the help of a tailor whom De Niro knew from Little Italy in New York, so that the attire conformed exactly to the photographs of Capone.

There was one more sublime, yet ridiculous, act. He learned from his research that Capone also wore silk underwear, supplied by a particular shop, A. Sulka & Co., which was still in existence. So he ordered for himself sets of silk underwear which would be worn exclusively during filming – regardless of the fact that there was not a single second when his silk knickers would be seen. He discovered Capone's particular brand of cigar and found photographs of his shoes. When all these external props were assembled he spent hours in front of mirrors, trying on the suits and the coats, and then even studied himself with different-sized cigars in his mouth to achieve the most effective look.

Now, to the average observer – and to older hands like Sean Connery, even though he was himself a meticulous researcher – all this for a mere six scenes may have seemed completely over the top. When producer Linson began receiving the bills he began to get worried until he saw the revamped De Niro looking, sounding, walking and smoking like Al Capone. At first bemused, he was finally jubilant that they had a secret weapon on their picture. He ordered a black-out of still pictures on De Niro, and no film of him was released in the trailers. Linson wanted to turn the whole thing to PR advantage – let no one see him in advance, leak out the change and then let the whole thing build up, just as had happened with Brando's appearance in *The Godfather*.

The hype certainly worked, aided by De Niro's own electrifying performance: the critics mostly agreed that it was one of his best. Backstage, among the profession and the students of the performing arts, he had once again raised the issue of not so much his style, which was a one-off, but the extent of his obsessive preparation to the point of becoming the character. Was his acting artificially inspired? How much external propping did he require to bring himself into the part? Was it a form of professional cheating? If he was playing an arsonist, would he go around setting buildings on fire just to get into the man's mind? These were good debating points in film schools and campus drama departments.

An actor who does not research is dead. Everyone has to study, write their little theses, read their lines for the beats and the nuances, mark and underscore, study and explore the actions and mind of the character, whether fictional or real. But then most will stand back, take a deep breath and begin acting. And, as De Niro demonstrated yet again, that was simply not his way. Those around him may look on aghast at the change, physically and orally. In five weeks he goes from a thin, shy, inarticulate man to a fat, brash, fast-talking gangster. He's that person all the time, and stays clear of all situations that might destroy the magic. What he served up in *The Untouchables* was a monster of a man, a psychopath, everything that Al Capone was and more – because De Niro also showed us that the man had intelligence and ability, that he was a politician and a businessman. He came right to the edge of turning his performance into burlesque, but pulled back just in time. It required absolute precision to achieve that effect and to make an unforgettable impact on the film.

It was interesting to compare De Niro's performance with that of Sean Connery – equally enigmatic, sometimes even more so. Connery's acting technique stemmed from a misspent youth and self-taught Shakespeare, followed by a few British B-movies and the tuition of innate discovery by a former Swedish ballet dancer who taught him the organic approach. Like De Niro he has a particular style and quality of his own. He is, however, always totally recognizable as Sean Connery, give or take the beard, the occasional toupee or costume as required by the movie. What he carried from one movie to the next was his charisma, not a suitcase full of disguises. He very seldom relies upon physical elements to create his character, to the degree that his costume or attire are fairly unimportant; the actor himself is always in focus. In his early days, he would write long essays on the meaning and his understanding of a particular play or story, and a deep analysis of the part he was playing, a technique used by many actors.

Connery has never altered. His good friend Robert Hardy once told me,

He has never attempted to disguise his Scottish accent. I can't think of a single instance of any of his roles when he has done so. It has mellowed somewhat from when I first worked with

him, when he was an unknown and we were playing
Shakespeare. It became softer, more readily understandable,
but he never really changed it from one character to the next.
He is just a bloody good actor. Sean Connery is Sean Connery,
but maintains the ability to suspend disbelief every time.

Connery only saw De Niro working on one day during the entire
shoot of *The Untouchables* and never had much to do with him, but
he was impressed. It was also Connery's picture by a mile. He out-
played the deliberate, low-key performance of Kevin Costner who in
the end was so laid back he was dull. De Niro's brilliant cameo came
as a pleasant surprise to the audience, but it was Connery who deservedly won his first Oscar for Best Supporting Actor. This was also the
most commercially successful film that De Niro had ever been
involved in, taking $15 million in the first week of screening after a
massive publicity hype. Since De Niro owned a couple of percentage
points of the net, he took more than a passing interest in its wellbeing.

He turned up at the star-spangled première in New York in 1987
with Toukie on his arm, publicly demonstrating their friendship for
the first time. She had come through a traumatic time recently, with
the death of her brother Willi from AIDS that spring. De Niro had
been at her side throughout and had also volunteered to appear in an
AIDS information television commercial. The camera lights shone
brightly as they hurried in, followed by the equally private but less
fraught Sean Connery and his wife, who joked and laughed with the
photographers on their way into the cinema.

Then De Niro joined a glittering array of talent jetted in for the
fortieth Cannes Film Festival, graced by the Prince and Princess of
Wales in the final throes of the pretence of their own togetherness.
Diana's brother Charles, then a television reporter for NBC, made
contact with De Niro's aides in the hope of getting an exclusive interview. But De Niro was having none of it. He flew in on Concorde,
joined the opening jamboree, then left again before anyone had a
chance to collar him.

Later, back in the USA, De Palma did manage to persuade him to
join him on a television chat show, but the event turned into an
uninformative exchange of mutual admiration:

De Niro: Oh, Brian . . . he's terrific. Always has been. He's
very easy and he's a great audience.

177

De Palma: Bobby . . . he's a chameleon. And that's absolutely a compliment. What I've found so remarkable about his performances is his ability not only to become the person he's playing, but physically to change the way he looks so that you don't recognize him from part to part. . . .

The greatness of 'America's finest actor' and the merits of his new picture were well and truly hammered home. Some critics wondered if De Niro had run out of steam and intended to do a Brando, making brief appearances in other people's movies. And by the time those reviews appeared the question was already out of date.

Another small time bomb had been ticking away in the De Niro soul. He had long been thinking of doing something else, by which he meant tackling different parts from the psychopaths and malcontents of the seventies. It was clearly an ongoing topic in the self-analysis of his career. He was thinking of comedy. He desperately wanted to play the body-change boy in *Big* and Penny Marshall, the movie's director, wanted him to do it too; but the studio thought that De Niro had too many skeletons in the cupboard from past movies that the critics and commentators would latch on to. This, they felt, would give *Big* the wrong image and detract from its intention to be seen as wholesome, family entertainment. De Niro could unconsciously give it darker tones with those looks and stares that he doesn't know he is doing until he sees it on film, which spell spit-in-your-eye menace. *Big* needed wide-eyed innocence, a big kid who could play with a train set or a space-walking doll. Could De Niro? The studio said no and signed Tom Hanks instead. Probably no one could have done it better; different, but not better.

Fortunately, at around the same time a comedy was on offer. Director Martin Brest, looking for a follow-up to his runaway blockbuster *Beverly Hills Cop*, the rough-and-tumble comedy filled with bad language that became the hit of 1984, had settled on another hard-edged comedy from the pen of George Gallo. He sent the script of *Midnight Run* to De Niro. Brest, producer as well as director, made no secret of his wish for a commercial slant rather than the character studies that De Niro usually looks for. There were no deep and meaningful sub-plots or intensity here, just a straightforward action comedy targeted for its mass entertainment value.

Though it was no *Beverly Hills Cop*, *Midnight Run* offered De Niro the chance to relax and have fun. 'It was a scary experience meeting him for the first time,' said Brest. 'But he had no attitude – just a down-to-earth guy. In fact, it was like making a movie with my film school friends. Sometimes I'd let the camera run after finishing a scene to see if he did any bits, and invariably he did.'

De Niro accepted, along with the highest fee of his life. He thus became Jack Walsh, the tough but honest detective who leaves the Chicago police force to become a modern bounty hunter, bringing back criminals who have skipped bail. Although the plot sounded formulaic it was adroitly inventive in its development, aided by a striking and rare screen partnership which De Niro formed with his co-star Charles Grodin.

Jack is hired to trace and capture Jonathan Mardukas, a wimpish, softly spoken accountant who has fled Los Angeles. His bondsman will have to forfeit $100,000 if he is not returned within four days. Jack picks him up in New York, and then discovers there is more at stake: Jonathan is not being sought only by the man who put up his bail. He turns out to be a book-keeper for the Mafia and has embezzled $15 million which he then gave away to charity. The gangsters are in hot pursuit, as are the FBI who want him to testify. So with Jonathan handcuffed to Jack, the pair set off to return to Los Angeles. It should have been a straightforward journey, but the accountant has a fear of flying and so the adventure turns into a cross-country chase thriller by train, bus and car.

The story is full of quirks and gags which provide De Niro with perhaps his best-ever opportunity of lifting the mask of grimness that his face so often mirrors. He and Grodin perform an on-the-road equivalent of Neil Simon's *The Odd Couple*, and their immediate rapport was evident in exchanges of improvised dialogue.

But there had been some pre-production background to the making of this film which had almost put Grodin out of the running. Paramount, who had initially taken an interest in Brest's production, wanted to put another major-league star alongside De Niro. Interestingly, they argued that De Niro was not a strong enough draw to carry a $30 million picture on his own. Their production executives suggested that the Grodin character should be changed to a woman, and that Cher should be offered the part, thus providing the opportunity to inject some sexual overtones into what was really a film about male bonding. Brest was not amused by the idea, and rejected it.

Other big names were mentioned and Robin Williams, having heard that De Niro was up for the role, actively promoted himself as

his screen partner. Williams even agreed to do an audition – highly
unusual for an actor of his stature. Brest remained unmoved. He still
wanted Grodin – so Paramount backed out, and Universal stepped in
and gave the producer-director what he had wanted all along.

Grodin, meantime, had overcome his own reservations about co-
starring with De Niro, whom he knew well from social encounters,
but had never worked with. 'I knew the reputation,' said Grodin, 'and
I know people are always worried that working with him is going to
be a depressing experience. You know very well that if he has a scene
driving a bus, he's going to spend five days on the road driving a bus.
But it turned out well. He was having fun. He's kind and sensitive, a
gentleman.'

Although Grodin is a highly competent actor with many similarities
to De Niro, it is probable that a bigger name would have produced a
better commercial result. But Brest stuck to his guns, and so in the
end took less money than he might otherwise have done. Anxious to
talk up the movie, when launch time came around Brest managed to
do what few have achieved in the past, which was to drag De Niro
before a roomful of journalists for a press conference. The event was
staged in the luxurious surroundings of the Plaza Hotel in New York,
then under the flamboyant supervision of Ivana Trump. The press
were keen to see what nuggets they could glean from this phantom of
the cinema, but there would be few surprises. He answered the barrage
of questions in unsteady but measured responses, either monosyllabic
or replying with a question.

The difficulties faced by anyone attempting to hold a sensible discussion on his work, let alone his private thoughts, were once again
frustratingly evident. The first question unknowingly struck a nerve,
and referred to a scene in the movie which was an almost exact rerun
of the moment when De Niro met his alleged daughter by Helena
Springs: 'We can believe the Jack Walsh character when he gets choked
up seeing his young daughter for the first time in years . . . how do
you achieve that? Is it instinctive?'

De Niro's face took on a look of quizzical fear. His thoughts were
almost visible. What do they know? Is this a trick question? What's
coming next?

'Ah . . . well . . . uh . . . humm. . . .'

Next question, and a journalist tried to turn him towards his well-
known role rehearsal.

'How did you prepare for this part?'

180

'Every part is different. One I approach one way, one another.'

No secrets there, either.

'Did you spend time with bounty hunters?'

'Going out with bounty hunters is not so easy . . . I had more luck going out with the police, but there was a lot of waiting around. Then you get a phone call. Then you look. The drama is in little spurts. Sometimes it's there. Sometimes it's not. . . .'

Oh well . . . the questioners pressed on.

'What was the challenge of this particular role?'

'There weren't many challenges. There weren't things that were that hard. . . .'

Frustrated, one tried a different tack.

'Did you like the idea of playing someone more like a normal guy?'

'Who's normal once you get to know them? To me, to get to know a person is more interesting, to know the other sides of people than those we usually see in public. People identify with it, these other sides. But you see these other sides more in novels than in movies.'

Oh. Right.

'What side of yourself did you draw on for this character?'

'In everything you do, there's a part of you. You draw on that. It doesn't mean you become that person.'

'Do you find it easier, feel less exposed, when you're emphasizing physical characteristics, as in *Raging Bull*?'

'I like to approach roles physically. Sometimes it's easier. Sometimes it isn't.'

'Of the roles you have played, which one approximates closest to yourself?'

'That's a private thing . . .'

And so it went on. Questions and non-answers. De Niro's press conference barely lifted a corner on his true self.

16

Looking for Control

The summer months of 1987 presented a mass of mixed emotions. There was the feelgood factor induced by the acclaim for his portrayal of Al Capone, along with a certain warmth derived from his relationship with Toukie Smith which, according to close friends, looked as if it had finally reached a point where he was clearing the decks for marriage. He was also invited to Moscow to chair a panel of jurors at the fifteenth Moscow Film Festival, a prestige appointment and the first time he had been a leading participant in such an event. In front of many international stars and film-makers, including his good friend Gerard Depardieu, Warren Beatty, Nastassia Kinski and directors Federico Fellini, Stanley Kramer, Arthur Penn and Milos Forman, he found himself making speeches and coming close to looking like an establishment figure. 'It is a great honour,' he explained, 'and I am a little nervous.' He took his son Raphael and adopted daughter Drina along for the experience.

As a sign of the mellowing times, the Russians opened the festival with a showing of *The Deer Hunter* which had once been politically castigated and banned in the Soviet Union as racist propaganda. There was still a touch of Communist idealism in the questioning, though, as he faced a large and enthusiastic crowd of Russian journalists who were enjoying certain freedoms in the first days of glasnost. Had he, as a steadfastly principled actor, compromised his conscience by acting in and promoting a film which dealt with young Americans of Russian origin (as in *The Deer Hunter*) participating in the Vietnam War?

'No,' he replied with considerably more directness than he had displayed on his own territory against semi-hostile questions, 'It was a film against war. From that standpoint, I certainly do not regret playing it.' Indeed, he looked far more relaxed in Russia than at home, giving interviews to local journalists and even one to a writer from a German magazine to whom he allowed far more latitude in his questions than probably any Western journalist to date had enjoyed.

During the festival he also met director David Jones, who had recently made the successful *84 Charing Cross Road* and was by coincidence working on a film script with a post-Vietnam theme. De Niro expressed his interest, and they would meet when they got back.

In fact, his return to the USA was marked by ambitions of his own in the business of film production; he began scribbling plans and casting his net for a distant project to build his own film centre and restaurant somewhere close to his apartment. He had talked about it often enough to Martin Scorsese, having seen producers of several of their films walk away with the lion's share even when the movie had not been a financial success. But money, he would insist, was not the driving force. He wanted artistic control over two great loves of his life – food (by way of owning a restaurant) and films, some of which he would not personally appear in.

It was not exactly an unknown diversion for movie stars when they have a few millions stuffed away in bank accounts and become afflicted with the Irving Thalberg syndrome or some other business ambition: actors from way back had formed their own production companies. The most famous, of course, was the creative alliance led by Charlie Chaplin, Mary Pickford and Douglas Fairbanks, who formed United Artists which came to a sticky end half a century later and was absorbed into MGM. The most successful of all actor-producers of the modern age was Warren Beatty, who after the mid-1960s seldom appeared in anything that he did not either produce or direct and aimed his films directly at the commercial jugular. He had made a reported $60 million – and secured a record number of Oscar nominations – from just three of the movies he initiated, *Bonnie and Clyde*, *Shampoo* and *Heaven Can Wait*, along with lesser sums from a string of others including *Reds*, *Dick Tracy* and *Bugsy*.

Michael Douglas did much the same, moving into the arena of producer when no one would hire him as an actor. He did not appear in *One Flew Over the Cuckoo's Nest* but, as its producer, won an Oscar for Best Film; this was followed by *The China Syndrome* which he produced with Jane Fonda, who also had her own company. Douglas then signed a three-year production deal with Columbia, didn't shoot a single foot of film and left to make his own movies. The highly successful *Romancing the Stone* and *The Jewel of the Nile* were aimed at promoting Michael Douglas, actor. Later, he formed another production company which turned out half a dozen reasonably successful movies in the late 1980s and beyond. It spawned a record label offshoot which also did well. Douglas, like his father Kirk, who was among the first Hollywood stars to move into production in a big way, turned in some impressive figures.

Robert Redford launched his own production company and film centre, which he called the Sundance Institute, from his ranch in Utah in 1980. He picked up Oscars for Best Director and Best Picture with his debut production *Ordinary People*, although he was not what might be termed prolific and waited years between projects.

By the mid-eighties Clint Eastwood too was to be found increasingly on the other side of the camera. Sylvester Stallone and Arnold Schwarzenegger had both involved themselves in production, and had also just joined forces with Bruce Willis to create a chain of hamburger restaurants which bore a passing interest in movie memorabilia. So there were plenty of precedents. For De Niro it all seemed a logical progression in spite of the financial traumas of his friend Martin Scorsese. Now, he was in the $5 million a picture bracket – though still cheap compared with Schwarzenegger and Stallone – and when a man of his nature and maturity gets to that position at a certain age he starts to think about doing those things that have been lodged at the back of his mind for years. He set the whole thing in motion that year, scouring the lower regions of Manhattan for suitable buildings. Eventually he found an abandoned coffee warehouse just below his apartment in Canal Street in the area known as TriBeCa, not ten minutes from his own childhood patch.

It would take two or three years to bring the project to fruition, but he was already pulling in the funds. That year he sold off the house in Brentwood, Los Angeles, which he had bought for himself and Diahnne in that brief period of the late 1970s when it looked as if they would become Hollywood people. It was bought by Lucille Ball's daughter, Lucie Arnaz, and her husband Laurence Luckenbill for $1.2 million.

He was in any case becoming seriously rich. Aggregate fees for his last two pictures, *The Untouchables* and *Midnight Run*, exceeded $7 million. In spite of mediocre box-office returns, he had developed what he described as a 'self-worth side to me'. In other words, he wouldn't sell himself short for the sake of getting a part. In fact, one producer who failed to negotiate terms used Sam Goldwyn's quote about Charlie Chaplin's financial abilities – 'all he knows about is that he can't take anything less'.

After many years of frugal existence compared to other stars, he was exceedingly comfortable financially. He spent very little money on cars or clothes and his housing remained unassumingly modest. Whenever he travelled on film business he carefully negotiated the terms of his expenses to ensure that he got his dues, although he never went over the top by demanding penthouse suites, private aircraft and round-the-clock chauffeur-driven limos, as some did. He was still happy living in the Chateau Marmont when in Los Angeles and using a self-drive Mercedes. He had millions sitting in his investment accounts but he was careful with it. What was his was his, period.

Helena Springs discovered that when she popped up again that summer. She was in Los Angeles when De Niro telephoned her to say he had heard that she wanted to speak to him. That was true, said Helena. She explained that Tony, to whom she had been married for four years, had said that they could not be a complete family until Nina's situation was resolved. Helena reckoned Tony complained that De Niro was ever-present in their lives even though he had little contact. He was hovering in the background, making occasional acknowledgements of Nina's existence – but otherwise ignoring her – which in turn caused uncertainty and distrust between Helena and Tony.

Although De Niro had only seen the child once in her life, his presence was still a factor to be dealt with as she grew older, especially as he did not seem interested in forming a father–daughter bond. Tony wanted to formally adopt Nina, just as De Niro had done with Diahnne's daughter Drina.

Helena said De Niro went 'crazy' at the suggestion and refused point-blank to discuss it. He said that if Nina was his daughter, he would not accept any other man taking over as her father even if it was not possible to do so himself at the time. Helena then said that if he would not let Tony adopt Nina, he should begin making formalized payments towards her education.

De Niro refused on the basis that if he were the father he wanted to take responsibility for his actions.

The issue remained unresolved. Nina, as far as anyone knew, was the daughter of Helena and De Niro, but was effectively fatherless because he refused to have contact with her. After four years of marriage to her mother, Tony Lisandrello loved the child and wanted to adopt her. But in rejecting this possibility De Niro made no suggestion as to how the situation might be resolved.

He did not deny he could be Nina's father – indeed he adamantly defended that position when challenged by Lisandrello. Yet he refused to do anything about it. He refused further financial support. His response, according to Helena, was first to be angry and then to walk away as if the problem did not exist.

He needed everything to be straightforward – commitment without responsibility. That is the basis on which he established all his relationships, although it was one that happened to suit Toukie Smith, who had been in his life now for almost eight years. As for Helena and her child, they were out of sight, although perhaps not out of mind.

Developments in his professional life also fell back, and gave an indication that his concentration may have lapsed while he was dealing with other things. He had recognized that by continually playing schizophrenics and other freaks he was running the risk of repeating himself. He tried comedy with Charles Grodin. It had worked as a picture, but it was not one that audiences would still be watching in fifty years' time. His confusion about what to do next was quite apparent in his next few choices, a string of movies which, set against the De Niro score-charts of the past, were weak and offered him little in the way of a challenge.

The principle of creating impact was the one by which he had maintained his image and reputation as one of the finest actors around. Suddenly now it was the money that had become important as he strove to rake in funds for the TriBeCa project. His choices during the late 1980s severely tested the loyalty of his fans. His next movie, in which he had been 'immersed' when Helena Springs came back on to the scene, was typical.

Entitled *Jacknife*, it was a revisitation of *The Deer Hunter* – a virtual continuation of the story. The film begins fifteen years after the war and is set in a small town in Connecticut. It is based upon the premise – as in *The Deer Hunter* – that one of the buddies is left behind and has to be retrieved, except that in this story he is left behind not in Vietnam but in post-war America.

While the rest of the group return to jobs and families Dave, played by Ed Harris, is the odd one out. His life is lonely and empty, except for drink and the fussing of his sister Martha (Kathy Baker) who shares the house they inherited from their parents. De Niro plays the charac-

186

ter Megs who comes to rescue him and attempts to break the lethargic cycle in which his old war buddy has become trapped.

The film is hampered by an inept, slow script that centres on just three principal characters and plods with some effort towards creating drama. The flashbacks to the war are of no great interest to an audience left shell-shocked by the brutality and gore of Oliver Stone's block-buster *Platoon*, released a year earlier, and in any event that was not the point of *Jacknife*. The more compelling scenes are those of the Vietnam veterans' encounter group, whose message is one of living life for today and attempting to put memories of the war in the past. It is in these intimate performances that *Jacknife* is most effective, and De Niro's feisty Vietnam veteran carried the movie.

At the end of the day, however, there did not seem much point to it. Adapted by Stephen Metcalfe from his own play *Strange Snow*, *Jacknife* was more suited to a made-for-television movie, and eyebrows were raised that De Niro had even bothered to participate. Even some of his usual supporters in the brotherhood of film critics made the point that there came a stage in a movie star's life when laying off was better than doing something for the sake of it, and that surely must have been the case here. Or at least that is what you would think – but there was another reason.

According to the publicity people, De Niro had made the film as part of his commitment to campaign on behalf of the Vietnam vet-erans, who he believed were getting a raw deal. He said:

> When I was doing *The Deer Hunter* I spent a lot of time with
> veterans, but that was like eleven years ago. They didn't talk
> about certain things then – you know, feelings and so on. Now
> other things are coming to the surface. So in a sense, this
> movie is a continuation of the other, like what might happen
> to the guy after he was home for a while, and that's why I wanted
> to do it. The guys who get no attention are still the vets. They
> suffer in silence. It's their turn to be recognized now, but one
> thing I can tell you, absolutely, they do not like being portrayed
> as crazy all the time. . . .

This went some way to explaining his motives for making *Jacknife*, but his need to raise money for the TriBeCa project was not a matter for public consumption at the time. So his followers could see neither rhyme nor reason for his next film, which had nothing to do with

Vietnam. The movie was a remake of the 1955 black comedy *We're No Angels* which starred Humphrey Bogart, Peter Ustinov and Aldo Ray and was not especially notable first time round. Furthermore, De Niro has a particular aversion to the work of Humphrey Bogart.

Interviewers at a brief press conference about the film were instructed: 'Don't mention Humphrey Bogart – Mr De Niro is not a fan of his and thus does not wish to speak about him.'

'But Bogart's been dead these past thirty years. . . .'

'Yes, but Mr De Niro does not like to speak ill of people, dead or alive.'

Why, then, wondered those who knew nothing of TriBeCa, was he attracted to material that even Bogey regarded as something of a potboiler when he did it?

The movie also provided him with the opportunity of doing a good turn for his friend Sean Penn, the minor hellraiser and former husband of Madonna. Penn was finding some difficulty in attracting prospective employers to his front door after recent escapades of fisticuffs and feats with the bottle that had secured him worldwide headlines. In short, he had only made one picture in the previous three years. 'Bobby saved me from despair and saved my career,' he said later.

In many respects Penn was a young version of De Niro. They often used to hang around together, and De Niro enjoyed his company. He had already promised Penn that he would find a movie in which they could work together and mentioned it to producer Art Linson, still basking in the glow of a huge pile of cash from *The Untouchables*.

Linson racked his brains and from the pigeon-holes of his mind produced *We're No Angels*, which he remembered was owned by Paramount. He then telephoned David Mamet, the respected Broadway dramatist, director and screenwriter who had scripted *The Untouchables* and had a varied list of credits, including the Jack Nicholson version of *The Postman Always Rings Twice*, a compelling adaptation of *The Verdict* starring Paul Newman, for which Mamet had won an Oscar nomination, and the stylish *House of Games*, which had been his directorial debut. Mamet, though not thrilled by the idea, said he would give it a try and produced a screenplay based loosely upon the original.

Considering the collaborators, it sounded a promising idea – instigated by a major star, scripted by an award-winning author and backed by a leading producer who negotiated a $20 million budget from

Paramount to make it. But the law of averages proves quite the reverse in Hollywood, and this was no exception.

In his pre-production launch Art Linson announced that the movie would be based only loosely upon the original. But the basic premise remained: set on the US–Canadian border during the Depression, it concerns two escaped convicts (De Niro and Penn) who disguise themselves as priests to cross into Canada beyond the reach of pursuing lawmen. For this purpose Linson approved at a cost of more than $3 million the construction of a mock border town with almost two dozen fake buildings, the largest single film set ever constructed in Canada. It was one of the more interesting statistics connected with this picture!

Notable among the supporting players was Demi Moore, who had appeared in David Mamet's 1986 movie *About Last Night* and was now cast as a single mother who helps De Niro's character to do some religious thinking. She had fought tooth and nail for the role, and justified her selection with one of the few performances in this flawed movie which had some degree of conviction.

Little more can be said about this most forgettable of De Niro's modern works. He mugged his way through a sleep-inducing plot with an ineptitude which was only matched by the clip-clop nature of the script. It was an absolute let-down in that regard, though ironically it did not lose as much money as some of his more classic films.

One other fact which went unnoticed by many people was that De Niro was listed in the credits as executive producer. It marked the first time he had had a behind-the-camera role, and it was clearly in preparation for his own personal ambitions which were already taking shape.

At the time he finished making *We're No Angels*, in the summer of 1988, he was negotiating the purchase of the Martinson Coffee Building. It was owned jointly by property developer Paul Wallace and theatrical producer Stewart Lane, of *La Cage aux Folles* fame. When De Niro produced his idea to turn the place into a film centre and high-class bistro they agreed to sell him a 50 per cent interest in the building for $7 million and gave him the go-ahead. Over the next six months he interviewed architects until he found one he could tune into: Lo-Yi Chan, a quiet middle-aged Chinese emigré who had recently completed renovations to the sedate buildings of Harvard and Columbia.

Chan recalls that he had three meetings with De Niro, who seemed more concerned with 'the chemistry between us, finding someone he could get along with' than with his professional credentials. Next, friends of De Niro began to get invitations to dinner as he openly touted amongst his associates for investors in his project.

The costs in high-priced Manhattan, even for rich men like himself, were enormous and the high-class restaurant trade, which was the end of the market he would be aiming for, was notoriously fickle. The socialites swapped and changed their allegiances like the wind. As for the film business, any accountant consulted by potential investors might have considered that the whole idea possessed the impulsive qualities of a seaside sandcastle rather than those of a carefully crafted business venture.

A number of his friends who came to dinner listened to his plans, delivered with enthusiasm, and then politely backed away. They included Jeremy Irons, Danny DeVito, Penny Marshall and Barbra Streisand. Streisand had originally agreed to tip in a few hundred thousand until she discovered that, as part owner of a company which would be applying for a liquor licence, she would have to be finger-printed by the police. This was completely against her strong civil libertarian principles and she said no. However there were several who did come in, notably Christopher Walken, Mikhail Baryshnikov and Sean Penn. Later, a second level of investors was invited in through a financial brokerage; in the end twenty-three partners would stump up $2.8 million.

This was, however, nowhere near sufficient to cover the eventual costs; in fact, it represented less than a third of the architect's original estimates for the conversion work and basic installations, and did not include the more expensive film equipment that De Niro would eventually require. But TriBeCa Productions and the TriBeCa Grill were up and running and, like an epic movie, it would consume De Niro's time and thoughts for months ahead.

17

Changing Direction

Even though he was beginning to see his own ambitions for film-making materialize with the building of his film centre, De Niro remained uncompromising in his attitude towards Hollywood and made no attempt to reposition himself closer to the hub of the movie industry, as some of his friends had done. Brian De Palma was considered by some to have sold out in his pursuit of the blockbuster, and there was a good deal of guffawing and back-stabbing when he came unstuck in his cartoonish direction of Tom Wolfe's *Bonfire of the Vanities*. His own description of his work – 'My films deal with a stylized, expressionistic world that has a kind of grotesque beauty about it' – was taken down and used in evidence in the ensuing debate about what had happened to De Palma.

In any case, De Niro did not have the same kind of pull in Hollywood, where faces had changed over the past eighteen months: many of the people who had been around at the time of his more spectacular films had now gone. He was viewed by people who did not know him well as a moody, anarchical figure. His friends knew better, but he continued to have an indifferent opinion of Hollywood.

He moved in a circle that had no direct studio input and therefore, unlike Beatty, Redford, Douglas and Eastwood, all of whom had production deals with studios, he had no fast-track contacts with studio chiefs. Even at this late stage of his career, too, he had not met many major stars. His first meeting with Marlon Brando, for example, did not take place until 1989 – almost eighteen years after *The Godfather* trilogy began – when he accompanied Martin Scorsese to Brando's private island in Tahiti to discuss a possible film deal. The meeting, which in scriptwriter terms had such great possibilities, turned into a flat, low-key affair and soon they were gone again. Brando in fact turned down the deal but, in spite of the intertwining of their careers, he and De Niro found little to talk about. 'He was very nice,' said De Niro in his minimalist account of the visit. 'Marty was there talking about some project which I wasn't involved in. We had a good time. He's very funny, got a good sense of humour. I don't know what else I can say. . . .'

The situation in Hollywood also had a bearing on De Niro's view of it – and their view of him. By the late 1980s the money factor was a bigger consideration than ever. The big blockbusters were heading towards the $300 million target for gross takings, and big plots, big movies and big stars were needed to attract that kind of money.

De Niro was not in the running for many of them. The 'big event' socializing that he hated remained the arena of the 'big deal', and when acting talents were weighed against the bankability of his contemporaries there sometimes seemed no justice in the fact that Arnold Schwarzenegger, Bruce Willis and Sylvester Stallone were commanding fees and percentages which would take their earnings per picture into the stratosphere, between $10 million and $25 million. Bruce Willis, for example, provided purely his voice for the narration of *Look Who's Talking* in that year of 1990. It was two weeks' work, for which he was paid $4 million and 10 per cent of the profits. It became one of the biggest box-office hits of the year and Willis collected another $14.5 million. At the same time, incidentally, his new wife Demi Moore – fresh from her modest effort with De Niro and Sean Penn – went into *Ghost*. It became the year's biggest blockbuster, taking $203 million from which she collected her first multi-million fee.

De Niro had never seen that kind of money, nor even come close to it. He remained low-profile, selecting off-beat, and often off-beam, material that was almost guaranteed *not* to make money. In any event, none of the actors just mentioned would have risked playing the roles in which he had wallowed.

Nothing more classically illustrated his usual procedure of starting from the bottom up and pursuing a venture at a very personal level than his involvement with director Penny Marshall on *Awakenings*. Marshall and De Niro had been friends for a long time and had come close to working with each other in the past, but had never quite made it. Penny, a former actress, had long ago moved to the other side of the camera and had had De Niro in mind for the lead role in *Big* before she finally chose Tom Hanks. She was also a New Yorker, so

De Niro's long-running affair with the actress–singer Diahnne Abbott (*below, Yardley Collection*) resulted in their marriage when she became pregnant with their son Raphael. They separated after two years, and by then he was involved with the supermodel from New York, Toukie Smith (*left*). Later, his affections switched to Naomi Campbell.

(*Above*) As the would-be comedian Rupert Pupkin in *The King of Comedy* with co-star Jerry Lewis (*20th Century-Fox*); and (*Left*) with James Woods in Sergio Leone's *Once Upon a Time in America*, in which he aged 50 years. (*Warner Bros*)

OPPOSITE PAGE:

Changing faces, with Jeremy Irons in *The Mission*. (*Top, Warner Bros*)

(*Left*) He put on weight again to give a brilliant cameo as Al Capone in *The Untouchables*. (*Paramount Pictures*)

(*Right*) He learned the Catholic mass in Latin for *True Confessions* in which he appeared with Robert Duvall. (*United Artists*)

Odd Couple – playing the catatonic patient brought to life by Robin Williams in *Awakenings*. (*Columbia Pictures, Yardley Collection*)

De Niro as the illiterate brought out of his shell by Jane Fonda, in *Stanley and Iris*. (*MGM/United Artists*)

Madonna's former husband, Sean Penn, was a great fan and, eventually, a good friend of De Niro's, crediting him with saving his career. They appeared together in the remake of *We're No Angels*. (*Yardley Collection*)

GoodFellas marked the rebirth of De Niro's collaboration with his old friend director Martin Scorsese. This crime classic also featured Ray Liotta (*left of* De Niro), Paul Sorvino and another regular collaborator Joe Pesci. (*Warner Bros*)

Jessica Lange appeared with him in one of the first movies produced at TriBeCa, De Niro's major new film-making centre in New York – a remake of the *film noir* thriller of the 1950s, *Night and the City*.

De Niro was at his most evil in *Cape Fear*, another remake and another movie produced from his TriBeCa centre, this time in collaboration with Steven Spielberg's production company, and directed once again by Martin Scorsese. (*Universal Studios, Yardley Collection*)

The ultimate metamorphosis: in *Mary Shelley's Frankenstein*, directed by Kenneth Branagh. (*Capital Pictures*)

she and De Niro had been running into each other at the same social events for years. Both as an actress and as a director her work has been noted for a pleasant, if unassuming, mix of sentimental humour and warmth.

Born in the Bronx in the same year as De Niro, she had made her way across to the West Coast in the 1960s, studying first at the University of New Mexico and then going on to Hollywood where she appeared in numerous bit parts before becoming a household name through the hit television series *Laverne and Shirley*. In the meantime she married and divorced Rob Reiner (*When Harry Met Sally, Postcards from the Edge, Sleepless in Seattle*) and, although she remained a busy actress who appeared, for example, with John Belushi in Spielberg's *1941*, she made no great impact. She turned to directing in the mid-1980s with *Jumpin' Jack Flash*, which did nothing for her reputation, but then her fortunes blossomed with the smash hit *Big*. After that she could more or less name her own next movie.

She pulled *Awakenings* from the pending file, where it had been on the back burner for years. Said Marshall:

> I found it on my desk among piles of other scripts, and I just thought the story was wonderful. I didn't know it was a dead project at Fox, so I just read it and it stuck with me. My mother had Alzheimer's and during her last two years she was in a sort of vegetative state. Everything had shut down but her heart. She was lying there, and sometimes you didn't know if she could hear you or not hear you. So I'd go over and sometimes just talk to her, tell her what was going on in my life. She didn't respond. I'd say to my brother, 'Maybe she heard.' The doctors have no idea, either.

So, motivated by personal reasons, she desperately wanted to make *Awakenings*, although studio interest in a story based on the complex, rambling medical diaries of an eccentric neurologist – Oliver Sacks's 1973 best-seller *The Man Who Mistook His Wife for a Hat and Other Clinical Tales* – was understandably low-key. She struggled for months to get access to the script, still owned by 20th Century-Fox, and managed to persuade Columbia to take it over. Finally, aided by Dustin Hoffman's revival of medical matters with his Oscar-winning performance as an autistic savant in *Rain Man*, she got a positive response by promising a package of top stars in the leading roles. But who? What stars would risk their 'image' playing a nutty professor and a walking vegetable? Marshall intended to focus on the relationship between one particular patient, Leonard Lowe, with Sacks. In the film, Sacks's name would be changed to Dr Malcolm Sayer to allow fiction to interact with the factual account of his diaries and personality.

Previously a researcher with little hands-on experience of hospital work, Sacks conducted a series of controversial experiments with a number of catatonic patients who were regarded by the medical establishment as brain-dead. In spite of loud opposition from the medical fraternity, he administered to these patients a new and untested 'miracle' drug. Some did indeed come back to life and virtual normality, though it was only a temporary recovery and in due course the patients returned to their original state. And so it was that Penny Marshall set out to shoot on four months' location in New York a film about this largely unknown group of people whose plight had such heart-rending connotations.

Marshall's philosophy of movie-making is based upon the simple premise that the audience needs to identify with someone in a movie. She saw in Dr Sacks a man who was shy, withdrawn, working day and night, believing in something with such power that he made things happen. Sacks, she discovered, was a very eccentric character, one that an actor would have to pull away from because it would create a wrong impression of the central theme. The story, said Marshall, is about the doctor, his obsession, his bucking the system and, above all, the effect the patients had on him and vice versa.

When she approached De Niro with a screenplay he came back soon afterwards enthusing about the role. 'Compared to other things I'd been doing,' said De Niro, 'it seemed right to do the Leonard part, which was more challenging. I hate to use the word but in some ways, that's what it was.'

Once he had agreed, Marshall involved De Niro at every step, and they anguished together over who should play the doctor. Several names were mentioned, until one day Marshall telephoned De Niro and asked him if he had seen Robin Williams in *Dead Poets Society*. When he said he hadn't Marshall replied: 'Go to the movies tomorrow and see him.'

He did so, and called her back: 'I'd be happy to do it with him. It was one of the best things I've ever seen him do.'

Williams read the script on a plane journey to Los Angeles and was moved to tears. A stewardess even came up to ask if anything was wrong. 'It decimated me,' he recalled, 'and then after that, when I read Oliver Sacks's book and discovered it was all true, it was incredible. It reads like Greek drama. It's something like Sisyphus, to rise and then fall, the human struggle of it all.'

Now began the hard work. The three of them began going to mental hospitals to observe patients and study procedures. They had long conversations with Sacks who produced some home movies that he had taken while working with the patients, demonstrating the stages they went through from the point of their sleep-walking existence to when they were awakened by the drug.

They discovered that one of the patients about whom Dr Sacks had written was still alive. They were able to go and see her, and witness for themselves the effects of the drug. 'She had a kind of speech loop,' said Marshall. 'It is still a side-effect of the drug, so that she'd say, "I'm going to the movies, the movies, the movies." We went to see her, and we saw the drug wear off. She went for a walk in the hallway with a walker, and all of a sudden she froze. Out. They carried her back to her room.'

While the drug was wearing off she could still speak a little, though very quietly. Marshall and De Niro were standing around her chair and were about to take some Polaroid photographs of her as she reverted to her catatonic state. She kept saying something. 'I couldn't hear it,' said Marshall, 'and I bent down close, and she said, "My head above, my head above, my head above." Apparently she wanted to make sure her head was up for the picture.' And so the pathos and the sentiment were real, with De Niro absorbing everything in his usual manner and noting in his book what that woman had told him when she was under the influence of the corrective drug: 'We always have a sense of humour.'

Now the scene moves to a mental hospital in Brooklyn which was to be the central location of four months' filming in order to achieve total reality in terms of setting, in much the same way that Michael Douglas had used a state mental hospital to shoot *One Flew Over the Cuckoo's Nest*. There were all sorts of dangers and complications. First, the hospital was in a neighbourhood where at night the gunfire between rival gangs could be heard. Inside the building the patients had a tendency to scream and dream noisily and, since much of the filming was to be done at night, there were sounds which Marshall's crew could not eliminate. Robin Williams recalled: 'You're supposed to be doing a quiet scene, and the patients are flipping out . . . going nuts . . . it was incredible.' The night that De Niro's character awakens from his brain-dead state, for instance, was medication time at the hospital. Their dialogue was to be softly spoken, a conversation between doctor and patient. Yet screaming and shouting can be heard in the background of the film because there was nothing they could do to avoid it.

It was, as Williams described it, 'a most amazing day'. For the first few weeks of filming De Niro had been in his rock-like state, a shuffling, bumbling catatonic with an expressionless face and staring, unblinking eyes. To achieve this, De Niro had had to divest himself of every normal muscular function and physical reaction. If he betrayed any recognition of the world about him the whole melodrama they were constructing would fall like a house of cards.

Scenes were shot time and time again for him to keep that sleepwalking appearance. When Williams gave him the drug that finally enabled him to speak the moment was truly powerful. 'It was like his birth,' said Williams, 'that kind of awe.'

As filming progressed the scenes were becoming increasingly parallel to reality, and at one stage Williams and De Niro were performing a scene where there was physical contact between them. De Niro had to push Williams down and they had choreographed the sequence with a rehearsal. However, when they came to do it Williams accidentally elbowed De Niro in the face and broke his nose. The crack was heard across the set and on the soundtrack, but they kept on going.

Williams, realizing what he had done, said, 'Oh, no!' but De Niro went on with the scene. It was only when Marshall yelled 'Cut!' that they saw blood coming from his nose. Even so, they did nine more takes of the scene because De Niro said, 'No, let's keep going.'

He knew that the next day it would be worse and he would get black eyes. In fact, his face was so swollen that he was unable to film for a week. Apart from that incident, which inaccurately reached the newspapers as an altercation between Williams and De Niro, the actors were immensely satisfied with their work. 'De Niro achieved something marvellous,' said Williams. 'There's a wonderful thing in this movie that I don't think I've seen him do before – a kind of innocence, a shyness that people don't expect. And then when he smiles he's got this wonderful warmth, because normally he's playing very scary guys. All of a sudden, he's very gentle and warm.'

Williams' praise for De Niro's most unusual performance, in a way one of the strangest of his career, was taken up by the reviewers who were by and large impressed. However, there remained a certain schmaltziness about this picture that was in part due to Marshall's apparent desire to give her audiences a warm glow. There were obvious deviations from the truth, too, which might be considered a serious error when dealing with a story based upon facts of this nature, especially when the system is being indirectly criticized via the movie.

De Niro's portrayal of the central character, the patient who awakens into virtual normality, is flawed by a particular truth that is conveniently overlooked to make the movie itself more palatable. Leonard was not the lovable character into which De Niro turned him, and certainly not the man who is shown in the movie to enter a rather contrived romance with a charming young woman played by Penelope Anne Miller. The truth was that when awakened from his catatonic state Leonard, the once brilliant, Harvard-educated scholar, was a dangerous character who threatened nurses, masturbated in public and, when allowed into the street, harassed women and talked of raping one of them. But to retain these facets would have destroyed the image that Marshall had pursued.

When these facts are known De Niro's powerful performance becomes less convincing, because he knew even as he was playing it that another director – and certainly Scorsese – would have found a different route for this picture. The patients, after all, were not freaks but severely incapacitated human beings whose plight had been largely ignored. It could have been scripted so that the flaws as well as the miracles were explored, the darkness as well as the light, and the contrived happy ending – when in reality it was not – might have been a touch more truthful. Then it would have been more in keeping with what De Niro's followers expected of him.

One of the most curious aspects of De Niro's choice of films at this time of his life related to his own physical appearance. He was fit and trim from compulsive daily work-outs in his own gym. Entering his forty-fifth year he was a fine figure of a man, handsome and with more sexuality than he had been able to show on screen for years. Other actors of that certain age, when mid-life crisis is at its peak, would surely have wanted to be more overt about their physical attributes. He had the potential in looks and general demeanour to burst forth into some action-packed drama, and give the critics, who were becoming decidedly niggardly in their opinions of his selections, something to rave about.

Yet, for the time being, he ignored that possibility. Even in his next film, in which he would be teamed for what seemed a likely combustible match with Jane Fonda, seven years his senior, the story was a lukewarm potboiler. It also failed to resolve one of the great shortcomings of De Niro's career – that audiences have had very few chances to see him pitted against an actor of similar status, in particular of the opposite sex. Was it deliberate? Did he always select scripts that left him relatively unchallenged as the prime force on screen? Was he scared of the competition? Apart from his cameo role in *The Untouchables* there had been only three opportunities to observe De Niro with actors of similar strength: Meryl Streep in *Falling in Love*, Robert Duvall in *True Confessions* and, to a lesser degree, Jeremy Irons in *The Mission*. But none – apart from his early encounter with Harvey Keitel – had unleashed a real screen duel of acting talent.

The new partnership with Jane Fonda promised exciting possibilities, but in the event it was just another pleasant dissertation on a matter of social disability, a worthy, well-intentioned tale about illiteracy that carried a message more akin to a government information film than big picture entertainment. It was one of those situations where the job was staffed with supremely overqualified people.

Even their title was downbeat: *Stanley and Iris*. Since the movie quickly found its way to television, which was its more natural home, there can be few who are unfamiliar with the story. De Niro plays a handsome, seemingly intelligent man who holds a secret shared, apparently, by 32 million US adults who are classed as 'functionally illiterate'. Before turning to this problem, however, the movie tackles the social situation in New England mill towns in the 1980s, when the promise of jobs galore evaporates as factories close down.

And then we meet Iris, played by Fonda. She is a widow struggling to bring up her family. She works next to Stanley in a large bakery, but they barely exchange a nod until one day he saves her from a mugger and a friendship of sorts develops. Stanley, meanwhile, loses his job for the same reason that he had been booted out of a succession of previous short-term occupations: the boss discovers he cannot read or write.

Iris now has the opportunity of helping him – in addition to the family she is supporting – by teaching him to read. Having reached that point, and a potential romance, the plot zooms off into fantasy land, with Hollywood turning the worthy story into a fairytale. Stanley, having overcome his disability, becomes a successful businessman and, when he makes his first million, returns to ask Iris to marry him. The 20 per cent of the US population classed as being as educationally challenged as Stanley had been were now either heading for the nearest sickbag or planning to be millionaires this time next year.

It was easy to wonder how this film ever attracted De Niro and Fonda, but it is hard not to dislike it either. But then if two professionals of such quality could not achieve that relatively easy task, given the material, then no one could.

Elsewhere in De Niro's life there were other pressing matters in the months leading up to 1990, the year which saw three of his movies on the cinema circuit. He frequently had to dash back to New York, often still 'in character' either as Leonard in *Awakenings* or as Stanley, to supervise building work on the TriBeCa project and to calm restless neighbours who were picketing the building for fear of an intolerable increase in noise and traffic. Demonstrations denouncing De Niro as an uncaring soul brought city officials into urgent conference. To pacify them De Niro sent his company vice president, Jane Rosenthal, whom he had poached from Disney. She arranged tours of the building and attempted to reassure all the complainants that the place would be a reputable restaurant and a very respectable movie production centre.

By the late spring of 1990 the conversion was well on its way and the dining room of the TriBeCa Grill was nearing completion. De Niro had lured Drew Nieporent, a thirty-four-year-old restaurateur who also ran the fashionable Montrachet nearby, to oversee the operation. It was already being heralded as New York's equivalent of a Hollywood commissary at which all the stars in town would hang out, and the route to fame had been set in motion by a series of private parties.

Like an over-budget movie, however, the project had its teething troubles. The financial package which De Niro had put together relied upon funding from a corporate partnership which went under the name of Home Boy Restaurant. The twenty-three 'partners' who had invested the original $2.8 million to back De Niro's dream were a diverse group ranging from showbiz friends to a shy sixty-six-year-old chicken farmer from New Jersey named David Trenk. 'After selling chickens for forty-three years this is going to be very exciting, like a new start,' he said. Another investor was Robert Krasnow, chairman of Elektra Records, who said he was doing it for the fun and to be 'part of the club'. By the turn of 1990, however, the project was running out of cash, the original budgets had been exceeded and the financial package had to be renegotiated so that the original owners of the building were left with a larger mortgage.

The completion date fell behind schedule amid a continual flurry of publicity articles in the society magazines. The natives were getting restless. Hundreds of telephone calls were coming in demanding to know when the place would be opened. Between takes on the movie set De Niro had been busily involving himself in the preparations. In February he flew his entire kitchen staff to Toronto because he remembered dining in a Thai-owned Italian restaurant called Stelle. He had enjoyed the food and wanted his people to meet and talk to the chef. De Niro put both sides into a most embarrassing situation. Then Stelle chef produced a showpiece demonstration that Nieporent had to applaud, after which he quietly told De Niro: 'This isn't us.'

Next, he remembered a swank restaurant called Matsuhisa in Los Angeles that had a Japanese sushi bar in the corner. He thought that would be a good idea too and flew the owner to New York to advise them on a little sushi project of their own. Unfortunately De Niro was not aware that the Japanese gentleman spoke very little English, so they all stood around smiling at each other. The sushi bar idea, like the Thai-flavoured pasta, was quietly dropped. Nieporent was getting worried. The revised opening day was fast approaching, and the fickle New York dinner crowd could be mercilessly contrary about their patronage. With all the additional, unexpected costs the restaurant would have to become one of the busiest in New York to make it pay.

Certainly, it was attractive enough. The place had an airy, spacious feel and retained many of the building's original features. The old water and heating pipes were left untouched and painted green, while the original floors and the high ceilings all added to the character. New additions included a huge ornate mahogany bar in the centre of the room which was designed not only for its obvious practical purpose, but also as a customer attraction, so that diners could ogle famous names who dropped in for a drink. Nevertheless De Niro, having invested a sizeable chunk of his own funds in the restaurant-cum-film production centre, was nervous and apprehensive.

In the midst of this flush of activity one other lingering matter came back to haunt him. While he was in Los Angeles filming he discovered that Helena Springs had returned to live there. Her marriage to Anthony Lisandrello had ended, and she blamed De Niro's refusal to allow him to adopt her daughter Nina as a starting-point for its collapse. He had complained, she said, that they were unable to become a family. True or not, they separated in 1989 and were divorced the following year.

Aware of this situation, De Niro contacted Helena. Her daughter was then eight years old and it had been more than eighteen months since she and De Niro had last met. He was still under the impression that he could be the child's father, and was curious to meet her again. He arranged a visit to her house and took Nina out alone that afternoon. They drove around for a while and then went to the cinema. Later, he dropped the child at a party at the house of a friend.

Nina, however, certainly had the impression that De Niro was her father. A neighbour and close friend of Helena's who recalls the incident told me:

> Nina was a really happy-go-lucky child, lovingly cared for by her mother. The day of the party, when she returned with De Niro, she was full of it. She said she had just been to the movies with her daddy, and that he was very famous. There was no question by then, in her mind, who her real daddy was and I found it hard to believe that he could leave it so long between visits, or any kind of contact. It seemed very odd.

Helena would say that at the time De Niro called simply because he was attempting to revive their own affair for whenever he was in Los Angeles, which he in turn would deny. She said that he talked briefly about providing for the child's future, and he gave her some cash at various times to help with her expenses. But then he was gone again, back to New York.

He rang Helena from the airport just as he was leaving, and for the immediate future any contact was restricted to occasional telephone conversations with both her and Nina. Helena's friend commented,

> If De Niro believed he was Nina's father at that time, he was apparently not going to allow her existence to get in the way of his life in New York. He seemed determined to keep her and her mother at a distance, hidden almost. To the few of us who knew of the situation it looked like a very callous act, and you could only wonder at the effect it might have on the child to

have a man she believed to be her father flitting in and out of her life with great gaps between contact.

But another complication had now entered the scenario, which is why he did not want Helena's situation to become common knowledge. He had just begun an affair with the sensational twenty-year-old black model Naomi Campbell as she finished her romance with the boxer Mike Tyson. She had been tagged 'supermodel' for two years or more; travelled the world; showed off the haute couture of the world's leading designers; and made $10,000 a day. Naomi was now so famous that her arrival anywhere would cause more activity among the paparazzi than De Niro himself. Indeed, if it came to a choice they would walk away from De Niro. He had told her, as they began their relationship, definitely No Publicity, just as he had drilled his children – now out and about on their own – never to talk to reporters, writers or cameramen. And so for the time being, Helena was joined in the shadows of his life by the most sought-after super-model in the business. Publicly, Toukie Smith still commanded the high ground.

18

Quick-fire Solutions

They hadn't worked together for a decade, and aficionados of Robert De Niro and Martin Scorsese were wishing they would. They both needed the fire that their collaboration of the 1970s brought to their own work and to the cinema at large, although for some it was already in the past and should be left there. De Niro himself was already being described as a man who had lost his way, lost his grip, lost touch with his public. Those in the know, of course, realized that the rush of indifferent films in which he had been involved had been made for the money and not the kudos, to help fund his TriBeCa centre – and it showed.

Scorsese, too, had gone through a bad patch as he, like De Niro, attempted to widen his repertoire away from the rigidity of the American themes that he had explored so far. In the decade since *Raging Bull* he had directed only two movies worthy of the acclaim he received in the heyday of their partnership. *The Color of Money* was out-and-out entertainment, a slick sequel to *The Hustler* (and won Paul Newman an Oscar), while *The Last Temptation of Christ* (the movie offered by Scorsese that De Niro turned down) was an evocative, beautifully shot movie whose intentions were marred by its notoriety. Apart from those two *After Hours*, in 1985, was a typical Scorsese failure with moments of sheer brilliance, while the French-based *Round Midnight*, released the following year, was essentially one for jazz buffs. He had come through a difficult time financially, when his personal affairs went haywire, and he was, to put it bluntly, struggling.

And so, for more reasons than the creative urge, De Niro and Scorsese were back, ready to show the world that reports of their impending eclipse had been somewhat premature – even though they chose a decidedly old-fashioned vehicle to announce their return. The title says it all: *GoodFellas*. And the location would bring them back to the New York streets and stories they knew so well.

The project had been fermenting for almost four years before they finally went into production. It began back in 1985 when New York journalist Nicholas Pileggi wrote a book called *Wiseguy*, the biography of the boss of a middle-ranking Mafia family, Henry Hill, who had decided to talk after being arrested for his crimes. He turned state's evidence, was given a new identity and was hidden away in the FBI's witness protection programme.

As with so many of these 1980s Mafia informers, he wanted to earn some additional pension money by telling his life story. It was really a family history running from his childhood in the 1930s to the 1980s, and dealt incisively with the mafiosi well below the level of Vito Corleone – those who control the gangster life of New York's districts and to whom such criminality is a profession.

What Scorsese saw in Pileggi's book went beyond the mere biography of a relatively unimportant Brooklyn hood, of whom there were many. The story of Hill's rise to power was merely the starting-point for his evocation of a particular slice of American culture, the life and times of the community gangster through whose eyes would emerge one of the most authentic Mafia pictures since the *Godfather* trilogy.

Pileggi was away from his desk in the office of a New York magazine when he received the call, and someone left him a message: 'Martin Scorsese telephoned.' Pileggi assumed it was a joke and did nothing about it. A couple of nights later he answered the telephone at home and a voice said, 'This is Martin Scorsese. I am a film director. I've been looking for this book for years. It's like all the stuff I remembered people telling me when I was a kid growing up in Little Italy. I've never seen it written down before.'

They arranged to meet and, whereas Scorsese might have been expected to offer Pileggi a fee for the screen rights, he chose instead to invite him to collaborate on a screenplay, no doubt because he was short on cash at the time. Eleven drafts and four years later Scorsese was ready to move, and began assembling the old team who had made *Raging Bull* a decade earlier. Although, like most directors, Scorsese often uses tried and tested technicians, the line-up of old familiar faces revealed his intention of trying to make history repeat itself and restore his visibility in the nineties.

First he approached Irwin Winkler, who had produced *Raging Bull*, *The King of Comedy* and *Round Midnight* (not to mention *Rocky I*,

II, III, IV and V). Winkler began moving towards a deal immediately, sensing that Scorsese was heading for a winner. Next he called De Niro and received an immediate yes in a five-sentence conversation. Then came Joe Pesci, who had played Jake La Motta's brother in *Raging Bull* and would be co-star in *GoodFellas*. Costume expert Richard Bruno and editor Thelma Schoonmaker, who had both worked on *Raging Bull*, were also hired.

Apart from the personnel, there were also some striking similarities in the characters – parallels between the De Niro character of then and now, with traces of *Taxi Driver* and *New York, New York*. But perhaps that was to be expected. The point about *GoodFellas* was that it fell in with the style of Scorsese's past exploration of American themes in which he examines life in the margins, out of the mainstream of events. *Mean Streets, New York, New York, The King of Comedy* and *Taxi Driver* had all dealt with oddball characters to whom the American dream was alluring yet elusive.

In contrast to Coppola's *Godfather* movies, which dealt with the Mafia full on and glamorous, Scorsese had in the past skirted around the seedy, sharp and violent edges. In *GoodFellas* he saw an avenue that lay mid-way between the two extremes – raw power achieved, as he put it, through the nuts and bolts of organized crime. He also picked up the progression which had begun in the *Godfather* movies, the move away from the supposed code of loyalty and trust that existed among the 'old' gangland chieftains as the vicious new breed took over. Scorsese now developed that progression to the point where he was suggesting that the disintegration of those old codes would ultimately destroy those who pulled them down. And this, as any follower of criminal activity would appreciate, was what was happening in the city streets, where Mafia bosses, large, medium and small, were being picked off through either their own failings or the disloyalty of others such as Henry Hill.

De Niro, oddly enough, did not take the part of the subject of Pileggi's biography but played what was essentially a supporting role. Jimmy Conway guides Henry Hill through his early days of gangsterism and teaches him the first commandment, which is: 'Do unto others before they do it to you.' That statement, as Hill would eventually prove, was one that could be interpreted in two ways.

Hill was played by Ray Liotta, another of Scorsese's quirky decisions. He was having his lead character portrayed by an actor of limited cinema fame who was better known for his series on American television, *Our Family Honor*. Pesci, of course, was reaching the peak of his fame after *Home Alone*, while Lorraine Bracco, who was cast as Hill's wife, had only just come to the fore in Ridley Scott's 1987 movie *Someone to Watch Over Me*. Married to Harvey Keitel, she was at that point not a famous name.

Like his own, De Niro's character in the film is a man of Irish-Italian ancestry who guides his two friends, Hill and Tommy DeVito (played by Pesci), in their rise to local power. Tommy is a cold-blooded psychopath who is seen shooting a waiter in the foot for walking too slowly, then a week later killing a youth in cold blood when he glares at him. Tommy also shoots a fellow gangster during an argument in a bar; in a scene of terrible black humour, the three of them dispose of the body after a hefty meal prepared by Tommy's mother – played, incidentally by the director's own mother, Catherine Scorsese.

Throughout, however, De Niro's Jimmy Conway is seen as the architect of their increasingly violent criminality. He is a vicious, calculating killer and at that level forms a unique double act with Joe Pesci's Tommy, just as they did in *Raging Bull*. In the film, it is Conway who gives instructions after a $6 million robbery at Kennedy Airport that they should hide their proceeds of the raid until the heat is off. When they refuse, he sets out to have them murdered. At that point, Hill fears that he and his wife are about to be killed and turns himself over to the law, to be given a new identity and a fresh start. And so although his character is not the focal point of the story De Niro is a pivotal figure, a supporting actor in every sense of the word.

Naturally enough, the rebirth of the De Niro–Scorsese partnership attracted great attention, although not the universal acclaim that they had received in the past. Several critics complained that De Niro was running out of tricks, that he showed nothing new whatsoever. That was true to a certain degree, but it was also characteristic of De Niro's performances that whatever he did involved repetition.

The freshness of approach, those jolting, frightening expressions that had so aroused the passions of film reviewers a decade earlier had been pushed through the mangle so many times that at some point similarities with the past were bound to arise. Looked at a second and third time, it is more accurate to describe his acting in *GoodFellas* as reaching such a level of professionalism that it did not obscure the rest of the film and the characters as it had done in the past. In a strong film he is not seen to overpower the action, but his performance often looks outstanding and dominant when he is dealing with lesser material, as in *Guilty by Suspicion*. This, his next offering, was the first of a trio of films including *Backdraft* and *Cape Fear* to be released in 1991. His current output demonstrated the extent of his fund-raising. He was working non-stop, shooting movies back to back and piling some of the multi-million dollar earnings – reputedly approaching $20 million for the six films he completed in a two-year period – into his TriBeCa project.

The restaurant and grill were open and busy by the middle of 1990. 'It turned out just as Bob planned it,' said architect Lo-Yi Chan. 'He is the ultimate New Yorker, and he wanted the building to be very New York. No Hollywood veneer. He just wanted a place he could walk into and have a great meal and make good movies.' The exterior is certainly laid back, and a passing crowd would barely know of its existence. There is no nameplate, and a huge coffee scale remains in place as a reminder of a past era.

De Niro's spacious office was built right at the top of the building, on the eighth floor. Work on the seven storeys which would house the film workshops and studios was still not complete, but he had struck some very lucrative deals. He talked in terms of establishing a creative community from which exchanges of ideas would bristle, driven and motivated by individuals rather than conglomerate commit-tees. In a rare talkative few moments to gain some publicity for the restaurant, De Niro explained: 'I thought it would be nice to have a place where ideas can generate off each other, that come up because people are in proximity to each other. Who knows how it will evolve? All I know is that I am putting together something I have always dreamed of; I can't tell how it will turn out.'

He talked expansively of initiating major projects from his own production company, which he would produce, direct and/or star in. Meanwhile, to help pay the bills, there were some worthwhile tenants who had rented space or agreed production deals. Miramax Films, distributor of the hot property *Sex, Lies and Videotape*, made for $1.2 million and grossing $20 million in twelve weeks, was among the first to set up shop there. Columbia Pictures rented space for the duration of the making of *Awakenings*, and then De Niro signed a deal with Tri-Star Pictures in which they would guarantee $1 million a year towards the overheads in return for first refusal on his company's movie output.

His hopes of setting up a creative community, free of businessmen and from which ideas would flow, sounded like the Chaplin–

Pickford–Fairbanks statement of intent sixty years earlier when they formed United Artists. In the year that De Niro launched his bid for power that company was ironically in the midst of a takeover drama as an Italian businessman of, it proved later, limited funds took over MGM/UA.

If De Niro had extended his past record of preparation for his roles into the business arena, he would have studied the history of those creative people who turned businessmen and sought to cushion himself from taking a large personal hit in the event of the commercial failure of one of the movies he planned to produce. Many lessons have been learned from those early heady days when Coppola and others spoke of their great expectations for meaningful independent productions.

A good many actors who tried had fallen victim to their own creative principles, while the likes of Beatty and Douglas placed their trust in Mammon and produced commercial entertainment from which they prospered. They were cautious and selective: Beatty left months, sometimes years, between projects. Jack Nicholson avoided all such matters and was simply content to take $8–$10 million a picture, with the occasional blockbuster bonus such as around $40 million from his slice of the *Batman* action. Only the big studios could guarantee that kind of payday for major stars.

This highlighted a crucial problem for smaller companies like De Niro's, who had to compete with the cash-rich studios for everything from scripts to stars. At that time, too, the whole of the movie industry was in a state of change. The big studios had been changing hands like dollar bills at a racetrack. During the 1980s the mega-conglomerates from Japan and international businessmen had settled billions of investment dollars in the movie and entertainment industry. There would, in due course, be many casualties and some spectacular financial failures. Studio chiefs came and went with alarming regularity as predictions and reality failed to meet. But still the money poured in to back the ever-expanding Hollywood largesse of increased budgets and escalating fees to the top twenty actors.

To the independent film-makers – whose ranks De Niro had now joined – the handsome flow of foreign money was a welcome source of funding for their creative ambitions. As one movie industry analyst commented at the time: 'The community is rejoicing. Every producer, large or small, is wondering how he or she can make their own $100 million deal.' It was the kind of rat-race that De Niro had been avoiding all his life, and now he had plunged himself into the thick of it.

Veteran producer Irwin Winkler, who had hired De Niro on four occasions in the past, could pass on a few tips about spending other people's money but trying to keep your own in your pocket. But in 1991 even Winkler still had some experimenting to do, inspired by De Niro's ambition for a creative colony. That year, at the age of sixty, he made his debut as a writer and director with his original screenplay entitled *Guilty by Suspicion*. He managed to get Arnon Milchan, another veteran De Niro associate, to produce it, Warner Bros to put up some money and De Niro himself to play the lead – and so the wheels-within-wheels of this merry band of film-makers kept on turning. It was like a small private club whose members could be mixed and matched to suit various projects, although invariably they chose De Niro to head the cast list. They won some, they lost some, but the movies kept on coming.

Guilty by Suspicion took De Niro back to the heart of old Hollywood that he had not visited as a professional insider since *The Last Tycoon*. The story was set in the era of Senator Joe McCarthy's Communist purges at the helm of the Un-American Activities Committee in the fifties, and centred upon David Merrill, a writer employed by Darryl F. Zanuck at 20th Century-Fox. After working in Europe at the start of the 1950s, Merrill returns to Hollywood with little knowledge of the witch-hunt sweeping through the industry, when friendships and working relationships are torn apart and names are named to McCarthy's committee. Dozens of people are blacklisted and some never work in Hollywood again. Among those named as Communist sympathizers is Merrill himself, played in Winkler's film by De Niro. He is forced to appear before McCarthy's committee, denies that he was ever a card-carrying member and refuses to name others who were. Now he too is blacklisted, kicked out of his job and his home and asked to return a $50,000 advance for a new project.

Gradually Merrill's world falls apart in a case history that matched the story of several well-known writers, actors and directors of the 1950s. Winkler's script noticeably produces a figure with whom the audience can identify and sympathize, but regardless of the flaws in the material De Niro gives a fine performance, with compelling crises of conscience and powerful speeches delivered with reserve and dignity.

He managed that too, in a different way, in Ron Howard's *Back-draft*, which he shot soon after *Guilty by Suspicion*. This one was strictly for the money, and the cynics would record that the only reason De Niro appeared in it was to secure a deal with Howard who was renting space in the TriBeCa Center. De Niro was well down the cast list, in a supporting role, as was his old adversary Donald Sutherland with whom he had appeared in *Novecento*. They shared some of the best spoken scenes in the picture, with De Niro as an investigator to Sutherland's fire-raiser.

Ron Howard, who, like De Niro, had just moved into production – his company had signed a massive twenty-film financing deal with Paramount – was adamant from the start that he wanted De Niro. Howard explained: 'The character was a charismatic, very individualistic guy who totally understands fire as an almost mystical, living entity.' That character was based upon a real-life figure who worked in Chicago. In spite of his other pressures, De Niro found time to do his research. He telephoned the fireman in question and arranged to work with him for a couple of weeks. Among his first calls was a murder by fire, and De Niro had to observe the autopsy. 'He immersed himself in the role so much', said Chicago fire chief Pat Burns, 'that you could easily forget he was an actor. We came to regard him as just another fire investigator.' And so the director got the performance he was looking for – a foundation stone of realism on which to build a spectacular, if somewhat contrived, movie.

Despite all this work to earn money for TriBeCa De Niro still had to find time for personal matters. Back in Los Angeles during the autumn of 1991, he called Helena Springs. She invited him over for lunch and he arrived clutching gifts for Nina. He kissed Helena on the cheek and after chatting for a while the three of them, De Niro, Nina and Helena, sat around the dining table eating their meal like a 'charming little family', according to their neighbour who happened to observe this event.

Helena, however, was beginning to get angry. She wanted some kind of commitment from De Niro: either he should recognize Nina as his daughter and treat her as such, or he should stay away from them. Pressure was mounting for him to do something, and he did not like being pressured. The saga of De Niro and Nina was drawing slowly to a conclusion.

19

Modern Times

After two decades in which money, style and status seemed to take second billing to personal satisfaction and choice in the pursuit of his art, the mood had changed, the good intentions were being overlooked and the output suffered. The one-time superstar who said he only ever wanted to make movies that people would still be talking about in fifty years' time had become the foreman of a conveyor-belt operation producing, one after the other, films whose quality ranged from good to dire.

De Niro had his personal credibility and a lot of money riding on the success of TriBeCa Productions, and only now was it becoming apparent what lengths he would go to – or have to be prepared to go to – to ensure that his company was running profitably. Unlike those with direct access to studio funds, he was having to do it basically on his own – arrange his own deals, let his own studio production space, raise the money for his own films – and it was no shoestring operation. One false move and the whole lot could come tumbling down.

In 1991 De Niro announced his company's involvement in a string of films in the immediate future. Now the bottom line was not about De Niro the dedicated actor but about De Niro the film-maker and minor mogul. The whole scenario was an ironic and total reversal of a line he had spoken in *The Last Tycoon* as Monroe Stahr, alias Irving Thalberg, who was notoriously contemptuous of the creative artists in his employ: 'I will not give them power. I will give them money, but not power. They're not equipped for authority.' And now, over to De Niro for a quote he gave in a brief aside to a reporter from *Time* magazine when it featured his plans to deliver a convincing perform- ance as a real-life movie producer: 'I never had full responsibility for a film before and never wanted it. But now I do. Ultimately, it's to have control.'

The quick-fire fund-raising showed his determination to achieve that. Perhaps the best example was the sixth film he made during that time, *Cape Fear*. It was made in a hurry and the motives were evidently and outstandingly commercial.

Cape Fear emerged out of renewed contact with Steven Spielberg, his friend from early days. With TriBeCa on the move, De Niro and Spielberg had met to discuss a joint production and agreed upon a remake of this movie, originally filmed in 1962 by J. Lee Thompson when it had starred Robert Mitchum, Gregory Peck and Polly Bergen. It was intended that Spielberg's company, Amblin Entertainment, and De Niro's TriBeCa would finance the film, along with Universal who bought the US distribution rights. They planned a budget of around $25 million. Spielberg would direct and De Niro would star in the role of Max Cady, originally created in a superbly controlled performance by Mitchum.

Had that plan materialized, it would have provided an interesting perspective on their work. As was well known, their career objectives to that point could not have been more polarized. Spielberg always aimed for top-flight box-office appeal – the word 'entertainment' was even part of his company title; while De Niro plundered the murky depths of human nature without too much regard for pleasing a mass audience.

Their collaboration was halted, however, when Spielberg was detained on the direction of his latest intended blockbuster, *Hook*, with Dustin Hoffman in the title role. And since the production of *Cape Fear* was already booked and ready, Spielberg and De Niro agreed to hire Martin Scorsese to direct. Scorsese's wife of six years, Barbara de Fina, was already the producer, thus keeping the top jobs in the family, as it were. But this time De Niro was the boss.

The news that two men who had produced some awesome pictures together were to remake a movie which was considered a classic thriller attracted a good deal of attention. Remakes have traditionally been a fraught area for directors, but in this case it was widely anticipated that Scorsese, a modern Alfred Hitchcock – for whom the screenplay was originally written, though he never directed it – could actually improve upon the first version. In fact, it turned out to be one of the least favoured of the films made by Scorsese and De Niro.

Because he came late to the project, much of the preparatory work

212

in which Scorsese would normally have involved himself had already been done. Since *Cape Fear* is driven by the story and its central character in it, the parameters were already set. It had clearly been intended as a commercial suspense movie. The cast list showed that – the plan had been that Robert Redford would take the Gregory Peck role. For the first time in his life De Niro would have been cast against a man of comparable screen presence, with a charisma and star quality which, smiling and open, was totally opposite to his own image. It would have presented a unique and fascinating opportunity to observe De Niro in such company, and would have resulted in a completely different movie than the one they ended up with. But it was not to be; Redford dropped out.

Nick Nolte came in as Sam Bowden, and, fine actor though he is, the effect could never be the same. Nolte's qualities are too similar to De Niro's. His natural stance is one of power and menace; a softer, gentler persona like Redford would surely have created a more interesting confrontation. Jessica Lange as Leigh Bowden was also a Spielberg selection, and there were even return appearances by Gregory Peck and Robert Mitchum in cameo roles.

Filming on location in Florida, Scorsese battled with a genre piece that he did not seem to like very much. He was heard complaining about 'thin material', and tried to compensate by pumping up the violence of the De Niro character and heightening the visual effects. He knew that, as with all remakes, the story of *Cape Fear* would be familiar to many movie buffs, so some intriguing updates were added for the new version.

In the original, Sam Bowden is a lawyer in a small Southern town who witnesses an attack on a woman. It is his evidence that puts Max Cady behind bars. On his release, Cady seeks revenge and slowly imposes himself upon Bowden's family until finally, in a crescendo of action, he subjects them to a violent ordeal.

In the Scorsese film, Bowden was Cady's lawyer who withheld vital evidence at his trial that might otherwise have freed him. On his release from the prison term which he believes Bowden to be responsible for, Cady begins to stalk the family covertly and cleverly, so that he stays out of reach of the law. He first targets Bowden's former mistress, whom he seduces and savagely beats up. Then he moves in on Bowden's teenage daughter, tenuously winning her friendship until, as in the original version, the family is trapped in an inescapable and horrendous climax of violence and attempted rape.

Scorsese's central theme was that Bowden recognized the potential threat to his family, knew it was coming but could not stop it, either legally or by having Cady beaten up. He just kept on coming, no matter what. De Niro – looking super-fit after an intense period of pumping iron specially for this role – went to the very extremes of physical ability to pursue his terrifying ambitions of causing mayhem and mutilation in the Bowden family. It was seen by many as an over-the-top performance, far exceeding the subtlety of Mitchum's more laid-back approach which oozed a bleak sexuality but achieved the same effect of instilling fear.

There were some exceptional scenes in *Cape Fear* which were pure Scorsese invention, and others which came out of De Niro's own intensity. But they could not rescue the feeling that this story had been pushed far beyond its limits for the sake of making it more commercial. It proved to be a film which attracted a good deal of debate and extreme opinions, but by and large it did not leave its audiences with memories of special moments, as most Scorsese films do. They were left with a feeling that the terror had been incessant and far too drawn out, which was not especially liked. For once, however, the American Academy disagreed with the critics – and put De Niro in the frame for a Best Actor nomination.

No such accolade would derive from his decision to produce *Mistress*, the next movie from the TriBeCa stable. The project seemed to be motivated out of the kindness of his heart rather than sound business judgement. It had been unsuccessfully touted by his friend Barry Primus for years, but was turned down everywhere as having no potential. Primus and De Niro had been friends since appearing together in Roger Corman's *Boxcar Bertha* in 1972. Primus also had a small role in *New York, New York* and appeared in *Guilty by Suspicion*, though his career had never really taken off. His last movie perhaps summed up his current position: *Cannibal Women in the Avocado Jungle of Death*.

Like many actors, Primus had a burning desire to direct his own movie – and this one in particular. Written jointly by himself and his friend John Lawton (later author of the screenplay for *Pretty Woman*), it was based upon their own experiences in attempting to get an earlier short film into production. The result was a fairly nonsensical tale that has some measure of satirical truth.

A writer trying to get his beloved screenplay made into a film is corrupted by the power of the financiers. First he says he will not change a word of the script, but gradually he is forced to accommodate the three men backing the movie, as each injects his own ideas which are aimed at finding roles for their mistresses.

Even before De Niro formed TriBeCa he had shown Primus' script to some of his movie-making friends, but failed to arouse any interest. One day, while they were strolling down Broadway and Primus had had his umpteenth rejection, De Niro said, 'I'm going to start my own company soon, and if you haven't sold it by then I'll make it myself.' True to his word, as soon as he formed TriBeCa he took up the option. Primus would direct the film himself and De Niro would play one of the three money-men. Co-starring would be the redoubtable Eli Wallach, just celebrating his seventy-fifth birthday, Martin Landau and Danny Aiello.

But in spite of its cast De Niro found difficulty in getting the movie into the cinemas. It was turned down by all the leading distributors and finally came into the hands of Henry Jaglom, the independent producer-director of eccentric movies who agreed to release it in the slow, cottage industry way that he puts out his own productions in neighbourhood cinemas. In the trade, the move reeked of desperation and last-resort tactics by De Niro. One distributor was moved to comment, 'It is remarkable that De Niro could not get this film released in any other way. Of course, no one will say anything negative about it on the record because they don't want to jeopardize possible future deals.'

De Niro had to go out and try to talk up the movie. Pressed to say why he had got involved in the first place, he insisted, 'I thought that someone like Barry Primus, who is a real artist, who really cares and is compassionate about people, should have more than the right to direct his own movie compared to some people who are hacks and who do movies time and time again and they make money, enough money to keep moving from job to job, and they have nothing to say.'

When asked about the lack of interest from mainstream distributors he emphasized his own commitment to art in movies, although in this particular case he may well have been over-gilding the lily. 'They said it was not a high-concept movie,' he moaned. 'But it's a piece of art from beginning to end. Nobody can say it doesn't have honourable intentions. I suppose there's always the answer that people might not like to see themselves in it.' That may have been true and, regardless of the merits proclaimed by De Niro himself, *Mistress* quickly vanished into the ether.

The publicity curve would, however, have shot off the graph if, at the time the movie was being made, the tabloid press had been aware of the developments in De Niro's own tangled love life – which, incidentally, would involve Barry Primus and his wife Julie. His affair with Toukie Smith had faded as news of his latest passion, Naomi Campbell, hit the grapevine, although it did not necessarily mean that Toukie was out of the picture completely. They were seen together on several occasions before Christmas 1991. Meanwhile the former, if brief, love of his life, Helena Springs, knew of the closeness between Naomi and De Niro because her daughter Nina had telephoned his home in New York and Naomi had answered. But then came a development that surprised even Helena.

De Niro telephoned her from Vancouver at the end of January 1992. He said he was very busy and very tired, but would like to see Nina again. Helena said that was fine by her, but when? De Niro said he would like her to fly to Canada the following weekend.

At about the same time Naomi Campbell was giving *Hello!* magazine an exclusive interview in which she confirmed publicly for the first time her romance with De Niro.

'Are you in love right now, Naomi?' asked the interviewer.

'Very much so,' she replied.

'Will you tell us who with?'

'Robert De Niro. I'm not going to deny it any more.'

Asked what she most loved about him, the model, then twenty-one years old, replied: 'His understanding. That he is a true friend and a support to me. I'm somebody who needs a great deal of love. With love I'm a much happier person. Love to me is the most important thing to have in life. I know exactly what I want in life and I can't accept compromises.'

Oddly enough, the weekend the article appeared was the one when De Niro had arranged for Nina to fly to Canada to join him. De Niro was still curious about this child. He had decided to try to get to know her and arranged for her to fly to Vancouver. She was there from Friday night and returned to Los Angeles on Sunday morning.

De Niro's aide, Robin Chambers, was asked to meet her at Vancouver Airport. The child was very excited at having flown first-class and was telling him about the experience. He drove her to De Niro's hotel, where they waited for him. Nina was a very talkative child, Chambers recalled, and had brought with her a number of teen magazines containing illustrated articles on De Niro, which she showed to

Chambers. She seemed fascinated by him and kept asking about him and about his work. She seemed very impressed that she had travelled there alone to see him.

After about two hours De Niro arrived and Chambers left. He did not see Nina again until the end of her visit. De Niro, meanwhile, took her for a meal and showed her around Vancouver. He bought her some gifts, and that night before she went to sleep they chatted. They spent the following day together.

On the Sunday Robin Chambers took her back to Los Angeles. The telephone contact between De Niro and Nina now became more frequent, and eventually Helena raised the question of putting the whole situation on a firm basis for the child's sake. She wanted to let Nina recognize him as her father and begin a proper father–daughter relationship, or else stop the visits completely. De Niro agreed, but then suggested that they should have blood tests to confirm that she was truly his daughter. Helena said she had no objection to that, and pointed out that she had suggested that course of action years earlier but he had refused. Now he wanted it done.

The tests were carried out the following month, in March 1992, and to De Niro's absolute relief and Helena's total surprise eliminated him as Nina's father.

De Niro telephoned her in Los Angeles and told her the results. She was very upset and crying and insisted that the tests were wrong. He was angry and told Helena he felt betrayed. She said she had slept with only one other man at the time, whom she had known for some time. This other man, it later transpired, could not now be tested as he had since died in a boating accident. So the upshot of these exchanges was that De Niro agreed to get a second and then a third blood test.

Helena, meantime, consulted the famed Hollywood palimony lawyer Marvin Michelson, who advised her that regardless of the blood tests – which he said were not conclusive anyhow – there was precedent in American law which provided her with good grounds to fight for maintenance for Nina. De Niro had accepted the child as his own, had told her he still wished to remain in Nina's life even though he wasn't her father, and was continuing to make payments towards her upkeep.

In May 1992, De Niro received a letter from Michelson. Knowing the lawyer's modus operandi of fighting his case in the media before actually getting to court, and fearing the damaging effects of adverse publicity on some very sensitive TriBeCa deals and his restaurant, he asked Julie and Barry Primus to act as mediators.

Julie had known Helena for about three years. When the business of the blood tests blew up she had a long discussion with Helena, who was very upset. She always believed that Bob was the father of Nina and after the blood tests she was in a state of confusion as to what to do. . . .

Even so, Marvin Michelson advised Helena to initiate court proceedings against De Niro on the basis of inconclusive tests and that he had established a bond with Nina. On Helena's behalf, Michelson filed a claim for $100,000 a year maintenance.

Through all of this, De Niro had managed to turn out another TriBeCa movie. *Night and the City*, in which he starred with Jessica Lange, was a return match after their appearance together in *Cape Fear*. In fact, everybody was together again. He hired Irwin Winkler to direct the movie; it was produced by Jane Rosenthal, who was also vice-president of TriBeCa; and the cast list included Eli Wallach and Barry Primus. Few people picked up on the fact that it was virtually always the same team of people in these TriBeCa movies. Nor had anyone been cynical enough to record that De Niro and his various collaborators had taken an easy route to acquiring material by doing so many remakes: *We're No Angels*, *Cape Fear* and then *Night and the City*.

The original *Night and the City* had been a 1950s British-made *film noir* effort starring Richard Widmark and Gene Tierney, with a thin plot about crooked wrestling matches and low-life gangsters. The new version was scripted by Richard Price, who wrote *Color of Money* and *Sea of Love*. But like much of his work, the tale pokes around the dark and seedy corners of a male world in mid-life crisis. The women are unattractive portraits – not unusual, because De Niro's films have been always about male dominance and male bonding, and female reference is usually from the standpoint of misogyny.

De Niro clearly made an effort to make this film stand up. His own performance was pretty faultless but it was not a strong film, and certainly not one to cause queues at cinemas. Anyway, people were beginning to talk: they were suggesting that De Niro was in danger of spreading himself too thinly as he made this all-too-evident dash to establish TriBeCa.

Before the year was out he made yet one more, *Mad Dog and Glory*. But really, what was he doing? This was absolute second-division material, and he had even roped in Martin Scorsese in the ignominious role of co-producer with his wife Barbara de Fina, playing nursemaid to an uncertain director named John McNaughton (previously known only for the modern shockers *Henry: Portrait of a Serial Killer* and *Sex, Drugs, Rock and Roll*).

The thin plot – again scripted by Richard Price – about a Chicago police photographer who would rather be doing something else provided De Niro with a modest role that would have amply suited a television movie. It was not a dire picture by any means – he would not let it be so. It was just very small stuff. But after three in a row the fans were rightly wondering what he was playing at. He was playing at being the tycoon, and he had already lined up three more movies to be released in 1993–4. Too many, too soon, too small: the reviewers, the pundits and the aficionados were already saying it, but De Niro wasn't listening.

If these troubled public reactions weren't enough to cause him sleepless nights, the package of legal documents delivered to his home in midsummer certainly were. Marvin Michelson was claiming that De Niro had refused to take a blood test years earlier, had refused to allow Helena's husband to adopt the child and had been argumentative and obstructive whenever there was contact between them. De Niro's actions during the past few years, Michelson claimed, first in his relationship with Helena, next in his contributions to Nina's upbringing and finally in his self-initiated contacts with the child from the age of eight onwards, were sufficient to provide a basis for a court ruling that he had accepted Nina as his daughter, regardless of true parentage.

The action was defended and subsequently went to a court hearing in October 1992. Helena said she had suffered 'ten years of hell' from De Niro in his treatment of her, and that he would never commit to anything. At the beginning, she said, when she told him she was pregnant, he had tried to persuade her to have an abortion and had even suggested a potion of herbs that would induce one. She had refused, and from that time on the situation had grown increasingly fraught.

Helena would say that it was the possessiveness of De Niro's current girlfriend Naomi Campbell that had triggered the paternity action:

Naomi wants people to know that she is his girlfriend. We have a mutual friend in New York who told me Naomi was bragging about her affair with De Niro. She wanted everyone to know that she was his girlfriend and she was very jealous of Bobby's past connections – and they included me and my daughter Nina. That was because at the time we were briefly sexually active again when he came to Los Angeles. I admit he was my weakness, and I could never refuse him. He was always a fantastic lover but I also knew that he has tons of women.

This last statement was one which found a measure of agreement between both parties. De Niro said that 'women just throw themselves at me. That's just how it is.' He remained adamant, however, about his decision not to pay Helena any further money. His lawyers argued that she wanted to drag out the action and pursue the theory of paternity. They said it was a 'sham' and that De Niro should not be held responsible.

The court, however, did not agree that De Niro's action were wholly defensible, and the hearing was adjourned pending a further blood test and other reports. In the meantime, De Niro was ordered to make a temporary child support payment to Helena of $2000 a month.

20

Debut Director

Robert De Niro was running all the time because he had so much going on, and now he had decided that, apart from his film centre, his restaurant, producing his own movies and appearing in other people's, he was going to chalk up another 'first' – he was going to become a director. Between projects he had acquired a script which would eventually become a movie entitled A *Bronx Tale*, produced by his own company, starring and directed by himself. In the summer of 1992, he was conducting auditions for one of the roles and had a couple of dozen middle-aged men sitting in an ante-room, being called in one by one to see him. They each had about the same amount of time, eight to ten minutes, and usually emerged saying, 'He's a really nice guy.' Eventually, when he had seen them all, De Niro himself came out. He was holding his back with both hands and complaining that he was tired. Then he ordered a drink and went back to work. That was one of the balls in the air.

Another was doing deals to ensure the establishment of the key business operations of TriBeCa on which the success of the film centre rested. There were still acres of space to be rented out to ancillary companies and, of course, the restaurant drew his constant interest and attention.

It was perhaps ironic that, as De Niro's own decidedly low-key offerings from TriBeCa created confusion among his fans and gave rise to questions about judgement in the media, one of the most successful of the new young film tycoons, one at the very heart of the Hollywood system, set in motion events which put a few million in his back pocket at exactly the right moment. It also demonstrates once again the friendly, trusting relationship that exists between De Niro and a very tight-knit group of film people, in and out of Hollywood,

221

who managed to keep the wheels of his career turning regardless of the critical response to his recent string of duds.

Peter Guber, one half of the whizz-kid production partnership of Guber and Peters, had bought the rights to a semi-autobiographical novel by Tobias Wolff entitled *This Boy's Life*. As soon as he read it he saw it as a very filmable project, and one that would eventually be offered to De Niro.

Guber and his partner Jon Peters were the very model of success for those who, like De Niro, had formed their own production units. The young duo had teamed up in the early eighties, with borrowed money and high hopes, to form Polygram Pictures. They then produced a series of lower-budget movies, several of which, such as Alan Parker's *Midnight Express*, *An American Werewolf in London* and Paramount's top box-office earner of 1983, *Flashdance*, became cult classics. They sold their company that year and formed Guber–Peters Entertainment, dedicated to bigger-budget pictures which included *The Color Purple*, *Rain Man*, *The Witches of Eastwick* and their supreme, all-time blockbuster for Warners, *Batman*, for which they personally cajoled a reluctant Jack Nicholson into playing the Joker.

It was in 1989, when Guber–Peters Entertainment was still a production company resident on the Warner Bros lot, that Peter Guber had bought *This Boy's Life*. Before he could turn it into a movie, however, he joined Sony Pictures Entertainment and was appointed head of Columbia Studios, which they had just bought. So he passed his pet project to De Niro's friend, the producer Art Linson. Linson, struck by Guber's enthusiasm, asked screenwriter Robert Getchell to produce the script and decided that De Niro would be ideal to play one of the central characters, the stepfather. Thus the wheels keep on turning.

Wolff's book, though presented as a novel, was really a vivid memoir of his abused childhood in the late 1950s. He recounts how he and his mother Caroline (to be played by Ellen Barkin in the film) escape from her cruel boyfriend in Florida and move far away, eventually settling in Seattle in the hope of starting afresh. The boy Toby has become something of a young tearaway, running with a local gang and sinking into the ways of fifties' juvenile delinquency – until, that is, his mother moves in with Dwight Hansen (to be played by De Niro), a tough, conservative man with a typical-of-the-era crew-cut. Dwight makes clear his intentions to bring the boy to heel, and he can only do it by breaking his rebellious spirit. The result is a psychological battle of wits and wills that at times achieves incredible tension as man and boy slug it out for supremacy, with Caroline playing the piggy in the middle.

At first sight this story, although full of emotion and psychological insight, did not seem to be one that would attract De Niro. However, given the financial pressures of entrepreneurship his interest was aroused. He visualized – and would create – Dwight as a monster of a man who claimed to be the epitome of truth and justice but who was in reality a grotesque and self-deluding liar.

Despite the calls on his time from TriBeCa he began studying Wolff's book almost line by line, and gave it the research preparation which has become such a familiar feature of his work. Wolff himself was by that time professor of creative writing at Syracuse University in New York State, and De Niro turned up one day to talk about the project.

Wolff remembers the meeting with relish, and tells the story over and over again to his students because he had never before witnessed a man so intensely bound up in a subject; it was especially poignant because it was his own life that De Niro was absorbing:

> He arrived carrying this enormous notebook. It was filled with about two hundred observations about Dwight which he had noted while reading the book. De Niro was interested in the tiniest, smallest detail about the man. What did he wear when he came out of the bathroom? Did he walk around the house naked? Did he wear a T-shirt? He wanted to know everything, accumulating details like a scholar.

As usual, it was the minutiae that De Niro sought to discover. He paid particular interest, for instance, when Wolff mentioned the way Dwight used to light a cigarette with his Zippo lighter – the same movements of the hand every time, like some ritual. De Niro asked Wolff to show him how and then borrowed a video-camera and taped him, doing it over and over again, though he was never sure that he had got it right. But when Wolff saw De Niro doing the same thing in the film, it was perfect to the last detail.

Similarly, director Michael Caton-Jones, like all newcomers to De Niro's way of working, was intrigued by this need for perfection. He had never witnessed such a thing before, though in De Niro's defence it must be said that Caton-Jones had never before directed such an intense actor. The previous big-screen experience of the Scottish-born director comprised *Scandal*, the story of the Profumo scandal, David Puttnam's ill-fated *Memphis Belle* and the modest and sentimental Michael J. Fox vehicle *Doc Hollywood*. Even so, watching De Niro trying on perhaps two hundred jackets before deciding which one he would wear in a particular scene was an exercise in extremes of physical correctness that astounded him. The clothes, said Caton-Jones, represented De Niro's make-up, as vital to that scene as the spoken lines. But what Wolff and Caton-Jones did not seem to realize was that they were seeing De Niro's own compulsive ritual. Just as his character had that particular way of flicking open his Zippo lighter, so De Niro set about his particular way of portraying a role. Why, at this stage in his career, did he still have to do that?

When he started out it was necessary to follow Stella Adler's instructions to the letter, because he had nothing else to offer in the way of charisma or looks or personality. But here he was, three dozen films and thirty years later, still going through those same exercises of establishing his physical props just as he had done when he was a kid with two wardrobes full of clothes and costumes he had bought in second-hand shops. Was this the obsessive compulsion of a man without confidence? Or was he a man who had so tied himself to a method that, like a cripple, he could not do without the crutch?

To be fair, *This Boy's Life* was a nicely done picture that gave quite a powerful insight into what was, none the less, a pretty familiar situation of a disciplinarian stepfather faced with a tenacious youth. De Niro injected his particular style of dark humour and character exploration into the film, which carried it safely along to its conclusion. But the result was one more character, one more piece of acting that was neither a stunning work nor a dismal failure, neither art nor box office – just a pretty standard De Niro performance, and there had been a few too many of those in recent years. The fans surely could not wait to see him challenged again by something totally fresh instead of colourless variations on the mean theme.

In earlier years diversions into quirkiness could be excused as De Niro's attempt to establish a varied body of work; and of course he had always felt that box office did not matter because he was producing pieces of cinematic history. But De Niro had changed the rules of the game. It was he who altered the focus into a money-go-round to support his ambitions and perhaps even to seek more suitable projects in his maturing years.

It was still possible to offer explanations and admit that, although *This Boy's Life* was not a 'big' picture in either intent or impact, those who were keeping score could remind themselves that the very fact that De Niro took on this kind of material was in one sense a credit to him. It was also a serious risk. Few of his contemporaries in the so-called A-list of male actors would even try some of the movies he had done for fear of invoking that much-remembered exchange that Billy Wilder wrote for *Sunset Boulevard*, when William Holden says: 'Hey, I remember you. You used to be big', to which Gloria Swanson replies: 'I am big; it's the pictures that got small.'

De Niro's pictures were getting smaller, just as Brando's pictures got smaller, but not before Brando had shown us his range, from punk drunk boxer to Mark Antony. De Niro, on the other hand, had yet to convince a growing band of detractors that he even possessed that range. Indeed, *Godfather* author Mario Puzo reckons he is no more than a very good ethnic actor who only has one act. 'He can't do Shakespeare,' said Puzo, 'and he can't do comedy. How can you even begin to compare him with Brando?'

True, De Niro had not matched the sheer range of Brando, nor, perhaps, the diversity of some of his modern contemporaries. To see Dustin Hoffman in drag in *Tootsie* or as the autistic savant in *Rain Man*, to watch Jack Nicholson in *The Witches of Eastwick*, as the Joker in *Batman* or in his powerful performance in *A Few Good Men* confirms that point. And it must be conceded that De Niro had clocked up a fair list of duds, which others in his league had managed to avoid. Every actor has an occasional flop now and again, but when the films are also contemptuous of audience expectations of their favourite actor the motives must be studied. Brando earned contempt through his own rejection of the craft that made him famous and his so obvious dash for cash to keep him happily ensconced on his South Sea atoll with his ever-extending family.

As he entered the 1990s De Niro risked a different kind of contempt, bred, as the old saying goes, through familiarity. The people who once proclaimed him as one of the greatest actors of his generation were beginning to have second thoughts. The headlines were turning nasty, having given him the benefit of the doubt for quite some time. Even the supportive British film journal *Empire* reported in a profile of him:

'Some have cruelly inferred that . . . for every *GoodFellas*, there's a *Stanley and Iris* waiting to happen . . . that after *The Mistress*, *Night and the City* and *This Boy's Life*, the great Robert De Niro may even – heaven forbid – have started to lose what little box office clout he once possessed.'

As he approached the age of fifty, the raging ambitions of Robert De Niro had produced a man in turmoil. He was edgy and irritable about his work, made worse by the fact that for the first time in his life he had to give media interviews to promote his movies, because he was now at the very sharp end of the business and financial effort in promoting them. But, still as tight-lipped as ever about his inner thoughts, he was prepared to speak only about the movie, its plot and its development. He was protective of himself and even his image. Sometimes, when a fan has spotted him and taken his picture, he has approached that person and said: 'I am going to tell you, you shouldn't have done that.'

The attitudes of the media people, confronted with De Niro's familiar stone-walling which for years had allowed them only to write stories about *not* getting an interview with him, were already changing. These days, the idea of publishing interviews that feigned co-operation but in truth merely represented a straight puff for a movie (or a book or a disc), as in those cosy, old-fashioned chat shows of bygone days, is firmly rejected by writers and broadcasters. A meaningless, stuttering conversation with a film star no longer ranks high in the priorities of newspaper columnists and television presenters who are fighting their own ratings and circulation battles. The response to uncooperative, privacy-seeking showbiz major-leaguers is now: Well, who needs you anyway?

The new movie on whose behalf he had to suffer the angst of media interviews was going to be a particular milestone, the move that took him past the age of fifty and with which he would achieve a number of ambitions. It was also one which gave substance to Mario Puzo's remark that De Niro has repeatedly drawn from his own ethnic background for his inspiration and work.

The screenplay for *A Bronx Tale*, written by Chazz Palminteri, came to him in 1991. It is a story of growing up in an Italian-American community in the Fordham district of the Bronx in the 1960s. The hero is a young man, played first by Francis Capra at the age of nine and then by Lillo Brancata at seventeen, who has two rival mentors. Both seek to influence his life as he comes of age in a Mafia com-

226

munity, and the film focuses on his ambivalence about whose values he should adopt.

The first influence is his father, Lorenzo, an impoverished, incorruptible bus driver played by De Niro. The second is the local neighbourhood Mob hero named Sonny, played by the author, Chazz Palminteri, whom the boy sees commit a murder. He is torn between his father's vision of right and wrong and the glamorous life recommended by the gangster.

The project had one of those beginnings that writers dream of: Palminteri, a former singer, wrote his story as a five-minute monologue and then turned it into a play which was produced at Theater West in Los Angeles in 1989. It transferred to New York and in due course he was offered $250,000 by Universal Studios for a screenplay. But Universal insisted on casting a major star in the role of Sonny, which Palminteri had been playing, so he said: 'No deal.' They kept increasing their offer until eventually Palminteri accepted $1.5 million and Universal agreed to his conditions: he would write the screenplay and play Sonny, and his friend Peter Gatien, who had financed the first stage version, would be executive producer.

Universal still needed a star, and De Niro was approached. When he saw the play he immediately wanted to turn it into a movie. A deal was struck, the details of which demonstrate the behind-the-scenes manoeuvrings in which De Niro was now involved as head of TriBeCa. Universal had budgeted the movie at $12 million, which they assessed would show them a reasonable return on their investment. De Niro wanted his usual $4 million fee as lead actor, plus 10 per cent of the adjusted gross receipts – which meant that after the cinemas had taken their cut he would take the next slice. For that he would throw in the directing for nothing, thus forgoing an additional $150,000 fee, and guarantee to deliver within 55 days. Working to his projections, Universal upped the budget to $16.5 million, at which point the accountants said that that would be the absolute limit.

So now, from his film centre, De Niro set to work with his vice-president, Jane Rosenthal, on casting and pre-production. One of the built-in difficulties, however, was that apart from himself and Palminteri the roles were largely in the hands of amateurs, even down to the extras who were being hired from line-ups personally screened by De Niro.

As the film progressed it became clear that the production and finance targets would not be met. First there was a series of unfortunate accidents, ranging from the breakdown of the 1960s bus that the De Niro character drove to young Francis Capra losing a front tooth. But the failure was also due in part to De Niro's well-known pursuit of perfectionism. Palminteri admitted: 'He approaches directing in the same way that he approaches acting . . . meticulous to the point of obsession. He's never satisfied. It has to be right and, if it ain't, we do it over and over again.'

As the movie fell behind schedule, a new budget of $18 million was posted. But Universal pulled out when De Niro refused to guarantee any over-runs with his own money. Now TriBeCa took over production and arranged new financial backing. It came jointly through PentAmerica, an Italian funding partnership which included media tycoon Silvio Berlusconi (before he became Prime Minister of Italy), and a fledgeling US film company called Savoy Pictures. PentAmerica, which had bankrolled De Niro's other recent production *Night and the City*, from which it had so far received a minimal return, agreed to stump up $12.6 million for the foreign rights of *A Bronx Tale*, while Savoy Pictures put up the rest.

The new budget now extended to $21 million and later went up to $24 million. The production hit further troubles, and by then De Niro was pumping in his own money. When he finally called a wrap and took his 200,000 feet of film – almost twice the normal amount needed – into the editing room at TriBeCa, he was thirty days over schedule. His work was being monitored daily by a representative of the Film Guarantors Insurance Company, which had set a time limit on his delivery and would take over the final cut if he did not achieve it on time. Jane Rosenthal explained to nervous observers from the film's backers, 'This is a natural extension of how Bob works as an actor. His search for reality brings the same attention to detail he brings to his characters.' By then, he was working flat out, eighteen hours a day, to achieve his deadlines.

In the middle of these production traumas he was hit by personal matters once again. His son Raphael, then fifteen, was arrested for allegedly vandalizing a subway, but got off with a warning. Then, in the second week of May, De Niro was called back to court in his continuing defence of the paternity action brought by Helena Springs. Although De Niro claimed that the third blood test he had taken had proved that he was not the father of her child, Marvin Michelson continued to demand child support on behalf of his client.

Michelson still claimed that the blood tests were inconclusive, and stated that in any event De Niro's 'acceptance' of the child as his daughter over a period of years was sufficient grounds for him to continue paying towards her wellbeing. 'He cannot just end it,' said Michelson. The judge interviewed both parties separately in chambers. They failed to reach an agreed settlement, however, and De Niro instructed his lawyers to reject all Helena's claims. He even said that an agreement for him to visit Nina, which Helena had offered, would not be necessary because he had no desire to exercise visitation.

And so a decision in the case was further postponed for the judge to consider the verdict. One month later, on 5 April, the court in Los Angeles finally gave its ruling – in De Niro's favour. He had been paying monthly maintenance since September 1992, and the Los Angeles Superior Court ruled that this should be discontinued. Three blood tests had proved that he was not the child's biological father, although ultimately that was not the issue. The claim was based upon whether De Niro had accepted the child as his own over a ten-year period and, by virtue of his contact with her, should continue child support payments.

The court accepted the submissions of De Niro's lawyer, Ron Anteau, that no 'bonding' had occurred between De Niro and Nina. Anteau said his client's involvement with the child had been minimal, and it was his contention that it should not obligate him 'legally, morally or ethically' to supporting the child.

And so, after years of wrangling, the case was resolved and De Niro walked away from it without further obligation resulting from his liaison with Helena Springs. It was accepted that the singer herself had always believed De Niro to be the father, and was 'shocked and surprised' by the results of the blood test. But in spite of his success at pursuing the formal rejection of Nina as his daughter, the case had clearly left its mark on him, both personally and publicly. Some people suggested that De Niro himself should have resolved the situation. Typically, he had prevaricated from the outset. Instead of taking a firm decision at the beginning, by taking a blood test or facing up to his responsibilities as Nina's father, he posted her to the back of his mind and tried to hide her away until Helena Springs began to force the issue because of her changing circumstances. As for the child, a neighbour of Helena's reported:

Nina was quite obviously affected by all of this. It seemed clear to us at the time that De Niro was playing a two-handed game

– he was having her for the occasional visit, taking her out during his visits to Los Angeles, but at the same time keeping her at arm's length. As it turned out, he had good reason. But his handling of the whole business left this child with a great disappointment that she will carry for the rest of her life.

Back in New York, in the hi-tech editing suite, A *Bronx Tale* was taking shape. But in the middle of his most crucial time he was struck by further personal trauma: his father died in May 1993, a month after the Helena Springs case ended. De Niro had become very close to his father in recent years and he was a familiar figure in the TriBeCa grill, taking a regular corner table and obviously proud that his son had hung many of his paintings on the walls. De Niro junior felt a particular sadness that his father did not live to view his first directorial effort – his own very personal 'canvas'. He inserted a line at the beginning of the film dedicating it to Robert De Niro senior.

All summer long De Niro was in the editing rooms, although the intensity of his work was relieved briefly in August when his friends organized a fiftieth birthday party for him, staged naturally enough at the TriBeCa grill. The event also highlighted once again the closeness of his circle of friends, which had barely expanded beyond those who had gathered for his wedding to Diahnne Abbott. She was, of course, present at the birthday bash, along with her daughter Drina and their son Raphael. Other guests included his former girlfriend Toukie Smith, his long-time associates Martin Scorsese, Paul Schrader, Irwin Winkler, Francis Ford Coppola, Harvey Keitel, Brian De Palma and Robin Williams, and his newest friends Kenneth Branagh (who was about to work with him) and Emma Thompson.

After that it was straight back to work to complete the cut of his film. He did two versions of his edit of A *Bronx Tale* and sent cassettes to Martin Scorsese for his comments. Later that month the movie was shown in private screenings in the TriBeCa Center, and rumours that De Niro's first effort as director was a disaster gave way to more rumours that it was beautiful. Since the Italian backers required evidence that the final film would satisfy them and justify their patience, he took a print to show at the Venice Film Festival in September. All through the showing he sat there nervously, the tension mounting as the end approached. . . . He breathed a sigh of relief when the audience gave it a five-minute standing ovation. After flying straight back to New York for some colour corrections he took off again the following day for the Toronto Film Festival. The same happened – another standing ovation.

By then, TriBeCa was busy turning out a thousand prints to be distributed across America after simultaneous premières in New York and Los Angeles on 29 September. It did reasonably good business but it was not a runaway commercial success, and he failed to eradicate the red figures via the US box-office returns.

As a movie, A Bronx Tale was also a statement that De Niro could deal with the discipline of direction as well as performing a key role. For that reason the movie received particular attention from the critics and, though acclaim on both counts was by no means a matter on which they agreed, they rightly gave the film a decent rating. As a directorial debut, De Niro's film was entirely satisfactory.

It had a great deal of heart to it and a moving plot. De Niro, strong and believable as ever, slots another ordinary, nondescript character, of whom he provides an excellent character study, into his gallery of faces. He was always good in this territory, the badlands of New York's rotten borough. As a piece of 1960s' memorabilia A Bronx Tale presents a striking portrait of that colourful place and time, traduced though it was by De Niro's personal fascination with gangsters and killers. That's why the call from Kenneth Branagh was welcome. It provided him with an opportunity to diversify into what was for him an unusual arena, that of the horror movie.

Branagh had been hired by Francis Ford Coppola's American Zoetrope production company, working for Tri-Star Pictures, to star in and direct Mary Shelley's Frankenstein. It was a daunting project, not least because of the familiarity of the world's most famous horror story. Branagh also realized that he had not been first choice for director, either. It was a well-thumbed screenplay, first written by screenwriter Steph Lady in 1987 while she was still teaching English in the ghettos of Los Angeles. She admitted to a virtual obsession with the project: 'It was always my contention that the real story, as portrayed by Mary Shelley, had been passed by, time and time again, by film-makers. The true passions and emotions of Shelley's work had been ignored in favour of the horror.'

Tri-Star Pictures bought the script which finally made its way to Branagh after several other directors, and stars, had passed on it. Neither was De Niro their first choice to play the Frankenstein creation. Branagh and Coppola offered it first to De Niro's good friend Gerard Depardieu, who turned it down because he did not think he could better the Boris Karloff interpretation in James Whale's original 1931 production. At Coppola's suggestion Branagh contacted De Niro, who was wary not so much of playing the role as of working with Branagh himself.

At the time of the first approach, in 1992, Branagh was achieving much publicity in Britain and across the Atlantic as the latest blue-eyed boy of British film, a title which David Puttnam had taken years to live down. He personally had a good deal riding on the movie, not to mention a hefty budget of around $40 million. A star of De Niro's calibre was essential.

'Bob indicated he was, shall we say, interested,' Branagh recalled.

He then proceeded to suss me out . . . thoroughly. He looked at the movies I had done, talked to other actors and looked into my reputation. Then we started talking about the movie and my whole concept, which was to portray Frankenstein and his Creature as a kind of father and son relationship, and show the complexities of it all. Bob gave the view that the Creature should be pulled away from the vision of earlier films and back to the spirit of the book, which coincided exactly with my own feelings. I wanted – and he agreed entirely – to make this creature horrific, yet capable of inspiring sympathy for his plight. Bob, too, wanted a creature who could be intelligent, angry, and above all as credible as science could make him.

With their mutual respect for each other assured, Branagh and De Niro began working together. They were in touch for months, meeting occasionally between commitments and formulating their own vision of the Creature which, after all, was the central, most memorable feature of the movie.

De Niro, meantime, began his own research. He started with the original novel, watched a rerun of the Boris Karloff movie – for copyright reasons he had to avoid any resemblance to Karloff's monster, although none was intended anyway. He also began an intensive study of the scientific possibilities of re-creating life and even its moral aspects. He and Branagh studied the medical texts which were available to Mary Shelley at the time she wrote her novel. They re-created for themselves the scenario of the house party in Switzerland where her story was composed, and at which the guests, who included her future husband Percy Bysshe Shelley and Lord Byron, explored Gothic themes and traditions. Branagh and De Niro even composed the Creature's speech pattern from the vocabulary of Milton's *Paradise Lost* and Goethe's *The Sorrows of Young Werther*. Then they sought out victims of strokes and others who suffered from speech impediments so that De Niro could create a monster as believable as reality allowed, although they did not use the word 'monster' themselves because they wanted to keep away from the popular image.

All of this was proceeding while De Niro himself was engaged elsewhere with his own TriBeCa productions and latterly on the direction of *A Bronx Tale*. Even so, when they began to prepare for filming at Shepperton Studios in England De Niro had completed nine months of experimentation with the physical appearance of his creation, so vital in everything he does. Production designer Daniel Parker contrived to cover his entire body with a prosthetic skin which would allow him flexibility of movement and provide clues to his creation, and yet would be thin enough to allow Robert De Niro, actor, to show through recognizably.

When they got down to the business of filming, the myth and legend of working with Robert the Great had travelled ahead of him and there was more than a touch of apprehension among the actors who would be working with him. The line-up included some of Britain's finest, including John Cleese, Robert Hardy, Richard Briers and Helena Bonham Carter. Branagh admitted that the 'De Niro legend' could put other actors off their stride. In fact they found him relaxed and good-humoured, and not constantly 'in character' as the monster.

Early tensions were swept aside by laughter on set as a naked De Niro and a near-naked Branagh wallowed in a sexual lubricant jelly which was used to simulate amniotic fluid as the monster was created. But as the cameras rolled, the deadly seriousness of their work emerged. John Cleese, playing a doctor, experienced a certain unease when facing a scene with De Niro. Branagh noticed it too, but before he could do anything De Niro himself stopped the cameras, sensing that Cleese was unhappy. They disappeared off-set and had a private chat. 'Bob took John aside and geed him up a bit,' said Branagh. 'He kept hundreds of us waiting while the two of them had their tête-à-tête, and came back and did a perfect take.'

And so with all of the familiar De Niro tricks of the trade in place, coupled with the hopes and expectations of the director and star of the show, Kenneth Branagh, the company retired to await the critical reaction to one of the most talked about and hyped movies of modern times. Perhaps the publicity people should have taken heed of a cautionary remark made in the past by De Niro himself, who, realizing the deadening potential of wasted words, said, 'Don't talk it away.' It was the philosophy he had adhered to all his working life.

But hype was all that mattered, now. And because of it the première became something of an anti-climax, certainly in terms of critical reviews. It also provided an opportunity to take a potshot at what one critic called 'the expansive ego' of Kenneth Branagh. 'Branagh has indeed created a monster but not of the kind he originally intended,' said *Variety*. 'This lavish but overwrought melodrama is in many ways less compelling than a mini-series.' And the influential British critic Alexander Walker of the London *Evening Standard* said that 'the whole adds up to considerably less than the parts'. These were fairly typical comments.

De Niro himself was criticized for not making his Creature fearsome enough. Perhaps it could never have lived up to the vision established in the mind's eye of the critics and the public that De Niro – most recently so totally over the top and scary in *Cape Fear* – would come up with a horrific monster to outdo all previous Frankenstein creations.

The point seemed to have been missed, however, that this version of both the story and the monster was never intended to have schlock-horror qualities. This underrated movie aspired to something quite different and stylish, much closer to the spirit of Mary Shelley's novel. On that basis, it more or less succeeded. Clearly it would not please those fans who enjoy the sensation of being scared out of their seats, and neither did it meet the aspirations of the money-men who expected to profit handsomely from their original investment.

Thus it represented one more somewhat indifferent addition to Robert De Niro's body of work. It also failed to appease those of his old fans who point accusingly at the roller-coaster ride he has given them in the past few years, in which the highs have been overshadowed by the low-points of the fast-buck tendency. His venture into the business side of the movies has had an effect in both quantity and quality. All the old values by which De Niro's work was judged – his abject refusal to conform, his meticulous research, his frighteningly real characters, his creation of screen images that paid little regard to public taste or popular opinion – have been marginalized since the late 1980s by the importance of money.

Bernardo Bertolucci long ago told him that he became an actor to express certain emotions that he could not express in life. 'I thought about that for a long time,' De Niro once admitted. 'And, uh, uh, um . . . I think that's right.' It is probably still true. He has been widely accused of spending a professional lifetime hiding behind his characters, and when he emerged from that camouflage he was, like Peter Sellers, a rich celebrity who was also curiously at odds with the world he had chosen to inhabit.

Sellers also possessed as a natural talent what De Niro had learned with Stella Adler – the ability to assume the character he was playing and alter his complete physical appearance accordingly. There has been abundant evidence of a selfish dedication to his craft which Scorsese once said superseded all other relationships, and which Laurence Olivier described as a curse. Equally, however, there is some testimony to his selflessness and generosity to other members of his profession.

De Niro has always vetted his directors as well as his scripts and, looking down the column of box-office returns for his movies, it could be argued by those who judge success on this criterion that he has not done too well. But that is exactly what makes De Niro stand out. In the 1970s he did all those movies that other 'stars' would have turned down. He built himself prestige and acclaim, and in every acting class in any city around the world they all wanted to be Robert De Niro – just as past generations opted for Brando or Dean. He became one of the great film-makers of his age not merely through his own abilities but by virtue of the people he chose to work with, and who usually became his close friends. Just as aspiring actors wanted to be him, aspiring directors wanted to be his collaborators like Scorsese or De Palma, the people who were making the most interesting films of that particular time.

He showed us a great actor in roles that were carefully tailored to his own qualities. It is apparent, as Puzo said, that he never extended himself beyond a certain category of characterization, never tried heavy sexual themes, never went into searing romantic drama, never tried real comedy, westerns or the classics. He basically stayed in his own back yard.

There remained, however, a mystique which is as much to do with his own self-perpetuated myth as it is with the characters he plays . . . that there is something hidden, still, that he has not revealed. He kept silent, like Garbo, and stuck rigidly to Stella Adler's tenet that you should never reveal yourself 100 per cent. The difference was, though, that De Niro did not apply this rule to his acting roles. He gave his all in *Taxi Driver*, *Raging Bull*, *The Deer Hunter*, *The Untouchables*, *Cape Fear*, and in *This Boy's Life* he was the stepfather from hell. He applied it instead to his own self, so that there was always a feeling emerging from the mystique and the myth that he had not shown his hand fully. Some have argued that that is all there is, that De Niro shot his bolt on the movies that made him famous and will spend the rest of his life treading water on good but unastounding performances, the like of which have dogged his most recent past as he put one foot in the production department.

He has undoubtedly extended himself by becoming actor, producer, director, businessman and moneybroker all rolled into one; and his work from the early 1990s may not be regarded with the same awed admiration of the past. But there was also a time-of-life factor to bear in mind – that period around the age of fifty when actors can fall into a kind of no-man's-land. Lacking the onscreen sexuality of a Robert Redford (as in *Indecent Proposal*), De Niro was too old for some of the kind of roles that made him famous and too young for the earthy, grizzled character parts of later life that have produced some challenging material for the likes of Jason Robards and Paul Newman.

In time, the disappointments of the most recent past may well prove no more than a blip in his career history, and perhaps even a turning point. There were signs that he had himself realized that he needed to turn up the heat and step more boldly along the path of commerciality which, like it or not, is Hollywood's reason for being there. Bankability is, as always, the measure by which success is judged and today, in the even more competitive climate of Hollywood where new moguls and owners scrutinize every penny spent, it is becoming even more vital.

In May 1995, in an impressively researched page of statistics, Britain's *Empire* magazine compiled a list of the Top Thirty international stars, based upon the American grosses of the last three movies of each of the stars. Predictably, De Niro was not among them. The list was headed by Tom Hanks, Tom Cruise and Harrison Ford, with Demi Moore, Jim Carrey, Julia Roberts, Robin Williams, Michael Douglas, Clint Eastwood and Arnold Schwarzenegger completing the top ten. There is nothing new in this statistic as far as De Niro is concerned, of course, because as we have seen his movies have seldom made the block-buster league. However, with his own money riding on his TriBeCa venture, the commerciality of movies he is involved in, either as producer, director or star, becomes more crucial to his future. The probability is that he will respond in the most positive way.

In the spring of 1995 he was working on yet another collaboration with Martin Scorsese, returning once again to the gangster theme with a movie entitled *Casino*, set in Las Vegas. His old friend Joe Pesci joined him on the project, along with the hottest female star of the moment, Sharon Stone. Early reports promised some lively action and some allegedly 'disturbing' sex scenes.

Robert De Niro, as he passed his half century, entered a new phase. Another era is already beckoning. It is impossible to imagine that he will not meet the challenge, pluck out the roles that best suit him, serve up a range of new characters and re-establish that individualistic, metamorphic style that has brought him fame and at least a decent fortune.

The future, then, looks promising; and as for the past, no one can complain about his body of work which, like the paintings his father would have loved to create, will be viewed years ahead when much of the output of some of his more glamorous and populist contemporaries has been forgotten. And that is all De Niro has ever really wanted.

Filmography

The Wedding Party (made 1963, released by Ajar Film Company 1969). Directors/writers/producers Brian De Palma, Cynthia Munroe and Wilford Leach; photography Peter Powell; music John Herbert McDowell. Cast: Jill Clayburgh, Charles Pflugar, Valda Setterfield, Raymond McNally, John Braswell, John Quinn, Robert De Nero (*sic*), William Finley, Jennifer Salt.

Greetings (aka *The Three Musketeers*, West End Films/Sigma 111, 1968). Director/editor Brian De Palma; producer Charles Hirsch; screenplay De Palma/Hirsch; photography Robert Fiore; music The Children of Paradise. Cast: Jonathan Warden, Robert De Niro, Gerritt Graham, Megan McCormick, Ashley Oliver, Cynthia Peltz, Ruth Alda.

Sam's Song (aka *The Swap*, released and re-released in various forms in 1969, 1971, 1980 and 1983, Cannon Distributors). Director (*Sam's Song*) Jordan Leondopoules; producer Christer Dewey, photography Alex Phillips; editor Arlene Garson; music Gershon Kingsley. *The Swap* written and directed by John Broderick, using footage from *Sam's Song*. Cast: Robert De Niro, Jered Mickey, Jennifer Warren, Terrayne Crawford, and additionally for *The Swap*: Anthony Charnotta, Sybil Danning, James Brown, Lisa Blount.

Bloody Mama (American International Pictures, 1970). Director/producer Roger Corman; screenplay Robert Thom; photography John Alonzo; editor Eve Martin; music Don Randi. Cast: Shelley Winters, Pat Hingle, Don Stroud, Diane Varsi, Bruce Dern, Clint Kimbrough,

Robert Walden, Robert De Niro, Alex Nicol, Pamela Dunlap, Scatman Crothers.

Hi, Mom! (Sigma 111, 1970). Director/writer Brian De Palma; producer Charles Hirsch; photography Robert Elfstrom; editor Paul Hirsch; music Eric Katz. Cast: Robert De Niro, Charles Durnham, Allen Garfield, Peter Maloney, Abraham Goren, Lara Parker, Jennifer Salt.

Jennifer on My Mind (United Artists, 1971). Director Noel Black; producer Bernard Schwartz; screenplay Erich Segal (from Roger L. Simon's novel *Heir*); photography Andy Laszlo; editor Jack Wheeler; music Stephen J. Lawrence. Cast: Tippy Walker, Michael Brandon, Lou Gilbert, Steve Vinovich, Peter Bonerz, Renee Taylor, Cuch McCann, Bruce Kornbluth, Barry Bostwick, Jeff Conaway, Robert De Niro, Erich Segal.

Born to Win (United Artists, 1971). Director Ivan Passer; producer Philip Langner; screenplay David Scott; photography Jack Priestly and Richard Kratina; editor Ralph Rosenbaum; music William S. Fisher. Cast: George Segal, Karen Black, Jay Fletcher, Hector Elizondo, Marcia Jean Kurtz, Irving Selbst, Robert De Niro, Paula Prentiss, Sylvia Sims.

The Gang That Couldn't Shoot Straight (MGM, 1971). Director James Goldstone; producers Robert Chartoff and Irwin Winkler; screenplay Waldo Salt (from Jimmy Breslin's novel); photography Owen Roizman; editor Edward A. Bierty; music Dave Grusin. Cast: Jerry Orbach, Leigh Taylor-Young, Jo Van Fleet, Lionel Stander, Robert De Niro, Irving Selbst, Hervé Villechaize, Joe Santos.

Bang the Drum Slowly (Paramount Pictures, 1973). Director John Hancock; producers Maurice and Lois Rosenfield; screenplay Mark Harris (from his own novel); photography Richard Shore; editor Richard Marks; music Stephen Lawrence. Cast: Robert De Niro, Michael Moriarty, Vincent Gardenia, Phil Foster, Ann Wedgeworth, Patrick McVey, Heather MacRae.

Mean Streets (Warner Bros, 1973). Director Martin Scorsese; producer Jonathan T. Taplin; screenplay Scorsese and Mardik Martin; photography Kent Wakeford; editor Sidney Levin; music various. Cast: Harvey Keitel, Robert De Niro, David Proval, Amy Robinson, Richard Romanus, Cesare Danova, George Memmoli, Vic Argo.

The Godfather, Part II (Paramount Pictures, 1974). Producer/director Francis Ford Coppola; screenplay Coppola and Mario Puzo (based upon Puzo's novel *The Godfather*); photography Gordon Willis; editors Peter Zinner, Barry Malkin and Richard Marks; music Nino Rota. Cast: Al Pacino, Robert De Niro, Diane Keaton, Robert Duvall, John Cazale, Talia Shire, Lee Strasberg, Michael V. Gazzo, G. D. Spradlin, Richard Bright, Gaston Moschin, Bruno Kirby, Troy Donahue, Harry Dean Stanton, Roger Corman, Danny Aiello, Phil Feldman, James Caan.

Novecento (aka *1900*, Paramount Pictures, 1976). Director Bernardo Bertolucci; producer Alberto Grimaldi; screenplay Bertolucci, Franco Arcalli and Giuseppe Bertolucci; photography Vittorio Storaro; editor Franco Arcali; music Ennio Morricone. Cast: Robert De Niro, Gerard Depardieu, Dominique Sanda, Burt Lancaster, Donald Sutherland, Sterling Hayden, Stefania Sandrelli, Alida Valli.

Taxi Driver (Columbia/Italo-Judeo, 1976). Director Martin Scorsese; producers Michael and Julia Phillips; screenplay Paul Schrader; photography Michael Chapman; editor Marcia Lucas; music Bernard Herrmann. Cast: Robert De Niro, Cybill Shepherd, Jodie Foster, Harvey Keitel, Albert Brooks, Leonard Harris, Peter Boyle, Steven Prince.

The Last Tycoon (Paramount Pictures, 1976). Director Elia Kazan; producer Sam Spiegel; screenplay Harold Pinter (from F. Scott Fitzgerald's unfinished novel); photography Victor Kemper; editor Richard Marks; music Maurice Jarre. Cast: Robert De Niro, Tony Curtis, Robert Mitchum, Jeanne Moreau, Jack Nicholson, Donald Pleasence, Ingrid Boulting, Ray Milland, Dana Andrews, Theresa Russell, Peter Strauss, John Carradine, Jeff Corey, Anjelica Huston.

New York, New York (United Artists, 1977). Director Martin Scorsese; producers Irwin Winkler and Robert Chartoff; screenplay Earl MacRauch and Mardik Martin; photography Laszlo Kovacs; editors Irving Lerner, Marcia Lucas, Tom Rolf, B. Lovitt and David Ramirez; music Ralph Burns, with new songs by John Kander and Fred Ebb. Cast:

Liza Minnelli, Robert De Niro, Lionel Stander, Barry Primus, Mary Kay Place, George Auld, Dick Miller, Murray Moston, Diahnne Abbott.

The Deer Hunter (Universal Studios, 1978). Director Michael Cimino; producers Barry Spikings, Michael Deeley, Michael Cimino and John Peverall; screenplay Deric Washburn; photography Vilmos Zsigmond; editor Peter Zinner; music Stanley Myers. Cast: Robert De Niro, John Cazale, John Savage, Meryl Streep, Christopher Walken, George Dzundza, Chuck Aspegren, Shirley Stoler, Rutanya Alda.

Raging Bull (United Artists, 1980). Director Martin Scorsese; producers Irwin Winkler and Robert Chartoff; screenplay Paul Schrader and Mardik Martin (from the autobiography by Jake La Motta); photography Michael Chapman; editor Thelma Schoonmaker; music Pietro Mascagni. Cast: Robert De Niro, Cathy Moriarty, Joe Pesci, Frank Vincent, Nicholas Colasanto, Theresa Saldana, Frank Adonis, Mario Gallo.

True Confessions (United Artists, 1981). Director Ulu Grosbard, producers Irwin Winkler and Robert Chartoff; screenplay John Gregory Dunne and Joan Didion; photography Owen Roizman; editor Lynzee Klingman; music Georges Delerue. Cast: Robert De Niro, Robert Duvall, Burgess Meredith, Charles Durning, Ed Flanders, Cyril Cusack, Kenneth McMillan, Dan Hedaya.

The King of Comedy (20th Century-Fox, 1983). Director Martin Scorsese; producer Arnon Milchan; screenplay Paul D. Zimmerman; photography Fred Schuler; editor Thelma Schoonmaker; music Robbie Robertson. Cast: Robert De Niro, Jerry Lewis, Diahnne Abbott, Sandra Bernhard, Whitey Ryan, Catherine Scorsese, Fred De Cordova, Shelley Hack, Martin Scorsese, Charles Scorsese, Mardik Martin (with Tony Randall and Victor Borge playing themselves).

Once Upon a Time in America (The Ladd Company/ Embassy/Warner Bros, 1984). Director Sergio Leone; producer Arnon Milchan; screenplay Leone, Leonardo Benvenuti, Piero De Bernardo, Enrico Medioli, Franco Arcalli, Franco Ferrini and Stuart Kaminsky; photography Tonino Delli Colli; editor Nino Baragli; music Ennio

Morricone. Cast: Robert De Niro, James Woods, Elizabeth McGovern, Treat Williams, Tuesday Weld, Burt Young, Joe Pesci, Danny Aiello, William Forsythe.

Falling in Love (Paramount Pictures, 1984). Director Ulu Grosbard; producer Marvin Worth; screenplay Michael Cristofer; photography Peter Suschitzky; editor Michael Kahn; music Dave Grusin. Cast: Robert De Niro, Meryl Streep, Jane Kaczmarek, George Martin, David Clennon, Dianne Wiest, Harvey Keitel, Victor Argo.

Brazil (Universal Studios, 1985). Director Terry Gilliam; producer Arnon Milchan; screenplay Gilliam, Tom Stoppard and Charles McKeown; photography Roger Pratt; editor Julian Doyle; music Michael Kamen. Cast: Jonathan Pryce, Robert De Niro, Michael Palin, Kim Greist, Katherine Helmond, Ian Holm, Ian Richardson, Peter Vaughan, Bob Hoskins.

The Mission (Warner Bros, 1986). Director Roland Joffe; producers Fernando Ghia and David Puttnam; story and screenplay Robert Bolt; photography Chris Menges; editor Jim Clark; music Ennio Morricone. Cast: Robert De Niro, Jeremy Irons, Cherie Lunghi, Ray McAnally, Aidan Quinn, Liam Neeson, Ronald Pickup, Monirak Sisowath, Daniel Berrigan.

Angel Heart (Tri-Star Pictures, 1987). Director Alan Parker; producers Alan Marshall and Elliott Kastner; screenplay Alan Parker (from William Hjortsberg's novel *Falling Angel*); photography Michael Seresin; editor Gerry Hambling; music Trevor Jones. Cast: Mickey Rourke, Robert De Niro, Lisa Bonet, Charlotte Rampling, Stocker Fontelieu, Brownie McGhee, Michael Higgins.

The Untouchables (Paramount Pictures, 1987). Director Brian De Palma; producer Art Linson; screenplay David Mamet; photography Stephen H. Burum; editors Jerry Greenberg and Bill Pankow; music Ennio Morricone. Cast: Kevin Costner, Sean Connery, Charles Martin Smith, Andy Garcia, Robert De Niro, Richard Bradford, Jack Kehoe, Brad Sullivan, Billy Drago, Patricia Clarkson.

Midnight Run (Universal Studios, 1988). Director/producer Martin Brest; screenplay George Gallo; photography Donald Thorin; editors

Billy Weber, Chris Lebenzon and Michael Tronick; music Danny Elfman. Cast: Robert De Niro, Charles Grodin, Yaphet Kotto, John Ashton, Dennis Farina, Joe Pantoliano.

Jacknife (Cineplex Odeon/Kings Road Entertainment, 1989). Director David Jones; producers Robert Schaffel and Carol Baum; screenplay Stephen Metcalfe (from his play *Strange Snow*); photography Brian West; editor John Bloom; music Bruce Broughton. Cast: Robert De Niro, Ed Harris, Kathy Baker, Charles Dutton, Loudon Wainwright III, Tom Isbell, Elizabeth Franz.

We're No Angels (Paramount Pictures, 1989). Director Neil Jordan; producer Art Linson; screenplay David Mamet (from the original by Ranald MacDougall); photography Philippe Rousselot; editors Mick Audsley and Joke Van Wijk; music George Fenton. Cast: Robert De Niro, Sean Penn, Demi Moore, Hoyt Axton, Bruno Kirkby, Ray McAnally, James Russo, Wallace Shawn, Jessica Jickels.

Awakenings (Columbia Pictures, 1990). Director Penny Marshall; producers Walter F. Parkes and Lawrence Lasker; screenplay Steven Zaillian (based on Oliver Sacks's book); photography Miroslav Ondricek; editors Jerry Greenberg and Battle Davis; music Randy Newman. Cast: Robert De Niro, Robin Williams, Julie Kavner, Ruth Nelson, John Heard, Penelope Ann Miller, Alice Drummond, Judith Malina, Max Von Sydow.

Stanley and Iris (MGM/UA, 1990). Director Martin Ritt; producers Arlene Sellers and Alex Winitsky; screenplay Irving Ravetch and Harriet Frank junior (based on Pat Baker's novel *Union Street*); photography Donald McAlpine; editor Sidney Levin; music John Williams. Cast: Jane Fonda, Robert De Niro, Swoosie Kurtz, Martin Plimpton, Harley Cross, Jamey Sheridan, Feodor Chaliapin.

GoodFellas (Warner Bros, 1990). Director Martin Scorsese; producer Irwin Winkler; screenplay Scorsese and Nicholas Pileggi (based on Pileggi's book *Wiseguy*); photography Michael Ballhaus; editor Thelma Schoonmaker; music various. Cast: Robert De Niro, Ray Liotta, Joe Pesci, Lorraine Bracco, Paul Sorvino, Frank Sivero, Tony Darrow, Mike Starr, Gina Mastrogiacomo.

Guilty by Suspicion (Warner Bros, 1991). Director/writer Irwin Winkler; producer Arnon Milchan; photography Michael Ballhaus; editor Priscilla Nedd; music James Newton Howard. Cast: Robert De Niro, Annette Bening, George Wendt, Patricia Wettig, Sam Wanamaker, Luke Edwards, Chris Cooper, Ben Piazza, Barry Primus.

Backdraft (Universal/Imagine Entertainment, 1991). Director Ron Howard; producers Richard Lewis, Pen Densham and John Watson; screenplay Gregory Widen; photography Mikael Salomon; editors Daniel Hanley and Michael Hill; music Hans Zimmer. Cast: Kurt Russell, William Baldwin, Jennifer Jason Leigh, Scott Glenn, Rebecca De Mornay, Robert De Niro, Donald Sutherland.

Cape Fear (Universal/Amblin Entertainment, 1991). Director Martin Scorsese; producer Barbara de Fina; screenplay Wesley Strick (from the original by James R. Webb, from John D. MacDonald's novel *The Executioners*); photography Freddie Francis; editor Thelma Schoonmaker; music Bernard Herrmann. Cast: Robert De Niro, Nick Nolte, Jessica Lange, Juliette Lewis, Joe Don Baker, Robert Mitchum, Gregory Peck, Illeana Douglas.

Mistress (Rainbow/TriBeCa, 1992). Director Barry Primus; producers Robert De Niro and Meir Teper; screenplay Barry Primus and J. F. Lawton; photography Sven Kirsten; editor Steven Welsberg; music Galt MacDermot. Cast: Danny Aiello, Robert De Niro, Martin Landau, Eli Wallach, Robert Wuhl, Jace Alexander, Tuesday Knight, Laurie Metcalf, Sheryl Lee Ralph, Christopher Walken, Ernest Borgnine (as himself).

Night and the City (20th Century-Fox/TriBeCa, 1992). Director Irwin Winkler; producers Jane Rosenthal and Winkler; screenplay Richard Price (from Gerald Kersh's novel); photography Tak Fujimoto; editor David Brenner, music James Newton Howard. Cast: Robert De Niro, Jessica Lange, Cliff Gorman, Alan King, Jack Warden, Eli Wallach, Barry Primus.

Mad Dog and Glory (Universal Pictures/TriBeCa, 1993). Director John McNaughton; producers Barbara de Fina and Martin Scorsese; screenplay Richard Price; photography Robby Muller; editors Craig

McKay and Elena Magnani; music Elmer Bernstein. Cast: Robert De Niro, Uma Thurman, Bill Murray, David Caruso, Mike Starr, Tom Towles, Kathy Baker.

This Boy's Life (Warner Bros, 1993). Director Michael Caton-Jones; producer Art Linson; screenplay Robert Getchell (from Tobias Wolff's book); photography David Watkin; editor Jim Clark; music Carter Burwell. Cast: Robert De Niro, Ellen Barkin, Leonardo DiCaprio, Johan Blechman, Eliza Dushku, Chris Cooper.

A Bronx Tale (Rank/Price/TriBeCa, 1993). Director Robert De Niro; producers De Niro, Jon Kilik and Jane Rosenthal; screenplay Chazz Palminteri; editor David Ray; music Butch Barbella. Cast: Robert De Niro, Chazz Palminteri, Francis Capra, Lillo Brancanta, Taral Hicks, Joe Pesci, Katherine Narducci, Clem Caserta, Alfred Sauchelli junior.

Mary Shelley's Frankenstein (Tri-Star/American Zoetrope, 1994). Director Kenneth Branagh; producer Francis Ford Coppola; screenplay Steph Lady and Frank Darabont; editor Andrew Marcus; music Patrick Doyle. Cast: Kenneth Branagh, Robert De Niro, Helena Bonham Carter, Cherie Lunghi, John Cleese, Tom Hulce, Richard Briers, Robert Hardy.

Index